THE P(

KIERKEGAARD'S WRITINGS, XXII

THE POINT OF VIEW

ON MY WORK AS AN AUTHOR

THE POINT OF VIEW FOR MY WORK
AS AN AUTHOR

ARMED NEUTRALITY

by Søren Kierkegaard

Edited and Translated
with Introduction and Notes by

Howard V. Hong and
Edna H. Hong

PRINCETON UNIVERSITY PRESS
PRINCETON, NEW JERSEY

Copyright © 1998 by Postscript, Inc.
Published by Princeton University Press,
41 William Street, Princeton, New Jersey 08540
In the United Kingdom: Princeton University Press, 6 Oxford Street,
Woodstock, Oxfordshire OX20 1TW

Third printing, and first paperback printing, 2009
Paperback ISBN: 978-0-691-14080-3

The Library of Congress has cataloged the cloth edition of this book as follows

Kierkegaard, Søren, 1813–1855.
[Om Min Forfatter-Virksomhed. English. 1998]
The point of view / by Søren Kierkegaard ;
edited and translated with introduction and notes by
Howard V. Hong and Edna H. Hong.
p.   cm. — (Kierkegaard's writings ; 22)
Includes bibliographical references (p.   ) and index.
[Translation of: Om Min Forfatter-Virksomhed.]
Contents: On my work as an author — The point of view for my work as an author —
Armed neutrality.
ISBN 0-691-05855-5 (cl : alk. paper)
1. Kierkegaard, Søren, 1813–1855.   2. Philosophers—Denmark—Biography.
3. Theologians—Denmark—Biography.   4. Authors, Danish—Denmark—Biography.
I. Hong, Howard Vincent, 1912- .   II. Hong, Edna Hatlestad, 1913- .   III. Title.
IV. Series: Kierkegaard, Søren, 1813–1855. Works. English. 1978 ; 22.
B4372.E5   1998
198'.9—dc21   97-34909

British Library Cataloging-in-Publication Data is available

Preparation of this volume has been made possible in part by a grant from
the Division of Research Programs of the National Endowment
for the Humanities, an independent federal agency

Printed on acid-free paper. ∞

Designed by Frank Mahood

press.princeton.edu

3   5   7   9   10   8   6   4

CONTENTS

Part Two
THE AUTHORSHIP VIEWED AS A WHOLE, AND FROM
THE POINT OF VIEW THAT THE AUTHOR IS A
RELIGIOUS AUTHOR
39

Postscript to the "Two Notes"
125

Armed Neutrality
127

HISTORICAL INTRODUCTION

Either/Or was published pseudonymously February 20, 1843. *Two Upbuilding Discourses* was published under Kierkegaard's name May 16, 1843. For seven years thereafter, two series of writings continued, pseudonymous works and signed works.[1] Of the eight pseudonymous and seven signed books published (in editions of 250 to 525) by 1846, only *Either/Or* was sold out by 1849.[2] The publisher, Carl Andreas Reitzel, wanted to print a second edition in 1847, and another publisher, Philip Gerson Philipsen, was also very interested.[3] On May 14, 1849, over three years after *Either/Or* had gone out of print, Reitzel published the second edition.

Usually a writer welcomes subsequent editions of a work, and preferably without much delay. To Kierkegaard, however, it was of crucial importance to maintain the distinction between the two parallel series of pseudonymous (esthetic) works and signed (ethical-religious) works, those offered, as he said, with the left hand and those offered with the right,[4] and at the same time to document the dialectical coherence of the authorship as a whole. In 1848 he had maintained the two parallel series by publishing *The Crisis and a Crisis in the Life of an Actress*, by Inter et Inter (in *Fædrelandet*, July 24–27),[5] and *Christian Discourses* (April 26), and

---

[1] See, for example, Supplement, p. 288 (*Pap.* X⁶ B 145), and table of Kierkegaard's published works, pp. xxiii–xxvii.

[2] The first edition of 525 copies was sold out within three years. The second was an edition of 750 copies. During Kierkegaard's lifetime there were nine second editions out of thirty-six titles (excluding the two earliest works; see note 65): *Either/Or* (1849), *Works of Love* (1852), *For Self-Examination* (1852), *Two Discourses at the Communion on Fridays* (1852), *The Lily in the Field and the Bird of the Air* (1854), *Practice in Christianity* (1855), *This Must Be Said* (1855), *The Moment* (1855), and *The Concept of Anxiety* (1855). In 1845 the eighteen discourses of 1843–1844 were remaindered to Philip G. Philipsen, and in 1847 the other nine books in print at the time were remaindered to Carl A. Reitzel..

[3] See *Kierkegaard: Letters and Documents*, Letters 152–57, *KW* XXV.

[4] See Supplement, p. 193 (*Pap.* X¹ A 351).

[5] See Supplement, p. 164 (*Pap.* IX A 216).

now he was faced again with the task of keeping the two series parallel.

> It will never do to let the second edition of *Either/Or* be published without something accompanying it. Somehow the accent must be that I have made up my mind about being a religious author.

To be sure, my seeking an ecclesiastical post also stresses this, but it can be interpreted as something that came later. . ...

> But the second edition of *Either/Or* is a critical point (as I did in fact regard it originally and wrote "The Point of View" to be published simultaneously with it and otherwise would scarcely have been in earnest about publishing the second edition)—it will never come again. If this opportunity is not utilized, everything I have written, viewed as a totality, will be dragged down mainly into the esthetic.[6]

This time, however, the task was agonizingly complicated by protracted reflection on indirect communication (pseudonymity) and direct communication and by a concern for his readers' understanding of his authorship as a whole, issues that impinged on his need to decide what should be done with all the writings of 1848–49 that lay finished, "the most valuable I have produced."[7] The thought of imminent death gave special urgency to these issues.[8]

Kierkegaard's views on both indirect and direct communication were predicated on his conception of his task. "It is Christianity that I have presented and still want to present; to this every hour of my day has been and is directed."[9] With the Socratic method of indirection, he used a pseudonymous, esthetic approach because of what he regarded as the illusion of "Christendom."

> Thus in a certain sense I began my activity as an author with a *falsum* [deception] or with a *pia fraus* [pious fraud]. The situa-

---

[6] See Supplement, pp. 185–86 (*Pap.* X[1] A 147).
[7] See Supplement, p. 178 (*Pap.* X[1] A 95).
[8] See Supplement, p. 164 (*Pap.* IX A 216).
[9] See Supplement, p. 162 (*Pap.* IX A 171).

tion is that in so-called established Christendom people are so fixed in the fancy that they are Christians that if they are to be made aware at all many an art will have to be employed. If someone who otherwise does not have a reputation of being an author begins right off as a Christian author, he will not get a hearing from his contemporaries. They are immediately on their guard, saying, "That's not for us" etc.

I began as an estheticist—and then, although approaching the religious with perhaps uncustomary alacrity, I denied being a Christian etc.[10]

Within an illusion, the maieutic is the maximum,[11] and it also leaves the reader alone with the work, free from extraneous interest in the author's personality and personal life.[12]

Although indirect communication is not inferior to direct communication, it has limits defined by the communicator and the nature of the communication. There is "something daimonic—but not necessarily in the bad sense—about it, as, for example, with Socrates."[13] Socratic indirection presupposed that the learner was in possession of the truth and needed only to be prompted to recollection, but with regard to Christianity the method is properly only provisional.

> Yet the communication of the essentially Christian must end finally in "witnessing." The maieutic cannot be the final form, because, Christianly understood, the truth does not lie in the subject (as Socrates understood it), but in a revelation that must be proclaimed.
>
> It is very proper that the maieutic be used in Christendom, simply because the majority actually live in the fancy that they are Christians. But since Christianity still is Christianity, the one who uses the maieutic must become a witness.
>
> Ultimately the user of the maieutic will be unable to bear the responsibility, since the maieutic approach still remains

---

[10] See Supplement, p. 161 (*Pap.* IX A 171), and also pp. 163–64 (*Pap.* IX A 215).

[11] See *JP* II 1957; VI 6804 (*Pap.* IX A 221; X^4 A 558).

[12] See Supplement, pp. 161, 283–84 (*Pap.* IX A 171; X^6 B 4:3).

[13] See Supplement, pp. 248–50 (*Pap.* X^3 A 413).

rooted in human sagacity, however sanctified and dedicated in fear and trembling this may be. God becomes too powerful for the maieutic practitioner and then he is a witness, different from the direct witness only in what he has gone through to become a witness.[14]

In addition to acknowledging that the requirement of witness (direct communication) is intrinsic to Christianity, Kierkegaard had a concern for the eventual interpretation of the authorship as a whole. His situation in Copenhagen was scarcely encouraging; "I am regarded as a kind of Englishman, a half-mad eccentric, with whom we jolly well all, society people and street urchins, think to have their fun."[15]

He also realized that the "poetical" works of the pseudonymous writers lent themselves to myriad uses and misuses.

Anyone with just a fragment of common sense will perceive that it would be ludicrously confusing to attribute to me everything the poetized personalities say. Nevertheless, to be on the safe side, I have expressly urged once and for all that anyone who wants to quote something from the pseudonyms will not attribute the quotation to me (see my postscript to *Concluding Postscript*). It is easy to see that anyone wanting to have a literary lark merely needs to take some quotations higgledy-piggledy from "The Seducer," then from Johannes Climacus, then from me, etc., print them together as if they were all my words, show how they contradict each other, and create a very chaotic impression, as if the author were a kind of lunatic. Hurrah! That can be done. In my opinion anyone who exploits the poetic in me by quoting the writings in a confusing way is more or less either a charlatan or a literary toper.[16]

The felt need to communicate directly his conception of the entire authorship was heightened by his own deepened under-

---

[14] *JP* II 1957 (*Pap.* IX A 221). See also Supplement, pp. 164–66, 187, 246–47, 286–88 (*Pap.* IX A 218, 234; X^1 A 235; X^3 A 258; X^4 A 383; X^6 B 145).

[15] See Supplement, p. 168 (*Pap.* IX A 288), and also p. 162 (IX A 172).

[16] See Supplement, p. 288 (*Pap.* X^6 B 145).

standing of the inner coherence of the whole. The task had been to present "one idea, this continuity from *Either/Or* to Anti-Climacus, the idea of religiousness in reflection."[17] The fulfilling of this task was "also my religious upbringing and development," and therefore what he could now say about the authorship was a "little by little subsequently acquired understanding" expressive of his nature, "which essentially is reflection and therefore never proclaims, prophesies, but essentially understands itself first in what has gone before, in what has been carried out."[18]

Having decided that something about the authorship as a whole should be said directly, Kierkegaard considered at length what it should be and how it should be done. In 1847 he made a brief beginning on a defense [*apologie*], but he quickly dropped it because his accusers were gossip and rumors and because what would please the elite would displease the commoners and vice versa.[19] Then he contemplated giving "a little series of lectures on the organizing theme throughout my entire work as an author," and in a draft invitation warned that the auditors, limited to twenty, would find it to be hard work, at times boring, and, if they understood, their lives would be made more difficult.[20] In January 1848, he wrote a proposal for a series of small quarterly publications on a subscription basis,[21] but this idea, like the others, was soon abandoned.

The remaining possibility was a publication to accompany the second edition of *Either/Or*, but this involved the question of what it should be, a question with a number of possible answers. The first one was to publish "The Point of View for My Work as an Author,"[22] "as good as finished" in November 1848.[23] But of all the things that in 1849 were ready for publication, "The

---

[17] See Supplement, p. 283 (*Pap.* X^6 B 4:3).

[18] See Supplement, p. 288 (*Pap.* X^5 B 145); see also pp. 164, 184–85, 193–94, 261–63 (*Pap.* IX A 216; X^1 A 118, 351; X^5 B 201, 249).

[19] See Supplement, pp. 156–59 (*Pap.* VIII^2 B 179:1–6, 181).

[20] See Supplement, p. 159 (*Pap.* VIII^2 B 186).

[21] See Supplement, pp. 159–60 (*Pap.* VIII^2 B 188, 196).

[22] See Supplement, p. 186 (*Pap.* X^1 A 147).

[23] See Supplement, p. 169 (*Pap.* IX A 293).

Point of View for My Work as an Author" worried him the most.[24] Did it say too much about him so that he would appear as an extraordinary?[25] With his sense of guidance in the whole complex authorship, did he even have the right to use "I" in the book?[26] Was the idea of publishing it the fruit of melancholy impatience, as if he were to die tomorrow or had decided to stop writing? Would it be arbitrariness on his part to enter into conflict because of the publication?[27] The decision was simply that it could not be published: "And what melancholy impatience! It was written historically after a whole intermediate series of writings, which must be published first if there is to be any question at all of publishing it while I am alive."[28]

But the decision to postpone publication of "Point of View" was flawed: " . . . now for the first time I understand and comprehend the whole . . . if I do not do it myself, there is no one who can present it, because no one knows it the way I do. No one can explain the structure of the whole as I can."[29]

Therefore the old way was considered as a middle way: to use a pseudonym. A journal entry from early 1849 begins with: "'The Point of View for My Work as an Author' must not be published, no, no!"[30] and at the end it reads: "The book itself is true and in my opinion masterly. But a book like that can be published only after my death." The penultimate conclusion was that a pseudonym ("the poet Johannes de Silentio") must be used, but that in itself demonstrated the soundness of the opening line of the entry, because then it would no longer be the same book, since "the point of it was my personal story."

After abandoning the idea of a Johannes de Silentio publication, Kierkegaard once again, ten months later in November, entertained the idea of publishing "Point of View" under a pseu-

[24] See Supplement, p. 197 (*Pap.* X¹ A 501).

[25] See Supplement, pp. 174, 187–88, 212–14 (*Pap.* X¹ A 74, 250; X² A 106).

[26] See Supplement, p. 209 (*Pap.* X² A 89).

[27] See Supplement, p. 188 (*Pap.* X¹ A 250).

[28] See Supplement, p. 177 (*Pap.* X¹ A 79); see also pp. 174–77, 187–88, 201–02 (*Pap.* X¹ A 78, 250, 546).

[29] See Supplement, pp. 209–10 (*Pap.* X² A 89).

[30] See Supplement, pp. 174, 176, 177 (*Pap.* X¹ A 78).

donym, A-O, wrote an A-O preface, and discussed the merits of this ingenious idea.[31] Kierkegaard's wrestling with the yes-and-no of publishing anything direct about the authorship is again illustrated by another entry from the same month. "But it is not necessary to publish them ["Point of View," "Armed Neutrality," "A Note" ("The Accounting"),[32] and "Three Notes"[33]] pseudonymously; it is not even right to do so, inasmuch as the matter does not become sufficiently simple."[34]

For Kierkegaard, however, the publication of "Point of View" was not the only subject of persistent pondering. What should be done about the publication of all the other writings of 1848 and early 1849, "the most valuable I have produced"?[35] There were not only the additional writings on his authorship, "Three Notes," "A Note," and "Armed Neutrality," but also "The Sickness unto Death," "Practice in Christianity," and a variety of other pieces, including versions of "The Book on Adler."[36]

> The question is: When should all the latest books be published! Again I cannot adequately thank God that I have finished them, and if I had not had the tension with the addition of new pains I perhaps would never have completed them, because once I have come out of the momentum of writing, I never get into it again in the same way. This time I succeeded, and for me it is enough that they exist, finished in fair copy, containing the completion and the entire structure of the whole, going as far as I in fact could go in my attempt to introduce Christianity into Christendom—but, please note, "poetically, without authority," for, as I have always maintained, I am no apostle or the like; I am a poetic-dialectical genius, personally and religiously a penitent.

[31] See Supplement, p. 222 (*Pap.* X² A 171).

[32] See Supplement, pp. 193–96 (*Pap.* X¹ A 351, 422).

[33] See pp. 101–26 for "Two Notes." Part of the third note was used later in the preface to *Two Discourses at the Communion on Fridays.*

[34] See Supplement, p. 229 (*Pap.* X² A 192).

[35] See Supplement, p. 178 (*Pap.* X¹ A 95). On 1848–49, see also pp. 212–14 (*Pap.* X² A 106); *JP* VI 6801 (*Pap.* X⁴ A 545).

[36] See Supplement, pp. 206–07 (*Pap.* X¹ A 678).

But when should they be published? If I publish them while I am still in the position of heterogeneity maintained up till now—that is, independent, free, unrestricted, floating—if I publish them while still maintaining this mode of life, all the extremely exact dialectical categories and determinations in the books will be of little help in defending myself against unhappy confusions, and I will nevertheless be confused with such a one.

But if I had gotten myself a position in the established order first of all, then my life would be a hindrance to a misunderstanding like that. But if I had held such a position I would not have written the books; of that I am sincerely convinced, and it is really easy to understand. But now it is done and the delay is simply a matter of publishing.

By being situated this way, I myself, like everyone else, will be placed under the "judgment," if you please, the judgment upon Christendom contained in these books. It is precisely this that will prevent my being confused with an apostle or someone like that. The books are poetically written, as if by an apostle, but I have stepped aside—no, I am not the apostle, anything but, I am the poet and a penitent.[37]

With all the finished writings on hand, Kierkegaard pondered another publication possibility in 1849: to publish everything, "the fruit of the year 1848," in three volumes under his own name and with the common title "The Collected Works of Completion." Volume I would be "The Sickness unto Death," with "Armed Neutrality" as an appendix; volume II "Practice in Christianity" in three parts; and volume III "On My Work as an Author," consisting of "Point of View" ("N.B. perhaps not yet"), "Three Notes," "A Note" ("The Accounting"), and "The Whole in One Word."[38]

My intention was to publish all the completed manuscripts in one volume, all under my name—and then to make a clean break.

---

[37] *JP* VI 6317 (*Pap.* X^1 A 56).
[38] See Supplement, pp. 234–35 (*Pap.* X^5 B 143).

This was a drastic idea, but I suffered indescribably in persistently wanting to cling to it; I penciled notes here and there (especially in the books about the authorship), and at the same time I continually overtaxed myself on the whole project, especially on the added point that I should existentially alter my course and yet in a way conceal that there was something false about my stepping forth in character on such a scale—by withdrawing entirely. . . .

Then the idea came to me again that it might be unjustifiable for me to let these writings just lie there . . . .. Then I tackled the matter again—sent the first part of the manuscript to the printer under my name, so it would now be possible to arrange the whole project. . . . —I realized also that it was rash and excessive to instigate a *coup* of that nature—with the result that *The Sickness unto Death* was made pseudonymous.[39]

The new pseudonym Anti-Climacus, used for *The Sickness unto Death* (July 30, 1849) and again for *Practice in Christianity* (September 25, 1850), not only made possible the publication of two of the 1848 works, but it also took care of Kierkegaard's scrupulous concern lest he seemed or might seem to claim to represent the ideality presented in these works. "Anti-Climacus" means not "against Johannes Climacus" but "above Climacus."[40]

Another possibility had been considered for publishing the other manuscripts. Six of them had been intended for a volume planned under the title "A Cycle of Ethical-Religious Essays." When this idea had been set aside and two essays were published as *Two Ethical-Religious Essays* (May 19, 1849) under another new pseudonym, H. H., the other writings, related to "The Book on Alder," remained unpublished.[41]

There was still the persistent question of what should be done with the writings on the authorship: "Point of View," "Three Notes," "A Note," and "Armed Neutrality." Kierkegaard con-

[39] See Supplement, pp. 236–37 (*Pap.* X² A 147); see also p. 203 (*Pap.* X¹ A 567).

[40] See *Sickness unto Death*, pp. ix, xx-xxii, *KW* XIX.

[41] See Supplement, p. 174 (*Pap.* X¹ A 74) and note 25, and also pp. 181–84 (*Pap.* X¹ A 97, 116, 117).

tinued to think that he should say something directly, and yet he still hesitated. A journal entry from April 1849 reads:

> I have made one final attempt to say a word about myself and my whole authorship. I have written "An Appendix" that should be called "The Accounting" and should follow the "Discourses" [*The Lily in the Field and the Bird of the Air*, published on the same day as *Either/Or*, 2 ed., May 14, 1849]. I think it is a masterpiece, but that is of no importance—it cannot be done.
>
> The point is that I perceive with extraordinary clarity the infinitely ingenious thought present in the totality of the authorship. Humanly speaking, now would be just the right time, now when the second edition of *Either/Or* appears. It would be splendid. But there is something false in it.
>
> *For I am a genius of such a kind that I cannot just directly and personally assume the whole thing without encroaching on Governance.* Every genius is preponderantly immanence and immediacy, has no "why"; but again it is my genius that lets me see clearly, afterward, the infinite "why" in the whole, but this is Governance's doing. *On the other hand, I am not a religious person of such a kind that I can directly assign everything to God.*
>
> Therefore not a word. If anything is to be said, then just that. Or if the world wants to extort a statement and explanation from me, then this.
>
> I suffer indescribably every time I have begun to want to publish something about myself and the authorship.[42]

Over two years passed before Kierkegaard finally published *On My Work as an Author*[43]—on the same day, August 7, 1851, when *Two Discourses for the Communion on Fridays* appeared (and with part of the third of the "Three Notes" as the preface). After this very truncated version of "Point of View" was published, Kierkegaard held back "Point of View" and the remaining two notes. *The Point of View for My Work as an Author*, with an appendix of "Two Notes" and a "Postscript" to the "Two Notes,"

---

[42] See Supplement, pp. 188–89 (*Pap.* X^1 A 266), and also p. 251 (*Pap.* X^3 A 423).

[43] See Supplement, p. 284 (*Pap.* X^4 A 351).

was eventually published posthumously (1859) by Kierkegaard's brother Peter Christian. *Armed Neutrality* remained unpublished until it appeared in 1880 in volume V of *Efterladte Papirer* (the first edition of Kierkegaard's journals and papers).

Quite apart from the questions of whether or not and, if so, when to publish, Kierkegaard sensitively pondered for a long time the dedication of *On My Work as an Author*. All his life he cherished his Dante-Beatrice, Petrarch-Laura, Novalis-Sophie kind of relationship with Regine Olsen. Therefore when it seemed to be the time to say something direct about the authorship, he thought that the relationship should be acknowledged. On September 10, 1849, eight years after the termination of the engagement, Kierkegaard wrote a letter to Regine (and sent it with a covering letter to her husband, Johan Frederik Schlegel) with the opening quotation, "'There is a time to be silent and there is a time to speak.'" He thanked her for "everything I owe to you."[44] Schlegel returned the letter unopened and with an indignant reply. Besides journal references to an "enigmatic dedication"[45] to Regine, there are versions of such a dedication.[46] Because of possible misunderstanding and journalistic misuse, the plan was abandoned. The intention was fulfilled, however, by the dedication, "To One Unnamed . . . the entire authorship, as it was from the beginning,"[47] in *Two Discourses at the Communion on Fridays*.

Presumably the ordinary edition of 525 copies of *On My Work* was printed. The second printing was made, together with the second printing of *Point of View*, in the first edition of the collected works (1901–06). The reception of *On My Work* in 1851 was rather quiet and meager. Himmelstrup's bibliography[48] lists only three items: an anonymous brief laudatory announce-

---

[44] *Letters*, Letter 235, *KW* XXV. Cf. *JP* VI 6332 (*Pap.* X⁵ A 153).

[45] See Supplement, pp. 230, 242 (*Pap.* X² A 215, 427).

[46] See Supplement, pp. 256–58 (*Pap.* X⁵ B 261, 262, 263, 264).

[47] *Two Discourses at the Communion on Fridays*, in *Without Authority*, p. 163, *KW* XVIII (*SV* XII 265).

[48] *Søren Kierkegaard International Bibliografi*, ed. Jens Himmelstrup (Copenhagen: Nyt Nordisk Forlag Arnold Busck, 1962), p. 12.

ment,[49] a reprinting of the same in another paper,[50] and Johan Ludvig Heiberg's publication in 1856 of Kierkegaard's letter[51] that accompanied his gift of the work to the actress Luise Heiberg. The little announcement called the work "an overview of this highly gifted man's work as an author" and stated that the work and the preface of the simultaneously published *Two Discourses* indicated that the author seemed to have ended his writing career. A later anonymous piece in *Flyve-Posten* warned readers against being confused by the book.[52]

Bishop Mynster was a more important audience, and Kierkegaard sent him copies of *On My Work* and *Two Discourses*. When he visited Mynster on August 9, 1851, Mynster had read the first but not the second. His response was, "'Yes, it is a clue [*Traad*, literally "thread"] to the whole, but spun later, but, after all, you do not say more than that yourself.'" To which Kierkegaard replied that "the point to bear in mind was this, to have been so devoted, over many years and in much writing, to one thing, that my pen had not made one single deviation."[53]

Reviews of *Point of View* (1859) were more numerous and more substantial. Two are of particular interest because of their authors, Andreas Gottlob Rudelbach and Jørgen Victor Bloch, both of whom had been polemically involved with Kierkegaard.[54] Readers of the works, said Rudelbach, know that Kierkegaard was a "poetic and religious genius." "But there are two things we certainly would like to know about and which only the writer himself can present in an adequate way: It is the life-

---

[49] *Flyve-Posten*, 175, August 7, 1851.

[50] *Byens-Avis*, 187, August 9, 1851.

[51] *Kjøbenhavnsposten*, 1, January 2, 1856; *Letters*, Letter 283, *KW* XXV (*SV* X 322). Luise Heiberg was the subject of *The Crisis and a Crisis in the Life of an Actress*, by Inter et Inter. In *On My Work* (p. 8), Kierkegaard acknowledged authorship of the piece and therefore sent her a copy.

[52] *Flyve-Posten*, 215, September 16, 1851. See Supplement, p. 287 (*Pap.* X[4] A 408).

[53] See Supplement, p. 285 (*Pap.* X[4] A 373).

[54] On Rudelbach, see "An Open Letter," in *The Corsair Affair and Articles Related to the Writings*, pp. xxxvi–xxxviii, 51–59, *KW* XIII (*SV* XIII 436–44). On Bloch, see Kierkegaard's "What Cruel Punishment," (a reply to an article by Bloch), in *The Moment and Late Writings*, pp. 56–59, and Supplement, pp. 367–71, *KW* XXIII (*SV* XIV 66–69 and 62–65).

key to his authorship and its internal coherence; it is what could be called his dedication and his plan, and it is this that he has given in the present work . . .." The value of the work will depend on "the extent to which he, the very subjectively disposed author, succeeds in making himself the object."[55] Kierkegaard did succeed in this regard, Rudelbach thought, but in reviewing the work he maintained that Kierkegaard's indirect method was Socratic enough but not Christian, that his emphasis on the individual amounted to "absolute isolation,"[56] and that his dismissal of apologetics was a mistake. We should, he concluded, read these works of "true inwardness, ethical energy, psychological perspicuity, everything that on the whole manifests itself in these writings as great, noble, sublime . . . .. But on the other hand we will not ignore what Luther testifies, 'that one drop of poison spoils the whole cask of wine.'"[57]

Bloch's long review article[58] years later centered on *For Self-Examination* and *Point of View*. Most of the article was a synopsis, with occasional critical comments, of the works. Of *Point of View*, Bloch had mixed opinions, and of the following observations Kierkegaard had expected the first, most likely would have felt that the postponement of publication was vindicated by the second, and would have rejected the third as a misrepresentation of his basic position and as a mistake in judgment.

> What is interesting in the eyes of the world, the interesting, is lost through this "direct communication." The riddle is solved; the author's part is disclosed to the eyes of all; the movement "from the interesting to the simple, to what it means to become a Christian," the world finds boring.[59]

> Yes, the author undeniably knows how to compel his reader to "become aware." The above-named work is one of his

[55] Andreas Gottlob Rudelbach, "*Synspunktet for min Forfatter-Virksomhed*," *Evangelisk Ugeskrift*, 4–5, January 20, 1860, p. 50.

[56] Ibid., p. 63.

[57] Ibid., pp. 65–66.

[58] Jørgen Victor Bloch, "*To Skrifter af S. Kierkegaard paany fremdragne*," *Dansk Kirketidende*, 28–29, 31–32, 34, July 12, 26, August 23, 1885, col. 451–58, 501–11, 538–43.

[59] Ibid., col. 538.

most engaging and captivating and as a real "Report to History" can be most warmly recommended to everyone who
wishes to gain an insight into S. Kierkegaard's personality and
an overview of the coherence in his great authorship, to which
it certainly is . . . a "primary key." If it had been published
while he was living, he no doubt would have found deeper
understanding and sympathy in his contemporaries, although
the general interest in 1848 was bent in another direction. But
conditions now are more favorable for understanding and
evaluating him without overvaluing him.[60]

How good it would have been if this melancholy disciplinar-
ian, in whom the human had died, had come into a living
association with *Grundtvig*, who more than anyone else had
emphasized the humanity of Christianity, and if this peniten-
tial hermit, who, without a confidant on earth, sought only the
single individual as his reader, had been led into the *Lord's*
congregation that was the homestead of all Grundtvig's discourse and song.[61]

When Kierkegaard's writings had been discovered by the
larger world, some readers compared, mutatis mutandis, *On My
Work as an Author* and *Point of View* to Augustine's *Confessions*
and Newman's *Apologia pro Vita Sua*.[62] Kierkegaard most likely
would decline any exalted literary association, although he did
call "Point of View" "masterly."[63] To him it was, like "On My
Work as an Author," not a literary work but an act, and his
characterization of the "significance of this little book" applies
also to the larger work published later.

The state of "Christendom" is as follows: the point of view of
Christianity and of what Christianity is has been completely

[60] Ibid., col. 541.

[61] Ibid., col. 542.

[62] See, for example, Walter Lowrie, Introduction, *The Point of View* (London: Oxford University Press, 1939), p. xiii. Lowrie, in *Kierkegaard* (London:
Oxford University Press, 1938), p. 392, says of *Point of View*: "a religious autobiography so unique that it has no parallel in the whole literature of the world."

[63] See Supplement, p. 176 (*Pap.* X¹ A 78).

shifted, has been cast in terms of the objective, the scholarly, and differences such as genius and talent have been made crucial.

This little book reverses the whole thing. It says (precisely because this enormous productivity preceded it): Forget genius, talent, scholarship, and all that—Christianity is the existential, a character-task. And now it is turned that way.

For that reason this little book is not a literary work, a new literary work, but an act, and therefore it was important that it be as short as possible, that it not mark a new productivity that people could then discuss. This little book is μετάβασις εἰς ἄλλο γένος [a shifting from one genus to another] and makes clear the extent to which it was already present in my total work as an author.[64]

KIERKEGAARD'S PUBLISHED WORKS[65]

Pseudonymous		Signed	
1843		**1843**	
Feb. 20	*Either/Or*, I-II, ed. Victor Eremita	May 16	*Two Upbuilding Discourses*
Oct. 16	*Repetition* by Constantin Constantius	Oct. 16	*Three Upbuilding Discourses*
Oct. 16	*Fear and Trembling* by Johannes de Silentio		
		Dec. 6	*Four Upbuilding Discourses*

[64] See Supplement, p. 286 (*Pap.* X⁴ A 383). For a brief overview of the "total work," see Historical Introduction, The Moment *and Late Writings, KW* XXIII.

[65] Kierkegaard excluded from the authorship proper the first two works (*KW* I, II) that bore his name: *From the Papers of One Still Living* (September 7, 1838, a review of Hans Christian Andersen's *Only a Fiddler*) and *The Concept of Irony, with Continual Reference to Socrates* (September 16, 1841), his university dissertation.

Pseudonymous 1844		Signed 1844	
June 13	*Philosophical Fragments* by Johannes Climacus, ed. S. Kierkegaard	March 5	*Two Upbuilding Discourses*
June 17	*The Concept of Anxiety* by Vigilius Haufniensis	June 8	*Three Upbuilding Discourses*
June 17	*Prefaces* by Nicolaus Notabene [written: *Writing Sampler*]	Aug. 31	*Four Upbuilding Discourses*
1845		**1845**	
April 30	*Stages on Life's Way* pub. by Hilarius Bookbinder	April 29	*Three Discourses on Imagined Occasions*
May 19–20	"A Cursory Observation Concerning a Detail in *Don Giovanni*" by Inter et Inter		
1846		**1846**	
Feb. 28	*Concluding Unscientific Postscript* by Johannes Climacus, with an appended "A First and Last Explanation" by S. Kierkegaard		

Pseudonymous		Signed	
1846		**1846**	
		March 30	*Two Ages: A Literary Review*
			[written: fair copy of version I of *The Book on Adler*]
1847		**1847**	
		March 13	*Upbuilding Discourses in Various Spirits*
		Sept. 29	*Works of Love*
1848		**1848**	
		April 26	*Christian Discourses*
July 24–27	*The Crisis and a Crisis in the Life of an Actress* by Inter et Inter	November	[*The Point of View for My Work as an Author* "as good as finished"]
1849		**1849**	
May 14	*Either/Or*, 2 ed.	May 14	*The Lily in the Field and the Bird of the Air*
May 19	*Two Ethical-Religious Essays* by H. H.		[written: *Armed Neutrality*]
July 30	*The Sickness unto Death* by Anti-Climacus, ed. S. Kierkegaard		
		Nov. 14	*Three Discourses at the Communion on Fridays:* "The High Priest"—

Pseudonymous		Signed	
1849		**1849**	
		Nov. 14	"The Tax
		cont.	Collector"—
			"The Woman
			Who Was a
			Sinner"
1850		**1850**	
Sept. 25	*Practice in Christianity* by Anti-Climacus, ed. S. Kierkegaard		
		Dec. 20	*An Upbuilding Discourse*
1851		**1851**	
		Aug. 7	*Two Discourses at the Communion on Fridays*
		Aug. 7	*On My Work as an Author*
		Sept. 10	*For Self-Examination* [written: *Judge for Yourself!*]
1854		**1854**	
		Dec. 18, 30	Articles I-II in *Fædrelandet*
1855		**1855**	
		Jan. 12– May 26	Articles III-XXI in *Fædrelandet*
		May 24	*This Must Be Said; So Let It Be Said*
		May 24– Sept. 24	*The Moment* I-IX [written: X]

Pseudonymous		Signed
1855		1855
	June 16	*What Christ Judges of Official Christianity*
	Sept. 3	*The Changelessness of God*

Posthumously Published Works

	1859	*The Point of View for My Work as an Author*
	1872	*The Book on Adler* (*Efterladte Papirer*, II)
	1876	*Judge for Yourself!*
	1880	*Armed Neutrality* (*Efterladte Papirer*, V)
	1881	*The Moment*, X (*Efterladte Papirer*, VIII)

ON MY WORK AS AN AUTHOR

by S. Kierkegaard

Wer glaubet, der ist grosz und reich,
Er hat Gott und das Himmelreich.
Wer glaubet, der ist klein und arm,
Er schreiet nur: Herr Dich erbarm!

[Whoever believes is great and rich,
He has God and the Kingdom of Heaven.
Whoever believes is small and poor,
He only cries: Lord, have mercy!]

The Accounting

Copenhagen, March 1849.

When a country is little, the proportions in every relationship in the little land naturally are small. So, too, in literary matters; the royalties and everything else involved will be only insignificant. To be an author—unless one is a poet, and in addition a dramatist, or one writes textbooks or in some other way is an author in connection with a public office—is about the poorest paid, the least secure, and just about the most thankless job there is. If there is some individual who has the capability of being an author and if he is also fortunate enough to have private means, then he becomes an author more or less at his own expense. This, however, is quite appropriate; there is nothing more to be said about it. In that way the individual in his work will love his idea, the nation to which he belongs, the cause he serves, the language he as an author has the honor to write. Indeed, this is how it will be where there is harmony between the individual and the nation, which in turn in the given situation will be somewhat appreciative of this individual.

Whether the opposite of this has in any way been my experience, whether I have been treated shabbily by anyone or by some persons, is really not my concern but quite properly is their business. What is my concern, however—and I am so happy that it is my concern—is that I should and ought to give thanks for whatever favors and kindness and courtesy and appreciation have been shown to me in general or by particular individuals.[2]

---

[3]The movement the authorship describes is: *from* "the poet," from the esthetic—*from* "the philosopher," from the speculative—*to* the indication of the most inward qualification of the essentially Christian; **from** the *pseudonymous Either/Or,* **through**

Concluding Postscript, with *my name as editor,* **to** *Discourses at the Communion on Fridays,** of which two were delivered in Frue Church.

This movement was traversed or delineated *uno tenore,* in one breath, if I dare say so—thus the authorship, regarded as a *totality,* is religious from first to last, something anyone who can see, if he wants to see, must also see. Just as one versed in natural science promptly knows from the crisscrossing threads in a web the ingenious little creature whose web it is, so an insightful person will also know that to this authorship there corresponds as the source someone who *qua* author "has willed only one thing."[13] The insightful person will also know that this one thing is the religious, but the religious completely cast into reflection, yet in

---

*Later, however, there appeared a new pseudonym: Anti-Climacus.[4] But the very fact that it is a pseudonym signifies that he is, inversely, coming to a halt, as the name (*Anti*-Climacus) indeed suggests. All the previous pseudonymity is lower than "the upbuilding author"; the new pseudonym is a higher pseudonymity. But indeed "a halt is made" in this way: something higher is shown, which simply forces me back within my boundary, judging me, that my life does not meet so high a requirement and that consequently the communication is something poetical. —And a little earlier in that same year, there appeared a little book: *Two Ethical-Religious Essays* by H. H.[5] The significance of this little book (which does not stand *in* the authorship as much as it relates totally *to* the authorship and for that reason also was anonymous, in order to be kept outside entirely) is not very easy to explain without going into the whole matter. It is like a navigation mark *by* which one steers but, note well, in such a way that the pilot understands precisely that *he is to keep a certain distance from it.* It defines the boundary of the authorship. "The Difference between a Genius and an Apostle" (essay no. 2) is: "The genius is without authority."[6] But precisely because genius as such is without authority, it does not have in itself the ultimate concentration that provides the power and justification for accentuating in the direction of "letting oneself be put to death for the truth"[7] (essay no. 1). Genius as such remains in reflection. This in turn is the category of my whole authorship: to *make aware* of the religious, the essentially Christian—but "*without authority.*"[8] —And finally, to include even the smallest, there came out later *The Lily in the Field and the Bird of the Air, Three Devotional Discourses,*[9] which accompanied the second edition of *Either/Or;*[10] and "The High Priest"—"The Tax Collector"—"The Woman Who Was a Sinner," *Three Discourses at the Communion on Fridays,*[11] which accompanied Anti-Climacus's *The Sickness unto Death*—two small books, both of which in the preface repeat that first preface, the preface to *Two Upbuilding Discourses* (1843).[12]

October 1849

such a way that it is completely taken back out of reflection into simplicity—that is, he will see that the traversed path is: to *reach*, to *arrive at* simplicity.

And this is also (in *reflection*, as it in fact was originally) the **Christian** *movement*. Christianly, one does not proceed from the simple in order then to become interesting, witty, profound, a poet, a philosopher, etc. No, it is just the opposite; *here* one begins and then becomes more and more simple, arrives at the simple. This, in "Christendom," is *Christianly* the movement of reflection; one does not reflect oneself into Christianity but reflects oneself out of something else and becomes more and more simple, a Christian. If the author had been a richly endowed intellect, or, if he was that, if he had been a doubly richly endowed intellect, he probably would have needed a longer or a doubly long period in order to describe this path in literary production and to reach this point.

* *

*

But just as that which has been communicated (the idea of the religious) has been cast completely into reflection and in turn taken back out of reflection, so also the *communication* has been decisively marked by *reflection*, or the form of communication used is that of reflection. "Direct communication" is: to communicate the truth directly; "communication in reflection" is: to *deceive into the truth*. But since the movement is to arrive at the simple, the communication in turn must sooner or later end in direct communication. It began **maieutically**[14] with esthetic production,* and all the pseudonymous writings are *maieutic* in nature. Therefore this writing was also pseudonymous, whereas the directly religious—which from the beginning was present in the gleam of an indication—carried my name. The directly reli-

*The maieutic lies in the relation between the esthetic writing as the beginning and the religious as the τέλος [goal]. It begins with the esthetic, in which possibly most people have their lives, and now the religious is introduced so quickly that those who, moved by the esthetic, decide to follow along are suddenly standing right in the middle of the decisive qualifications of the essentially Christian, are at least prompted to become *aware*.

gious was present from the very beginning; *Two Upbuilding Discourses* (1843) is in fact concurrent* with *Either/Or*. And in order to safeguard this concurrence of the directly religious, every pseudonymous work was accompanied concurrently by a little collection of "upbuilding discourses"—until *Concluding Postscript* appeared, which poses the issue, which is *the issue* κατ' ἐξοχήν [in the eminent sense] of the whole authorship: *becoming a Christian.*"**[15] From that moment the gleam of the directly religious ceases, since now the exclusively religious writing begins:

Upbuilding Discourses in Various Spirits, Works of Love, Christian Discourses.[17] But in order inversely to recall the beginning (corresponding to what *Two Upbuilding Discourses* was at the beginning, when the voluminous works were esthetic), there appeared at the end (when for a long period the writing was exclusively and voluminously religious) a little esthetic article by Inter et Inter[18] in the newspaper *Fædrelandet*, no. 188–191, July 1848. The gleam of the two upbuilding discourses at the beginning meant that it was actually this that should advance, this at which it was to arrive; the gleam of the little esthetic article at the end was meant, by way of a faint reflection, to bring to consciousness that from the beginning the esthetic was what should be left be-

---

*This also serves to prevent the illusion that the religious is something one turns to when one has become older. "One begins as an esthetic author and then when one has become older and no longer has the powers of youth, then one becomes a religious author." But if an author *concurrently* begins as an esthetic and a religious author, the religious writing certainly cannot be explained by the incidental fact that the author has become older, inasmuch as one certainly cannot concurrently be older than oneself.

**The situation* (becoming a *Christian* in *Christendom*, where consequently one is a Christian)—the situation, which, as every dialectician sees, casts everything into reflection, also makes an indirect method necessary, because the task here must be to take measures against the illusion: calling oneself a Christian, perhaps deluding oneself into thinking one is that without being that. Therefore, the one who introduced the issue did not *directly* define himself as being Christian and the others as not being that; no, just the *reverse*—he denies being that and concedes it to the others. This Johannes Climacus does.[16] —In relation to pure receptivity, like the empty jar that is to be filled, *direct* communication is appropriate, but when illusion is involved, consequently something that must first be removed, direct communication is inappropriate.

hind, what should be abandoned. *Concluding Postscript* is the mid-point, and so exactly—something that of course only lays claim to being a curiosity—that even the quantities of what was written before and after it are more or less equal if one, and rightfully so, includes the eighteen upbuilding discourses[19] in the purely religious writing, and even the periods of the literary activity prior to and after *Concluding Postscript* are roughly equal.

Finally, this movement of the authorship is again decisively marked by reflection or is the movement of reflection. The direct way begins with individuals, a few readers, and the task or the movement is to gather a large number, to acquire an abstraction: the public. Here the **beginning is made**, *maieutically*, with a sensation, and with what belongs to it, the public, which always joins in where something is going on; and the movement was, *maieutically*, to shake off "the crowd" in order to get hold of "the single individual,"* religiously understood. At the very same time when the sensation *Either/Or* created was at its peak, at that very same time appeared *Two Upbuilding Discourses* (1843), which used the formula that later was repeated unchanged: "It seeks that single individual whom I with joy and gratitude call my reader."[20] And precisely at the critical moment when *Concluding Postscript*, which, as stated, poses "the issue," was delivered to the printer so that the printing could commence as soon as possible and the publication presumably quickly follow[21]—at precisely that moment a pseudonym, most appropriately in a

XIII
498

---

*This again is the dialectical movement (like that in which a religious author *begins* with esthetic writing, and like that in which, instead of loving oneself and one's advantage and supporting one's endeavor by illusions, one instead, hating oneself, removes illusions), or it is the dialectical method: in *working* also to *work against oneself*, which is reduplication [*Redupplikation*] and the heterogeneity of all true godly endeavor to secular endeavor. To endeavor or to work *directly* is to work or to endeavor directly in immediate connection with a factually given state of things. The dialectical method is the *reverse*: in working also to work against oneself, a redoubling [*Fordoblelse*], which is "the earnestness," like the pressure on the plow that determines the depth of the furrow, whereas the direct endeavor is a glossing-over, which is finished more rapidly and also is much, much more rewarding—that is, it is worldliness and homogeneity.

newspaper article,[22] made the greatest possible effort to alienate the public* and after that began the decisively religious production. For the second time I religiously affirmed "that single individual," to whom the next substantial book** (after *Concluding Postscript*), *Upbuilding Discourses in Various Spirits*, or the first part of the same book, "Confessional Address," was dedicated. Perhaps nobody paid much attention to the category "that single individual" the first time I used it, nor was much notice paid to its being repeated unchanged in the preface to every volume of upbuilding discourses. When I the second time or in the second potency repeated the message and stood by my first message, everything was done that I was able to do to make the whole weight of emphasis fall upon this category. Here again the move-

XIII
499

ment is: *to arrive at* the simple; the movement is: *from* the public *to* "the single individual."[25] In other words, there is in a *religious sense* no public but only individuals,†[26] because the religious is earnestness, and earnestness is: the single individual; yet every human being, unconditionally every human being, which one indeed is, can be, yes, should be—the single individual. Thus it was and is a joy to me, the upbuilding author, that also from that moment the number of those increased who became aware of[29] this about *the single individual*. It was and is a joy to me, for I certainly do have faith in the rightness of my thought despite the whole world, but next to that the last thing I would surrender is my faith in individual human beings. And this is my faith, that

*Just one thing more, the press of literary contemptibility had achieved a frightfully disproportionate coverage. To be honest, I believed that what I did was a public benefaction; it was rewarded by several of those for whose sake I had exposed myself in that way—rewarded, yes, as an act of love is usually rewarded in the world—and by means of this reward it became a truly Christian work of love.[23]

**The little literary review of the novel *Two Ages*[24] followed *Concluding Postscript* so closely that it is almost concurrent and is, after all, something written by me *qua* critic and not *qua* author; but it does contain in the last section a sketch of the future from the point of view of "the single individual," a sketch of the future that the year 1848 did not falsify.

†And insofar as there is the *congregation* in the religious sense, this is a concept that lies on the other side of *the single individual*,[27] and that above all must not be confused with what *politically* can have validity: the public, the crowd, the numerical, etc.[28]

however much confusion and evil and contemptibleness there can be in human beings as soon as they become the irresponsible and unrepentant "public," "crowd," etc.—there is just as much truth and goodness and lovableness in them when one can get them as single individuals. Oh, to what degree human beings would become—human and lovable beings—if they would become single individuals before God!

XIII
500
[30]This is how I *now* understand the whole. From the beginning I could not quite see what has indeed also been my own development. This is scarcely the place for a lengthy account. Here it is just a matter of being able very briefly to fold together in simplicity what is unfolded in the many books or what unfolded is the many books, and this brief communication is more immediately prompted by the fact that the first book in the authorship now comes out the second time, the new edition of *Either/Or*,[31] which I earlier was unwilling to have published.

Personally—also when I consider my own inner sufferings, which I personally may have deserved—personally, one thing absorbs me unconditionally, is more important to me and lies more upon my heart than the whole authorship: to express as honestly and as strongly as possible something for which I can never adequately give thanks and which I, when I at some time have forgotten the whole authorship, will eternally recollect unchanged—how infinitely much more Governance has done for me than I had ever expected, could have expected, or dared to have expected.

––––––––––

XIII
501
[32]*"Without authority"* **to make aware** of the religious, the essentially Christian, is the category for my whole work as an author regarded as a totality. From the very beginning I have enjoined and repeated unchanged that I was "without authority." I regard myself rather as a *reader* of the books, not as the *author*.

[33]"Before God," religiously, when I speak with myself, I call my whole work as an author my own upbringing and development, but not in the sense as if I were now complete or completely finished with regard to needing upbringing and development.[34]

Appendix[35]

1

MY POSITION

Copenhagen, November 1850.

Never have I fought in such a way that I have said: I am the true Christian; the others are not Christians, or probably even hypocrites and the like. No, I have fought in this way: *I know what Christianity is*; I myself acknowledge my defects as a Christian— but I do know what Christianity is. And to come to know this thoroughly seems to me to be in the interest of every human being, whether one is now a Christian or a non-Christian, whether one's intention is to accept Christianity or to abandon it. But I have attacked no one, saying that he is not a Christian; I have passed judgment on no one. Indeed, the pseudonymous writer Johannes Climacus, who poses the issue of "becoming a Christian," does even the opposite, denies being a Christian[37] and accords this to the others—surely the greatest possible distance from passing judgment on others! And I myself have from the start enjoined and again and again repeated stereotypically: I am "without authority." Finally, in the last book by Anti-Climacus[38] (who has tried to disturb the illusions, especially in No. I, with the aid of the poetical that dares to say everything and the dialectical that shuns no consequences), again no one, not one, is judged. The only person mentioned by name, on whom the judgment falls that in the striving for ideality (see the thrice-repeated preface[39]) he is only a very defective Christian, the only person judged is myself—to which I willingly submit, since it is of infinite concern to me that the requirements of ideality at least be heard. But this, again, is surely the greatest distance possible from passing judgment on others.

2

MY STRATEGY

XIII
506

For a long time the strategy employed was to utilize everything to get as many as possible, everyone if possible, to accept Christianity—but then not to be so very scrupulous about whether what one got them to accept actually was Christianity. My strategy was: with the help of God to utilize everything to make clear what in truth Christianity's requirement is—even if not one single person would accept it, even if I myself might have to give up being a Christian, which in that case I would have felt obliged to acknowledge publicly. From the other side this was my strategy: instead of even in the remotest manner suggesting that Christianity is nevertheless beset by such difficulties that a defense is necessary if we human beings are to enter into it, instead of that, to present it, which is the truth, as something so infinitely high that the defense lies somewhere else, is up to us, so that we dare to call ourselves Christians, or changes into a contrite confession, that we thank God if we only dare to regard ourselves as Christians.

But this must not be forgotten either. Christianity is just as gentle as it is rigorous, just as gentle, that is, infinitely gentle. When the infinite requirement is heard and affirmed, is heard and affirmed in all its infinitude, then *grace* is offered, or grace offers itself, to which the single individual, each one individually, can then have recourse as I do; and then it works out all right. Yet it certainly is no exaggeration for infinity's requirement, the *infinite* requirement, to be presented—*infinitely* (it is indeed also in the very interest of *grace*). In another sense, it is an exaggeration only when the requirement alone is presented and grace is not introduced at all. Christianity is taken in vain, however, when the *infinite* requirement is either made finite (perhaps in view of the opinion that "this won't do at all in practical life"—something that together with their *practice* presumably must be able to impress both God in heaven and Christianity and the apostles and martyrs and truth-witnesses and the fathers) or it is even left out completely and *grace* is introduced *as a matter of course,* which, after all, means that it is taken in vain.[40]

But never, not even in the remotest way, have I made any move or attempt to carry the matter into pietistic rigor, something that is foreign to my soul and being, or to overtax the lives of people, something that would grieve the spirit in me. No. What I have wanted has been to contribute, with the aid of confessions, to bringing, if possible, into these incomplete lives as we lead them a little more truth (in the direction of being persons of ethical and ethical-religious character, of renouncing worldly sagacity, of being willing to suffer for the truth, etc.), which indeed is always something and in any case is the first condition for beginning to exist more capably. What I have wanted to prevent is that someone, confining himself to and contented with the easier and lower, thereupon goes further, abolishes the higher, goes further, sets the lower in the place of the higher, goes further, makes the higher into fantasticality and ludicrous exaggeration, the lower into wisdom and true earnestness; I have wanted to prevent people in "Christendom" from existentially taking in vain Luther and the significance of Luther's life—I have wished, if possible, to contribute to preventing this.

What was needed, among other things, was a godly satire. This I have represented, especially with the help of pseudonymous writers, who did not let me get off unscathed either. But lest any confusion could occur, lest this satire could be confused with what all too readily wants to pass itself off as satire—the profane revolt of the most deeply sunken profane powers—then I, who have represented this godly satire, then I was the very one who hurled myself against and exposed myself to that mob-revolt's profane satire.[41] In this way I have devoutly striven from the very beginning to be honest. Furthermore, even if the presentations have a sting of truth, the whole thing is nevertheless done as gently as possible inasmuch as it is only a matter of admissions and confessions, admissions and confessions that are left up to each individual to make by oneself before God. Yet perhaps this very gentleness is in another sense an inconvenience to some people; it would be much easier to dispose of the whole thing if the author were an addlepate who at every point exaggerated both the indictment and the requirement. Now, since this is not the case, presumably someone or other could get it into his head

XIII
507

to spread the story that this is the case. Yet by the help of God the attempt will surely come to naught. Yes, if I were a strong ethical-religious character—alas, instead of being hardly anything but a poet!—and therefore justified and duty-bound in proceeding more rigorously on behalf of the truth, it would no doubt be possible that I would only encounter opposition instead of finding access to my *contemporaries*. But since I am not that strong, I will surely succeed in finding access to my *contemporaries*, therefore not on the basis of my perfection, a confession I think I owe to the truth.

With regard to an "established order," I have consistently— since my position has indeed been *the single individual*, with polemical aim at the numerical, the crowd, etc.—always done the very opposite of attacking. I have never been or been along with the "opposition" that wants to do away with "government" but have always provided what is called a *corrective*, which for God's sake wishes that there might be governing by those who are officially appointed and called, that fearing God they might stand firm, willing only one thing—the good.[42] I have thereby managed to have a falling out with the opposition and the public; yes, at times I have in addition even had to put up with disapproval by some perhaps less informed public official. —Provided an ecclesiastical established order understands itself, it will to the same degree understand the latest book, *Practice in Christianity*, as an attempt to find, ideally, a basis for an established order. I was not immediately willing to state this (which, incidentally, the preface expresses directly by stating how I understand the book) as directly* as I do here, in order, in the interest of truth, not to spare myself with regard to what, reasonably or unreasonably, was still a possibility, in order not to evade the difficulties and dangers that could arise if the established order had taken it upon itself to

XIII
508

---

*It cannot be said *directly* that the book (except for the editor's preface, which stands by itself) is a defense of the established order, since the communication is doubly reflected; it can also be just the opposite or be understood as such. This is why I directly say only that an established order that understands itself must understand it in this way; all doubly reflected communication makes contrary understandings equally possible; then the one who passes judgment is disclosed by the way he judges.

XIII
508

change the communication into opposition, which would have opened an alarming glimpse into the religious condition of the established order, but, praise God, this did not happen. It was, however, possible that the trivial, the comical, could still happen, that some well-informed public official, for whom it alone is enough that I am not a public official, comes rushing to defend and protect the established order against this—yes, against what at present is certainly the potential defense for an established order if it understands itself.[43]

In the year 1848[44] the threads of sagacity broke; the shriek that announces chaos was heard![45] "It was the year 1848; it was a step forward." Well, yes, if "government" is achieved for which not a single new official is needed or the dismissal of any older official,[46] but perhaps an internal transformation in the direction of becoming steadfast by fearing God. Certainly the mistake from above was that on the whole the strength throughout the government from top to bottom was essentially secular sagacity, which essentially is precisely the lack of strength. The fault from below was to want to do away with all government. The punishment, since the mode of the sin is always the mode of the punishment, the punishment is: that which comes to be most bitterly missed is precisely—government. Never as in our century have any generation and the individuals within it (the ruler and those ruled, the superiors and the subordinates, the teachers and those taught, etc.) been so emancipated as now from all the inconvenience, if you will, of something standing and necessarily standing unconditionally firm. Never have "opinions" (the most diverse and in the most various spheres), "in freedom, equality, and fraternity," felt so unconstrained and so blissfully happy with the free pass "to a certain degree"; never will a generation so deeply come to sense that what it and every individual in it needs is that something stands and must stand unconditionally firm, needs what the deity, divine love in love, invented—the unconditional, for which humankind, sagacious to its own corruption, in self-admiration substituted this much-admired "to a certain degree."

Command the seaman to sail without ballast—he capsizes; let the generation, let every individual in it try to exist without the unconditional—it is and remains a vortex. In the intervening period, for a longer or shorter time, it may seem otherwise, that there is steadfastness and security—fundamentally it is and remains a vortex. Even the greatest events and the most strenuous lives are nevertheless a vortex or like sewing without fastening the end[47]—until the end is once again fastened by the application of the unconditional, or by the single individual's relating himself to an unconditional, even though at ever so great a distance. To live only in the unconditional, to breathe [*indaande*] only the unconditional—the human being cannot do this; he perishes like the fish that must live in the air. But on the other hand a human being cannot in the deeper sense *live* without relating himself to the unconditional; he expires [*udaande*], that is, perhaps goes on living, but spiritlessly [*aandløst*]. If—to stick to my subject, the religious—if the generation, or a great number of individuals in the generation, has outgrown the childishness that another human being is the one who represents the unconditional for them—well, nevertheless one cannot thereby do without the unconditional; rather, one can all the less do without it. Thus *the single individual* must personally relate himself to the unconditional. This is what I to the best of my ability and with maximum effort and much sacrifice have fought for, fighting against every tyranny, also the tyranny of the numerical. This endeavor of mine has incurred opprobrium as enormous pride and arrogance—I believed, and[48] I do believe, that this is Christianity and love for "the neighbor."[49]

THE POINT OF VIEW
FOR MY WORK AS AN AUTHOR

A DIRECT COMMUNICATION,
REPORT TO HISTORY

by S. Kierkegaard

In jedem Dinge muss die
  Absicht
mit der Thorheit auf die
Wagschale gelegt werden
[In everything the purpose
must be placed on
the scale with the folly].
  SHAKESPEARE

What shall I say? No weight
My poor words have, like
  crumbs.
O God, your wisdom is so great,
Your goodness, power, your
  royal realm.
  BRORSON

Published by P. Chr. Kierkegaard [1859]

A point has been reached in my authorship where it is feasible, where I feel a need and therefore regard it now as my duty: once and for all to explain as directly and openly and specifically as possible what is what, what I say I am as an author.[2] The moment, however unfavorable in another sense, has come, partly because, as stated, this point has been reached, and partly because I now will meet for the second time my first work in literature, the second edition of *Either/Or*,[3] which I previously was unwilling to allow to be published.

There is a time to be silent and a time to speak.[4] As long as I religiously considered the strictest silence as my duty, I strove in every way to preserve it. Nor have I hesitated—as is consistent with silence and mysteriousness and doubleness—in a *finite* sense to work against my effort. What I have done in this regard has been misunderstood, interpreted as pride, arrogance, and God knows what. Since I have religiously considered silence as my duty, I have not done the least thing to remove this misunderstanding. But I considered silence as my duty, because the authorship was not yet at hand in its totality and thus the understanding could be only a misunderstanding.

The content, then, of this little book is: what I in truth am as an author, that I am and was a religious author, that my whole authorship pertains to Christianity, to the issue: becoming a Christian, with direct and indirect polemical aim at that enormous illusion, Christendom, or the illusion that in such a country all are Christians of sorts.

I request everyone who truly has the cause of Christianity at heart, and I request more urgently him who has it at heart more earnestly, to become acquainted with this little book, not inquisitively, but thoughtfully, as one reads a religious book. Because I am a religious author, it of course is on the whole a matter of indifference to me whether a so-called esthetic public has found or would be able to find some enjoyment through reading the esthetic works, or through reading the esthetic in the works, which is the incognito and the deception in the service of Christianity. If it is assumed that such a reader perfectly understands and judges the particular esthetic work, he totally misunderstands me, since he does not understand it in the religious totality of my work as an author. If, however, it is assumed that someone who understands my work as an author in its religious totality perhaps does not understand a particular esthetic work, then this misunderstanding is only incidental.

What I write here is for orientation and attestation—it is not a defense or an apologetics. If in nothing else, on this point I truly believe that I have something in common with Socrates. Just as the daimon of Socrates, when Socrates was accused and about to be sentenced by "the crowd," he who felt himself to be a divine gift,[5] forbade him to *defend* himself[6]—indeed, what an impropriety and self-contradiction it would have been!—so also there is in me and in the dialectical nature of my relationship something that makes it impossible for me and impossible in itself to conduct a "defense" of my authorship. I have put up with a great deal; I hope—yet who knows, the future may be more gentle than the past—to be able to put up with more without losing myself. The only thing I could not put up with and could not do without losing myself and the dialectical in my relationship (which is precisely what I could not put up with) is to *defend* myself *qua* author. It would be an untruth, which even if it meaninglessly helped me to gain the whole world[7] would eternally become my downfall.

Humble before God, also before people, I know very well what offenses I *personally* may have committed. But I also know with God that precisely my work as an author was the prompting of an irresistible inner need, the only possibility for a depressed person, an honest indemnifying attempt by one deeply humbled, a penitent, to make up, if possible, for something by means of every sacrifice and effort in the service of the truth. Therefore I know with God, before whose eyes the undertaking found and finds favor as it rejoices in his assistance, that in connection with my authorship I am not one who must defend myself before my contemporaries, because, if I am anything in this regard, I am not the guilty party, nor counsel for the defense, but counsel for the prosecution.

Yet neither do I accuse my contemporaries, just because I have religiously understood it as my duty to serve the truth this way in self-denial, that it was my task in every way to keep from becoming the esteemed, the beloved. Only the one who personally understands what true self-denial is, only he can solve my riddle and see that it is self-denial. The one who does not personally understand it may rather call my conduct self-love, pride, eccentricity, madness, for all of which I, consistently, do not indict him, because in my service of self-denial I myself have indeed contributed to it. There is unconditionally one thing that can be understood neither by a noisy assembly nor by an esteemed public, nor in a half-hour, and that is: what Christian self-denial is. In order to understand this, much fear and trembling, quiet solitude, are required, and for a long time.

That I have understood the truth I am presenting—of that I am absolutely convinced. I am just as convinced that my contemporaries, insofar as they do not understand the same thing, will be forced by fair or foul means to understand it when in eternity they have been freed from many of the disturbing worries and hardships from which I have been freed and in eternity they have found the stillness of earnestness, solitude, and time enough to think. Therefore, however much misunderstanding I have suffered (from this it does not follow that because I voluntarily exposed myself to it I cannot *actually* suffer, for in that case all true Christian suffering, which is voluntary, is annulled; nor from this does it follow summarily and plainly that "the others" have no guilt; then surely it is true that I am suffering this in the service of truth), I cannot do anything else than to thank God— not because I am suffering in this way, but for what infinitely occupies me—that he allows me to understand the truth.

And then just one more thing. It is self-evident that I cannot present completely an explanation of my work as an author, that is, with the purely personal inwardness in which I possess the explanation. In part it is because I cannot make my God-relationship public in this way, since it is neither more nor less than the universally human inwardness, which every human

XIII
520

being can have without any special call, which it would be a crime to suppress and a duty to stress, and to which I could not lay claim or make an appeal. In part it is because I cannot wish (and no one, I am sure, could desire that I do so) to press upon anyone something that pertains solely to my private character, which of course for me contains much of the explanation of my author-character.[8]

Part One

The Equivocalness or Duplexity
in the Whole Authorship,*
Whether the Author Is an Esthetic or
a Religious Author

Accordingly, what is to be shown here is that there *is* such a duplexity from beginning to end. It is not, then, as is ordinarily the case with a supposed duplexity, that others have discovered it and it is the task of the person concerned to show that it *is not*. By no means, just the opposite. Insofar as the reader might not be sufficiently aware of the duplexity, it is the author's task to make it as obvious as possible that it is there. In other words, the duplexity, the equivocalness, is deliberate, is something the author knows about more than anyone else, is the essential dialectical qualification of the whole authorship, and therefore has a deeper basis.

But is this really the case, is there such a sustained duplexity? Can the phenomenon not be explained in another way, that it is an author who was first an esthetic author and then in the course of years *changed* and became a religious author? I will not now discuss the point that if this were so the author certainly would not have written a book such as the present one, would scarcely, I dare say, have taken it upon himself to give an overview of the writing as a whole, at least would not have chosen to do so at

---

*In order to have them at hand, here are the titles of the books. First division (esthetic writing): *Either/Or, Fear and Trembling, Repetition, The Concept of Anxiety, Prefaces, Philosophical Fragments, Stages on Life's Way*—together with eighteen upbuilding discourses, which came out successively. Second division: *Concluding Unscientific Postscript*. Third division (only religious writing): *Upbuilding Discourses in Various Spirits, Works of Love, Christian Discourses*—together with a little esthetic article: *The Crisis and a Crisis in the Life of an Actress.*⁹

the very time he meets his first work again.[10] Nor will I discuss the point that it would indeed be odd that such a change would occur in the course of so few years. Ordinarily, when it is seen that an esthetic author becomes a religious author, at least a considerable number of years intervenes, so that the explanation of the change is not implausible, so that it is consistent with the author's actually having become significantly older. But I will not discuss this, since even if it were odd, almost inexplicable, even if it might make one inclined to seek and find any other explanation, it would still not be impossible that such a change could occur in the course of three years. On the contrary, I will show that it is impossible to explain the phenomenon in this way. If, namely, one looks more closely, one will see that three years are certainly not allowed for the occurrence of the change, but that the change is concurrent with the beginning, that is, that the duplexity is there from the very beginning. *Two Upbuilding Discourses* is concurrent with *Either/Or.* The duplexity in the deeper sense, that is, in the sense of the whole authorship, was certainly not what there was talk about at the time: the first and second parts of *Either/Or.* No, the duplexity was: *Either/Or*— and *Two Upbuilding Discourses.*

The religious is present from the very beginning. Conversely, the esthetic is still present even in the last moment. After the publication of only religious works for two years, a little esthetic article follows.* Therefore, at the beginning and at the end, there is assurance against explaining the phenomenon by saying that the writer is an esthetic author who in the course of time had changed and had become a religious author. Just as *Two Upbuilding Discourses* came out approximately two or three months after *Either/Or,* so also that little esthetic article appeared about two or three months after two years of exclusively religious writings. The two upbuilding discourses and the little article match each other conversely and conversely show that the duplexity is both first and last. Although *Either/Or* attracted all the attention and no one paid attention to *Two Upbuilding Discourses,* this nevertheless signified that it was specifically the upbuilding that should

---

***The Crisis and a Crisis in the Life of an Actress. Fædrelandet,* July 1848.

advance, that the author was a religious author who for that reason never wrote anything esthetic himself but used pseudonyms for all the esthetic works, whereas the two upbuilding discourses were by Magister Kierkegaard. Conversely, whereas the exclusively upbuilding books of the two years may have attracted the attention of others, perhaps no one in turn has noticed in the deeper sense the little article, what it signifies—that now the dialectical structure of this whole authorship is complete. The little article is an accompaniment precisely for documentation, for the sake of confrontation, in order at the end to make it impossible (as the two upbuilding discourses do at the beginning) to explain the phenomenon in this way—that it is an author who in the beginning was an esthetic author and then later *changed* and thus became a religious author—inasmuch as he was a religious author from the very beginning and is esthetically productive at the last moment.

The first division of books is esthetic writing; the last division of books is exclusively religious writing—between these lies *Concluding Unscientific Postscript* as the *turning point*. This work deals with and poses *the issue*, the issue of the entire work as an author: becoming a Christian. Then in turn it calls attention* to the pseudonymous writing along with the interlaced 18 discourses[11] and shows all this as serving to illuminate the issue, yet without stating that this was the object of the prior writing— which could not be done, since it is a pseudonymous writer[12] who is interpreting other pseudonymous writers, that is, a third party who could know nothing about the object of writings unfamiliar to him. *Concluding Unscientific Postscript* is not esthetic writing, but, strictly speaking, neither is it religious. That is why it is by a pseudonymous writer, although I did place my name as editor, which I have not done with any purely esthetic production**—a hint, at least for someone who is concerned with or has

---

*See pp. 187–227 [*SV* VII 212–257; *KW* XII.1, pp. 251–300], a section with which I would ask the reader to become familiar.

**The literary review of *Two Ages* is no argument against this, both because it is not, after all, esthetic in the sense of being a poet-production but is critical, and because it has a totally religious background in its understanding of "the present age."

a sense for such things. Then came the two years in which there appeared only religious writings under my name. The time of the pseudonyms was over; the religious author had extricated himself from the disguise of the esthetic—and then, then for documentation and by way of a precaution came the little esthetic article by a pseudonymous writer: Inter et Inter. In a way it at once calls attention to the whole authorship; as said previously, it calls to mind conversely *Two Upbuilding Discourses*.

XIII
524

B

The Explanation: That the Author Is and Was a Religious Author

It might seem that a simple declaration by the author himself in this regard is more than adequate; after all, he must know best what is what. I do not, however, think much of declarations in connection with literary productions and am accustomed to take a completely objective attitude to my own. If in the capacity of a third party, as a reader, I cannot substantiate from the writings that what I am saying is the case, that it cannot be otherwise, it could never occur to me to want to win what I thus consider as lost. If I *qua* author must first make declarations, I easily alter all the writing, which from first to last is dialectical.

Consequently I am unable to make any declaration, at least not until I in some other way have made the explanation so obvious that the declaration in that sense is entirely superfluous, because then it can be *admitted* as a lyrical satisfaction, insofar as I feel a need for it, and it can be *demanded* as a religious duty. In other words, *qua* human being I may be justified in making a declaration, and from the religious point of view it may be my duty to make a declaration. But this must not be confused with the authorship—*qua* author it does not help very much that I *qua* human being declare that I have intended this and that. But presumably everyone will admit that if it can be shown that such and such a phenomenon cannot be explained in any other way, and that on the other hand it can in this way be explained at every point, or that this explanation fits at every point, then the correctness of this explanation is substantiated as clearly as the correctness of an explanation can ever be substantiated.

But is there not a contradiction here? If it is substantiated in the preceding that the equivocalness is present to the very last, to the same degree as this succeeds, to the same degree it is made impossible to substantiate which is the explanation, then to that extent a statement, a declaration, seems here to be the only way to break the dialectical tension and knot. This seems very perspicacious [*skarpsindig*] and yet is actually only subtle [*spidsfindig*]. If, for example, someone in a certain situation found a mystification necessary, it is perfectly consistent with subtlety for him to do it in such a way that—the comic emerges—that he himself cannot make head nor tail of it. But this is also a lack of earnestness and an infatuation with mystification in and for itself instead of having its teleological truth. Thus where a mystification, a dialectical redoubling [*Fordoblelse*], is used in the service of earnestness, it will be used in such a way that it only wards off misunderstandings and preliminary understandings, while the true explanation is available to the person who is honestly seeking. To use the supreme example: Christ's whole life here on earth would indeed have become a game if he had been so incognito that he had gone through life totally unnoticed—and yet he truly was incognito.

So also with a dialectical redoubling, and the dialectical redoubling is that the equivocalness is maintained. Once the requisite earnestness takes hold, it can also solve it, but always only in such a way that the earnestness itself vouches for the correctness. Just as a woman's demureness relates to the true lover, and then, but only then yields, so also a dialectical redoubling relates to true earnestness. Therefore the explanation cannot be communicated to a less earnest person, since the elasticity of the dialectical doubleness is too great for him to manage; it takes the explanation away from him again and makes it dubious for him whether it is indeed the explanation.

Let us make the attempt; let us try to explain this whole authorship on the assumption that it is the work of an esthetic author. It will readily be seen that from the beginning this explanation is not in accord with the phenomenon but promptly runs aground on *Two Upbuilding Discourses*. If, however, we attempt to explain the authorship by assuming that it is the work of a religious author, we will see that step by step it tallies at every point. The only thing inexplicable is how it ever occurred to a religious author to use the esthetic in this way. That is, we are once again face-to-face with the equivocalness or the dialectical redoubling. The difference is only that the assumption that it is a religious author will have been established and the task is to explain the equivocalness. Whether another person can do this, I do not decide; but the explanation is what becomes the content of the second part of this little book.

XIII
526

Just one more thing—which, as stated, both can lyrically satisfy me *qua* human being and is for me *qua* human being my religious duty: namely, a direct declaration that the author was and is a religious author. When I began *Either/Or* (of which, speaking *in parenthesi* [parenthetically], there existed literally only about one page, namely, a few Diapsalmata,[13] whereas the whole book was written in eleven months and the second part first), I was *potentialiter* [in potentiality] as deeply influenced by the religious as I ever became. I was so profoundly shaken that I basically understood that I could not possibly succeed in finding the calm, secure middle course in which most people have their lives—I either had to plunge into despair and sensuality or absolutely choose the religious as the one and only—either the world on a scale that would be dreadful or the monastery. That it was the latter I would and must choose was basically decided. The eccentricity of the first movement was only the expression for the intensity of the second, that I had come to understand how impossible it would be for me to be sort of religious to a certain degree. Here lies *Either/Or*. It was a poetical emptying, which did not, however, go further than the ethical. Personally, I was far from tranquilly wanting to summon existence back to marriage, I who religiously was already in the monastery—an idea concealed in the pseudonym *Victor—Eremita* [the Hermit].

This is how it stands. Strictly speaking, *Either/Or* was written in a monastery, and I can attest (a declaration that is addressed especially to such persons, if they should happen to see this little book, who perhaps have neither the capacity nor the opportunity to survey such a production but who may yet be disturbed by my authorship's odd merging of the religious and the esthetic), I can attest that the author of *Either/Or* regularly and with monastic scrupulousness spent a certain period of each day reading devotional writings for his own sake, that in fear and much trembling he considered his responsibility. He particularly had in mind "The Seducer's Diary" (how strange!). And then what happened? The book was an enormous success, especially "The Seducer's Diary" (how strange!). The world opened up, even to a remarkable degree, to the admired author, who, however, was not "seduced" or changed by all this—for that he was an eternity too old.

Then followed *Two Upbuilding Discourses*—what is most important often seems so insignificant. The big work, *Either/Or*, which was "much read and even more discussed"—and then *Two Upbuilding Discourses*, dedicated to my late father,[14] published on my birthday (May 5),[15] "a little flower under the cover of the great forest, sought neither for its splendor nor for its fragrance nor its food value."* There was no one who in the profounder sense paid any attention to or cared about the two discourses; indeed, I even recall that one of my acquaintances came to me and complained that he had in good faith gone and bought them, thinking that since they were by me they must be something rather witty and clever. I also recall that I promised him that he would have his money back if he so desired. With my left hand I passed *Either/Or* out into the world, with my right hand *Two Upbuilding Discourses*; but they all or almost all took the left hand with their right.**

Before God I had made up my mind what I wanted; my preference was for the two upbuilding discourses, but I certainly understood that very few understood this†—and here for the first

---

*See the Preface to *Two Upbuilding Discourses*, 1843.[16]

**See the preface to *Two Upbuilding Discourses* (1844): It seeks *my* reader, who with the right hand accepts what is offered with the right hand.[17]

†This accounts for the sadness in that preface when it says of the little book: "Inasmuch as in being published it is in a figurative sense starting a journey, I let my eyes follow it for a little while. I saw how it wended its way down solitary paths or walked solitary on public roads. After a few little mistakes, through being deceived by a fleeting resemblance, it finally met that single individual whom I with joy and gratitude call *my* reader, that single individual it is seeking, to whom, so to speak, it stretches out its arms" etc.[18] See the preface to *Two Upbuilding Discourses* (1843). On the whole, this first preface had and has for me an utterly unique intimate meaning, which of course cannot be communicated as such.

time comes the category: that *single individual*,[19] "that single individual whom I with joy and gratitude call *my* reader," which was repeated unchanged in the preface to every collection of upbuilding discourses. I cannot truly be charged with having changed, with perhaps having at a later time judged the public differently than previously because I possibly was not on such good terms with it. No, if I have ever been on good terms with the public, this relation was highest or at its peak in the second or third month after the publication of *Either/Or*. This very situation—for many perhaps tempting, but to my thinking advantageous only for being able to get a good showing for what I had to do—I used in the service of truth to introduce my category *that single individual*. It was at that very moment that I made a break with the public, not out of pride or arrogance etc. (and certainly not because the public was unfavorable toward me at the time, since, the very opposite, it was altogether favorable toward me), but because I had made up my mind that I was a religious author whose concern is with *the single individual*, an idea (*the single individual* versus *the public*) in which a whole life- and worldview is concentrated.

XIII
528

From now on, that is, as early as *Fear and Trembling*,[20] the earnest observer who himself has religious presuppositions at his disposal, the earnest observer to whom one can make oneself understood at a distance and to whom one can speak in silence (the pseudonym: *Johannes—de Silentio*), became aware that this surely was a very singular kind of esthetic production; and here the most worthy firm Kts[21] placed the proper emphasis, which pleased me very much.

Part Two

THE AUTHORSHIP VIEWED AS A
WHOLE, AND FROM THE POINT OF
VIEW THAT THE AUTHOR IS A
RELIGIOUS AUTHOR

A

THE ESTHETIC WRITING

WHY THE BEGINNING WAS MADE WITH ESTHETIC WRITING, OR WHAT THIS

WRITING, UNDERSTOOD IN THE TOTALITY,* SIGNIFIES

§1

"Christendom" Is an Enormous Illusion

Everyone who in earnest and also with some clarity of vision considers what is called Christendom, or the condition in a so-called Christian country, must without any doubt immediately have serious misgivings. What does it mean, after all, that all these thousands and thousands as a matter of course call themselves Christians! These many, many people, of whom by far the great majority, according to everything that can be discerned, have their lives in entirely different categories, something one can ascertain by the simplest observation! People who perhaps never once go to church, never think about God, never name his name except when they curse! People to whom it has never occurred that their lives should have some duty to God, people who either maintain that a certain civil impunity is the highest or do not find even this to be entirely necessary! Yet all these people, even those who insist that there is no God, they all are Christians, call themselves Christians, are recognized as Christians by the state, are buried as Christians by the Church, are discharged as Christians to eternity!

XIII
530

That there must be an enormous underlying confusion here, a dreadful illusion, of that there can surely be no doubt. But to touch on this! Yes, I am well aware of the objection! There

---

*Once and for all I must urgently request the kindly disposed reader continually to bear *in mente* [in mind] that the total thought in the entire work as an author is this: becoming a Christian.

surely are this one and that one who understand what I mean but who then with a certain good-naturedness would pat me on the shoulder and say, "My dear friend, you are still rather young—and then to want to begin such a project, a project that, if it is to have any success at all, would require at least a dozen well-trained missionaries, a project that amounts to neither more nor less than wanting to introduce Christianity again—into Christendom. No, dear friend, let us be human beings; such a project is beyond both your power and mine. This project is just as insanely grandiose as wanting to reform 'the crowd,' which no sensible person gets involved with but lets it be what it is. To begin on such a thing is sure disaster." Perhaps, but even if it is or would be sure disaster, it is also certain that the objection has not been learned from Christianity, because when Christianity entered into the world it was even more decidedly sure disaster to begin on it—yet it was begun; and it is also certain that this objection was not learned from Socrates, because he involved himself with "the crowd" and wanted to reform it.

This is just about the way things are. Every once in a while a pastor makes a little fuss in the pulpit about there being something not quite right with all these many Christians—but all those who hear him and who are present there, consequently all those he is speaking *to*, are Christians, and of course he is not speaking to those he is speaking *about*. This is most appropriately called simulated motion. —Every once in a while a religious enthusiast appears. He makes an assault on Christendom; he makes a big noise, denounces nearly all as not being Christians—and he accomplishes nothing. He does not take into account that an illusion is not so easy to remove. If it is the case that most people are under an illusion when they call themselves Christians, what do they do about an enthusiast like that? First and foremost, they pay no attention to him at all, do not read his book but promptly lay it *ad acta* [aside]; or if he makes use of the Living Word,[22] they go around on another street and do not listen to him at all. Then by means of a definition they smuggle him outside and settle down quite securely in their illusion. They make him out to be a fanatic and his Christianity to be an exag-

XIII
531

geration—in the end he becomes the only one, or one of the few, who is not a Christian in earnest (since exaggeration, after all, is a lack of earnestness); the others are all earnest Christians.

No, an illusion can never be removed directly, and basically only indirectly. If it is an illusion that all are Christians, and if something is to be done, it must be done indirectly, not by someone who loudly declares himself to be an extraordinary Christian, but by someone who, better informed, even declares himself not to be a Christian.* That is, one who is under an illusion must be approached from behind. Instead of wanting to have for oneself the advantage of being the rare Christian, one must let the one ensnared have the advantage that he is a Christian, and then oneself have sufficient resignation to be the one who is far behind him—otherwise one will surely fail to extricate him from the illusion; it can be difficult enough anyway.

If, then, according to the assumption, most people in Christendom are Christians only in imagination, in what categories do they live? They live in esthetic or, at most, esthetic-ethical categories.

On the assumption, then, that a religious author has from the ground up become aware of this illusion, Christendom, and to the limit of his ability with, note well, the help of God, wants to stamp it out—what is he to do then? Well, first and foremost, no impatience. If he becomes impatient, then he makes a direct assault and accomplishes—nothing. By a direct attack he only strengthens a person in the illusion and also infuriates him. Generally speaking, there is nothing that requires as gentle a treatment as the removal of an illusion. If one in any way causes the one ensnared to be antagonized, then all is lost. And this one does by a direct attack, which in addition also contains the presumptuousness of demanding that another person confess to one or face-to-face with one make the confession that actually is most beneficial when the person concerned makes it to himself secretly. The latter is achieved by the indirect method, which in

XIII
532

---

*One recalls *Concluding Unscientific Postscript*, whose author, Johannes Climacus, directly declares that he himself is not a Christian.[23]

the service of the love of truth dialectically arranges everything for the one ensnared and then, modest as love always is, avoids being witness to the confession that he makes alone before God, the confession that he has been living in an illusion.

Therefore the religious author first of all must try to establish rapport with people. That is, he must begin with an esthetic piece. This is earnest money. The more brilliant the piece is, the better it is for him. Next, he must be sure of himself, or rather he must in fear and trembling relate himself to God (the surest and the only surety), lest the opposite happen, so that he does not become the one who gives the others a start but the others become the ones who get power over him and then he ends up becoming stuck in the esthetic himself. Therefore he must have everything prepared in order, yet without any impatience, to bring forth the religious as swiftly as possible as soon as he has gained their attention, so that with the momentum of being engrossed in the esthetic the same people come face-to-face with the religious.

The point is to introduce the religious neither too speedily nor too slowly. If too long a time intervenes, there immediately arises the illusion that now the esthetic author has become older and therefore religious. If it comes too swiftly, the effect is not strong enough.

On the assumption that it is an enormous illusion that all these many people call themselves and are regarded as being Christians, there is no judgment and condemnation in this approach. It is a true Christian invention, cannot be practiced without fear and trembling, only in true self-denial. The helper is precisely the one who carries all the responsibility and has all the strain. But that is why this approach has intrinsic worth. Ordinarily it holds true that an approach has worth only in proportion to what is achieved by it. One judges and condemns, makes a big noise—this has no intrinsic worth, but one reckons on achieving a great deal thereby. It is different with the approach described here. Assume that a person had devoted his whole life to using it, assume that he had practiced it all his life, and assume that he had achieved nothing—he nevertheless has by no means lived in vain, because his life was true self-denial.

§ 2

If One Is Truly to Succeed in Leading a Person to a Specific Place,
One Must First and Foremost Take Care to Find Him
*Where **He** Is and Begin There*

This is the secret in the entire art of helping. Anyone who cannot do this is himself under a delusion if he thinks he is able to help someone else. In order truly to help someone else, I must understand more than he—but certainly first and foremost understand what he understands. If I do not do that, then my greater understanding does not help him at all. If I nevertheless want to assert my greater understanding, then it is because I am vain or proud, then basically instead of benefiting him I really want to be admired by him. But all true helping begins with a humbling. The helper must first humble himself under the person he wants to help and thereby understand that to help is not to dominate but to serve, that to help is not to be the most dominating but the most patient, that to help is a willingness for the time being to put up with being in the wrong and not understanding what the other understands.

Consider a person who is impassioned about something, granted that he actually is in the wrong. If you cannot begin with him in such a way that it seems as if it is he who should teach you, and if you cannot do this in such a way that he, who impatiently refuses to listen to a word from you, is gratified to find in you a willing and attentive listener—if you cannot do that, then you cannot help him either. Consider an infatuated person who became unhappy in love; assume that it is actually indefensible, sinful, and unchristian to surrender to his passion as he does. If you cannot begin in such a way with him that he finds genuine alleviation in speaking with you about his suffering, in such a way that you, in what you add concerning his suffering, almost enrich him with a poetical view, you who still do not share the passion and specifically want to have him out of it—if you cannot do that, you cannot help him either. He shuts himself off from you, shuts himself up in his innermost being—and then you merely preach to him. Perhaps by personal power you will be able to force him to confess to you that he is in the wrong. Ah,

XIII
534

my dear fellow, the very next moment he sneaks around by another path, a secret path, to a rendezvous with the secret passion,
for which he now longs all the more; yes, he has almost become
afraid that it would have lost some of its seductive fervor—for
now by your behavior you have helped him to fall in love once
again, namely, with his unhappy passion—and then you only
preach!

So it is also with becoming a Christian, under the assumption
that it is a delusion on the part of the multitude in Christendom
who call themselves Christian. Denounce the bewitchery of the
esthetic—well, there have been times when you thereby might
have succeeded in coercing people. Yes, to what end?—to love
in their secret heart that bewitchery even more fanatically with
clandestine passion. No, let it come forward—and you earnest,
rigorous man, remember that if you cannot humble yourself you
are not the earnest one either—be the astonished listener who sits
and listens to what delights that other person, whom it delights
even more that you listen in that way. But above all do not forget
one thing, the number carried [*Mente*[24]] that you have, that it is
the religious that you are to have come forward. Or, if you are
able to do so, portray the esthetic with all its bewitching charm,
if possible captivate the other person, portray it with the kind of
passionateness whereby it appeals particularly to him, hilariously
to the hilarious, sadly to the sad, wittily to the witty, etc.—but
above all do not forget one thing, the number carried that you
have, that it is the religious that is to come forward. Just do it; do
not fear to do it, for truly it can be done only in much fear and
trembling.

If you can do it, if you can very accurately find the place where
the other person is and begin there, then you can perhaps have
the good fortune of leading him to the place where you are.

To be a teacher is not to say: This is the way it is, nor is it to
assign lessons and the like. No, to be a teacher is truly to be the
learner. Instruction begins with this, that you, the teacher, learn
from the learner, place yourself in what he has understood and
how he has understood it, if you yourself have not understood it
previously, or that you, if you have understood it, then let him
examine you, as it were, so that he can be sure that you know

your lesson. This is the introduction; then the beginning can be made in another sense.

This is why I continually have inwardly raised an objection to a certain party of the orthodox here, that they band together in a little circle and strengthen one another in thinking that they are the only Christians—and thus do not know anything else to do with all Christendom than to declare that they are not Christians. If it is true that there actually are so few true Christians in Christendom, then these are *eo ipso* [precisely thereby] obliged to be missionaries, even though a missionary in Christendom will always look different from a missionary in paganism. It is obvious that this objection quite properly comes from behind, because it takes for granted the admission or assumption that these orthodox actually are true Christians, the only true Christians in Christendom.

Consequently, in Christendom the religious author, whose total thought is what it means to become a Christian, properly starts out with being an esthetic author. For a time let it be an open question whether Christendom is an enormous illusion, whether it is a delusion on the part of the multitude who call themselves Christian. Let the opposite be assumed—well, then, this beginning is a redundancy based on something that does not exist, but that does no damage. The damage is far greater, or rather this is the damage, when someone who is not Christian pretends to be that. The damage is not so great, however, if one who is a Christian gives the appearance of not being that—on the assumption that all are true Christians, it can then at most only encourage them even more in being that.

§ 3
The Illusion That Religion and Christianity Are Something to Which One Turns Only When One Becomes Older

The esthetic always overrates youth and that moment of eternity; it cannot reconcile itself with the earnestness of the years, nor with the earnestness of eternity. Therefore the esthetic has always had a suspicion about the religious person, that he either has never had a sense for the esthetic or that basically he nevertheless

XIII
535

would rather have continued belonging to it, but time exercised its deteriorating power, he became older, and then he turned to the religious. One divides life into two ages: the age of youth is the age of the esthetic; the older age is the age of religiousness—but to tell the truth we all would surely prefer to have continued to be young.

How *can* this illusion be removed—whether it will succeed is something else, but it can be removed by concurrent esthetic and religious works. Here no dubiousness is possible, because the esthetic production testifies that youth is present—then the *concurrent* religious work cannot be explained on some incidental basis.

XIII
536

On the assumption that Christendom is an enormous illusion, that it is a delusion on the part of the multitude who call themselves Christians, in all probability the illusion we are discussing here is very common. But in turn this illusion is worsened by the very delusion that one is a Christian. One goes on living one's life in esthetic categories, and if at some time a person comes to think about Christianity, he dismisses the matter until he becomes older and sufficiently reassures himself—since, he says to himself, I am after all basically a Christian. It cannot be denied that there are those in Christendom who live just as sensately as any pagan ever did—indeed, even more sensately, because they have this confounded security that basically they are Christians. But the decision to become a Christian is shoved off as long as possible—indeed, an additional obstacle has been acquired, because one takes pride in being young as long as possible—and only when one becomes old does one turn to Christianity and religiousness. One is so reluctant to make the admission that one has become old—but only when one becomes old does one turn to Christianity and religiousness.

If, therefore, one could continually stay young, one would not need either Christianity or religiousness.

For all true religiousness this is an extremely pernicious error that has its basis in our confusing becoming older in the sense of time with becoming older in the sense of eternity. It certainly cannot be denied that we more often see the scarcely upbuilding spectacle of a youthfulness that with blazing passion was the interpreter of the esthetic and then, when the time of youth was over, changed into a religiousness, in one sense too relaxed, in another sense too high-strung, that had all the faults of old age. Nor can it be denied either that many who portray the religious, out of fear that it will not be earnest enough, make it both too rigorous and too morose. This and much else can contribute to making that illusion more common and establishing it more firmly—but what good does that do? What will help is precisely that which could contribute to removing the illusion.

If, then, a religious author wants to touch on that illusion, he must in one swoop begin with simultaneously being an esthetic and a religious author. But one thing above all he must not forget, the number carried, which is which, that it is the religious that is to come forward decisively. The esthetic writing becomes a means of communication and, for the person who may need it (on the assumption that Christendom is an enormous illusion, there are many of these), evidence that the religious writing cannot possibly be explained by the author's having become older, because it is indeed concurrent—and one certainly has not become older concurrently.

Perhaps it will not succeed at all in this way, perhaps; the damage cannot be great. At most the damage can be that one does not really believe in the religiousness of such a communicator. Well, then! Often enough a communicator of the religious can be too anxious about being regarded as religious himself. If so, this simply shows that he is not in truth religious. This is similar to the situation of someone who wants to be a teacher and is too much occupied with the thought of what those he wants to teach will judge of him and his teaching, his knowledge, etc. Such a teacher really has no elbowroom at all in teaching. Suppose, for example, that for the sake of the learner he thought it most appropriate to say he did not understand something he really did understand. Heaven forbid! Out of fear that the learner would actually believe that he did not understand it, he would not dare—that is, he is really not fit to be a teacher. Although calling himself a teacher, he is so far from being one that he really aspires to be cited for excellence—by the learner. Or it is similar to the situation of a preacher of penitence who wants to castigate rigorously the vices

XIII
537

of the age—but is very much occupied with how the age he is castigating judges of him—he is so far from being a preacher of repentance that he is more a New Year's Day caller who merely makes himself a bit interesting by wearing an outfit rather odd for a New Year's Day caller. So also with *that* religious person who, if worst comes to worst, could not endure being regarded as the only one who was not religious. To be able to endure this is in reflection the most accurate definition of essential religiousness.

§ 4
Even Though a Person Refuses to Go Along to the Place to Which One Is Endeavoring to Lead Him, There Is Still One Thing That Can Be Done for Him: Compel Him to Become Aware

XIII
538

A person may have the good fortune of doing a great deal for another, may have the good fortune of leading him to the place to which he desires to lead him and, to hold to what in essence is continually under discussion here, may have the good fortune of helping that person to become a Christian. But this is not in my power; it depends upon very many things and above all upon whether he himself is willing. Compel a person to an opinion, a conviction, a belief—in all eternity, that I cannot do. But one thing I can do, in one sense the first thing (since it is the condition for the next thing: to accept this view, conviction, belief), in another sense the last thing if he refuses the next: I can compel him to become aware.

That this is a good deed, there is no doubt, but neither must it be forgotten that this is a daring venture. By compelling him to become aware, I succeed in compelling him to judge. Now he judges. But what he judges is not in my power. Perhaps he judges the very opposite of what I desire. Furthermore, that he was compelled to judge perhaps makes him infuriated, ragingly infuriated—infuriated with the cause, with me—and perhaps I become the victim of my daring venture.

To compel people to become aware and judge is namely the law for true martyrdom. A true martyr has never used power but has contended by means of powerlessness. He compelled people to become aware. Indeed, God knows, they did become aware—they put him to death. Yet he was willing to have that happen. He did not think that his death halted him in his work; he understood that his death was part of it—that the momentum of his work began precisely with his death. Truly, those who had put him to death did indeed become aware; they began to think once again about the cause and in quite another way, and what the one living was not able to do the one dead was able to do: he won to his cause those who had become aware.

The objection I have repeatedly made privately against those who ordinarily proclaim Christianity in Christendom is that they, themselves surrounded and safeguarded by all too many illusions, do not have the courage to make people aware. That is, they do not have sufficient self-denial in relation to their cause. They are eager to win adherents, but they want to win them—because this strengthens their cause—and therefore are not scrupulously careful about whether they in truth become adherents or not. This in turn means that in a deeper sense they have no cause; they relate themselves selfishly to the cause they do have. Therefore they do not actually risk going out among the people or abandoning illusions in order to make a genuine idea-impression, because they have a dim notion that it is truly a dangerous matter to make people aware. Mendaciously to make them aware, that is, to bow and scrape before them, to flatter them, to ask for their attention and lenient judgment, to submit—the truth—to balloting well, this involves no danger, at least not here in the world, where on the contrary it involves every advantage; but yet it perhaps does involve the danger of eventually failing in eternity.

This, then, is the way it stands with what has been assumed, that it is indeed a delusion on the part of the multitude who call themselves Christians. If, then, a person lives in this delusion, consequently lives in completely different, in completely esthetic categories—if, then, one is able to win and capture him completely by means of an esthetic portrayal and now knows how to introduce the religious so swiftly that with this momentum of attachment he runs straight into the most decisive categories of the religious—what then? Well, then he must become aware. Yet what follows from this no one can predict, but he must

XIII
539

become aware. It is possible that he actually comes to sober reflection on what it was supposed to mean that he has called himself a Christian. It is possible that he becomes enraged with the person who has ventured to do this to him; but he has become aware, he is beginning to judge. In order to retrieve himself, he perhaps judges the other person to be a hypocrite, a charlatan, a half lunatic—it is of no avail, he must judge, he has become aware.

Ordinarily the relationship is reversed, and the relationship was truly reversed when Christianity came in contact with paganism. What is entirely overlooked, however, is how altered the situation is, that the category Christendom sets all relationships into reflection. Ordinarily, also in Christendom, the person who is striving to lead people to become Christians employs everything in order to establish securely that he himself is a Christian; he gives assurances and assurances. He fails to note that from the beginning there is an enormous confusion here, since, after all, those whom he is addressing are Christians. But if he is addressing Christians, what then does it mean to get them to become Christians? If, however, in his opinion they are not Christians although they still call themselves Christians, the very fact that they call themselves Christians makes manifest, of course, that here is a reflection-category. Thus we are in a situation in the sphere of reflection, but then also the entire strategy must be changed.

Here I cannot now develop further how that which Christendom needs first and foremost is a totally new science of arms; it is a science of arms that is completely permeated by reflection. In several of my books I have provided the crucial elements in regard to this. The whole thing can be stated in one phrase, the whole thing, which can indeed take days and years of work to develop, the most vigilant attention night and day, incessant scale finger-exercising in the dialectical every day, and a never-slumbering fear and trembling—the method must become indirect. In the communication of Christianity, when the situation is Christendom, there is not a direct relation, there is first of all a delusion to remove. The entire old science of arms, all the apologetics and everything belonging to it, serves instead, to put it bluntly, to betray the cause of Christianity. At every point and at every moment, the strategy must be constituted on the basis of having to contend with a delusion, an illusion.

So when in Christendom a religious author whose total thought is the task of becoming a Christian wants to make it possible to make people aware (whether it will succeed is of course something else), he must begin as an esthetic author and to a certain point he must maintain this possibility. But there must be a limit, since it is being done, after all, in order to make aware. And one thing the author must not forget, the number carried, which is which, the religious the crucial, the esthetic the incognito—lest the dialectical interaction end up in babbling.

§5
All the Esthetic Writing Seen in the Totality of the Writing Is a Deception, but Understood in a Singular Way

If someone wanted to consider the esthetic writing as the totality and from its point of view and on this assumption consider the religious writing, he would have to regard the latter as a defection, a decline. That the presupposition of this observation is wrong I have shown in the preceding, where it was substantiated that from the beginning and over my signature signs were provided that telegraphed, concurrently with the pseudonymous writing, in the direction of the religious.

But from the total point of view of my whole work as an author, the esthetic writing is a deception, and herein is the deeper significance of the *pseudonymity*. But a deception, that is indeed something rather ugly. To that I would answer: Do not be deceived by the word *deception*. One can deceive a person out of what is true, and—to recall old Socrates—one can deceive a person into what is true. Yes, in only this way can a deluded person actually be brought into what is true—by deceiving him.

The one who is of another opinion thereby betrays that he simply is not much of a dialectician, which is precisely what is necessary in order to operate in this way. In other words there is a great difference, that is, the dialectical difference, or the difference of the dialectical, between these two situations: one who

XIII
541

is ignorant and must be given some knowledge, and therefore he is like the empty vessel that must be filled or like the blank sheet of paper that must be written upon—and one who is under a delusion that must first be taken away. Likewise, there is also a difference between writing on a blank piece of paper and bringing out by means of chemicals some writing that is hidden under other writing. Now, on the assumption that someone is under a delusion and consequently the first step, properly understood, is to remove the delusion—if I do not begin by deceiving, I begin with direct communication. But direct communication presupposes that the recipient's ability to receive is entirely in order, but here that is simply not the case—indeed, here a delusion is an obstacle. That means a corrosive must first be used, but this corrosive is the negative, but the negative in connection with communicating is precisely to deceive.

What, then, does it mean "to deceive"? It means that one does not begin *directly* with what one wishes to communicate but begins by taking the other's delusion at face value. Thus one does not begin (to hold to what essentially is the theme of this book) in this way: I am Christian, you are not a Christian—but this way: You are a Christian, I am not Christian. Or one does not begin in this way: It is Christianity that I am proclaiming, and you are living in purely esthetic categories. No, one begins this way: Let us talk about the esthetic. The deception consists in one's speaking this way precisely in order to arrive at the religious. But according to the assumption the other person is in fact under the delusion that the esthetic is the essentially Christian, since he thinks he is a Christian and yet he is living in esthetic categories.

Even if ever so many pastors will find it indefensible, even if equally as many will be incapable of getting it into their heads—although all of them otherwise, according to their own statements, are accustomed to using the Socratic method—in this respect I calmly stick to Socrates. True, he was no Christian, that I know, although I also definitely remain convinced that he has become one. But he was a dialectician and understood everything in reflection. And the question here is purely dialectical—it is the question of the use of reflection in Christendom. Qualitatively two altogether different magnitudes are involved here, but formally I can very well call Socrates my teacher—whereas I have believed and believe in only one, the Lord Jesus Christ.

B
CONCLUDING POSTSCRIPT

forms, to repeat again, the turning point in the whole authorship. It poses the *issue*: becoming a Christian. After first having appropriated all the pseudonymous esthetic writing as a description of one way along which one may go to becoming a Christian—*back* from the esthetic to becoming a Christian, the book describes the second way—*back* from the system, the speculative, etc. to becoming a Christian.

C
THE RELIGIOUS WRITING

As early as *Concluding Postscript*, I could be very brief when the point of view for all the work as an author is that the author is a religious author; what needed explanation there was how the esthetic writing is to be interpreted on this assumption. And what needs no explanation at all on this assumption is of course the latter part, the purely religious writing, which specifically provides the point of view.

CONCLUSION

XIII
543

And what does all this mean when the reader now gathers together the elements developed in the various sections? It means: this is an authorship of which the total thought is the task of becoming a Christian. But it is an authorship that from the beginning has understood, with dialectical consistency has pursued, what the implications of this are that the situation is Christendom, which is a category of reflection, and therefore has cast all the Christian relationships into reflection. In Christendom—to become a Christian is either to become what one is (the inwardness of reflection or the reflection of inward deepening), or it is

first of all to be wrested out of a delusion, which again is a category of reflection. Here there is no vacillation, no ambiguity of
the usual sort, that one does not know and cannot ascertain
whether the situation is in paganism, whether the pastor in this
sense is a missionary, or where one is. Here one does not lack
what is usually lacking, a decisive categorical definition and a
decisive expression for the situation: to proclaim Christianity—
in Christendom. Everything is cast into reflection. The communication is in reflection—therefore is indirect communication.
The communicator is defined in reflection, therefore negatively,
not one who claims to be an extraordinary Christian or even
claims to have revelations (all of which is commensurate with
immediacy and direct communication) but the opposite, one
who even claims not to be Christian—in other words, the communicator is in the background, helping negatively, since
whether he succeeds in helping someone is indeed something
else. The issue itself is one belonging to reflection: to become a
Christian when in a way one is a Christian.

CHAPTER II

The Dissimilarity of My Personal Existing Corresponding to the Dissimilar Nature of the Writing

In these days and for a long time now we have utterly lost the idea that to be an author is and ought to be a work and therefore a personal existing. That on the whole the press, representing abstract, impersonal communication, is demoralizing, especially since the daily press, purely formally and with no regard to whether what it says is true or false, contributes enormously to demoralization because of all the impersonality, which in turn is more or less irresponsibility and impenitence; that anonymity, the highest expression for abstraction, impersonality, impenitence, and irresponsibility, is a basic source of modern demoralization; that on the other hand anonymity would be counteracted most simply, that a very beneficial corrective to journalism's abstraction would be provided if we turned back once again to antiquity and learned what it means to be an individual human being, no more and no less, which also an author certainly is, no more and no less—this is self-evident. But in our day, when that which is the secret of evil has become wisdom—namely, that one is not to ask about the communicator but only about the communication, only about "what," about the objective—in our day what does it mean to be an author? It means, often even when he is identified, to be an x, an impersonal something that, by means of printing, addresses itself abstractly to thousands upon thousands but itself is unseen, unknown, living as secretly, as anonymously, as impersonally as possible, presumably so that the contrast between the enormous means of communication and being an individual human being does not become obvious and glaring, perhaps also because he fears the supervision that life actually should have over everyone who wants to instruct others, that one sees him, his personal existing, and its relation to the communication. But with all this, to which someone who wanted to study the demoralization of the modern state should give great attention—with all this I cannot become further involved here.

A

PERSONAL EXISTING IN RELATION TO THE
ESTHETIC WRITING

So now to my work as an author and the first period of my existing. Here was a religious author, but one who began as an esthetic author, and this first part was the incognito, was the deception. Very early and very thoroughly initiated into the secret that *mundus vult decipi* [the world wants to be deceived],[25] I was unable at that time to choose to pursue this strategy. Quite the opposite, it was a matter of deceiving inversely on the largest possible scale, of using all my familiarity with people and their weaknesses and their obtusities—not in order to profit from them but in order to annihilate myself, to weaken the impression of myself. The secret of the deception that indulges the world, which wants to be deceived, consists partly in forming a clique and all that goes with it, in joining one or two of those mutual admiration societies whose members assist each other by word and pen for the sake of worldly gain, and partly in hiding from the human throng, never being seen, in order in this way to produce an effect on the imagination. Therefore the very opposite had to be done. I had to exist and safeguard an existence in absolute isolation, but I also had to make a point of being seen at every time of the day, living, so to speak, on the street, associating with every Tom, Dick, and Harry and in the most casual situations. This is truth's way of deceiving, the ever-sure way to weaken the impression of oneself in the world, furthermore certainly also the way of self-renunciation taken by men quite different from me in order to make people aware. Those highly esteemed, the "deceivers," who want the communication to serve them instead of their serving the communication, are

XIII
545

merely intent on winning esteem for themselves; the despised, the "truth-witnesses," who deceive inversely, have always followed the practice of sacrificing themselves in a worldly sense, of being nothing, although working night and day, and among other things also without the support of the illusion that the work they are doing is their official career or livelihood.

So this had to be done, and it was done, not now and then but every blessed day. I am convinced that a sixth of *Either/Or*,[26] a little clique, and then an author one never managed to see—this would have become, especially over a long period, something extraordinary in quite another way. I had, however, made sure I could work as hard as I pleased, and as the spirit prompted me, without being afraid of gaining too much esteem, because in a certain sense I worked just as hard in another direction—against myself. Only an author will really be able to understand what such a task is: to work *qua* author, that is, with intellect and pen, and then practically be at everybody's service. It is a criterion for criticism (even though it did also give me extraordinary enrichment with observations) that would bring most people to despair, since it means taking away completely even the least illusion and providing the pure idea-relationship—and truly it is not truth that rules the world but illusions. Even if an achievement were eminent to a degree never seen before—if the author just lives in this way, he will in a very short time have safeguarded himself against worldly esteem and against the bestial flattery of the crowd. The crowd has no ideality and therefore no power to hold on to an idea despite appearances; the crowd always falls into the trap of appearances. To be seen day after day and to be seen in the most casual company are enough to make the crowd lose the idea and very soon become sick and tired of a person. It does not even take very much time to manage to be seen every day if only one ingeniously (i.e., humanly speaking, insanely) uses the time properly—that is, walks to and fro in the same but the most frequented place in the city.

Anyone who conserves his esteem in a worldly way does not return by the same way he went out, even if it is his path, lest he be seen twice in so brief a time—then people might think that he did not do anything, which would not occur to anyone if he sat at home in his parlor and loafed two-thirds of the day. On the other hand, an hour spent properly, devoutly understood, an hour lived for eternity, spent in walking to and fro among the common people, is already not a little. It is truly pleasing to God that truth is served in this way; his spirit witnessed powerfully with my spirit[27] that it had his complete and highest approval. All the truth-witnesses nod to one their approval that it is the truth, the idea one wants to serve, not the truth one wants to betray and then wants to profit from the illusions. It was a purely Christian satisfaction for me to dare to carry out on Monday a little bit of what on Sunday, when the pastor preaches and in so doing even sheds tears, one sheds tears over—and on Monday quite rightly laughs at. It was a purely Christian satisfaction for me that if ordinarily there was no one else there was definitely one in Copenhagen with whom any poor person could without ceremony speak and associate on the street; that if ordinarily there was no one else, there was one who, in whatever social circles he otherwise moved, did not slink by but acknowledged every maidservant, manservant, and every day laborer he knew in other contexts. It was a purely Christian satisfaction to me that if ordinarily there was no one else there was one who (several years before existence again assigned the lesson to the generation) in action tried a little to do the doctrine about loving the neighbor—alas, one who precisely by his act also received a frightful insight into what an illusion Christendom is and indeed, particularly later, also into how the common people let themselves be seduced by wretched journalists, whose striving and fighting for equality can only lead, if it leads to anything, since it is in the service of the lie, to making the elite, in self-defense, proud of their aloofness from the common man, and the common man brazen in his rudeness.

XIII
547

To develop in more detail this sketch of my personal existing cannot be done here, but I am convinced that rarely has any author used as much cunning, intrigue, and ingenuity to win honor and esteem in the world in order to deceive it as I have done for the opposite reason—to deceive it into an understanding of the truth. By just a single episode, for which I have the proofreader of *Either/Or*, my friend Giødwad,[28] as witness, I shall attempt to give an idea of the scale on which this deception was carried out. When I was reading proof pages of *Either/Or*, I was so busy that it was impossible for me to spend the usual time strolling up and down the street. I did not finish until late in the evening—and then in the evening I hurried to the theater, where I literally was present only five to ten minutes. And why did I do that? Because I was afraid that the big book would bring me too much esteem.* And why did I do that? Because I knew people, especially in Copenhagen; to be seen every night for five minutes by several hundred people was enough to sustain the opinion: So he doesn't do a single thing; he is nothing but a street-corner loafer.

That was the way I existed, shoring up the esthetic writing (in addition breaking with all cliques) and entirely with the polemical aim of regarding every eulogy as an attack, but every attack as something to which no attention was to be paid. That was the way I existed publicly. I almost never made visits, and at home one thing was strictly observed—unconditionally not to receive anyone except the poor who asked for help. There was no time for visits at home, and in a visit someone could easily come to suspect what he was not supposed to suspect. That is the way I existed. If Copenhagen was ever of one single opinion about someone, I dare say it has been of one opinion about me: I was a street-corner loafer, an idler, a *flâneur* [lounger], a frivolous bird, a good, perhaps even brilliant pate, witty, etc.—but I completely lacked "earnestness." I represented the worldly mentality's irony, the enjoyment of life, the most sophisticated enjoyment of life—but of "earnestness and positivity" there was not a trace; I was, however, tremendously interesting and pungent.

As I think back on this form of existence, I could indeed decide to make a kind of apology to the distinguished and esteemed members of society. True enough, I truly was fully aware of what

XIII
548

---

*For the same reason, at the moment *Either/Or* was all finished and ready for making a fair copy, I also put in *Fædrelandet* a little article in my name, "Open Confession," in which I altogether gratuitously disclaimed authorship of the many interesting newspaper articles in various newspapers, admitted and confessed my inactivity, and requested only one thing: that in the future no one would regard me as the author of anything that did not bear my signature.

I was doing, but from their point of view they were still justified in censuring me because by weakening myself in this way I was on the whole contributing to weakening power and esteem, however conservative I have otherwise always been in this regard and with however much respect, veneration, and admiration I have been happy to give the distinguished and esteemed person what he deserved. But it did not follow from my conservative nature that I myself in any way participated in the same thing. And just because the esteemed in society have in so many ways shown me not only sympathy but even preference, in so many ways have tried to do what from their side was no doubt honest and well-intentioned—to draw me to themselves—I feel impelled to make an apology to them, even though I naturally cannot repent of what I have done, since I was serving my idea. Yet the esteemed have always proved to be consistent in comparison with the common people, who not even from their own point of view have been in the right toward me, inasmuch as, in consequence of the foregoing, they did indeed attack me— because I was not elitist, which is very odd and ludicrous of the common people.

This is the first part. By means of my personal existing, I attempted to support the pseudonymous writers, all the esthetic writing. Depressed, incurably depressed as I was, sorely afflicted in my innermost being, after having in despair broken with the world and what is of the world, rigorously brought up from childhood in the view that the truth must suffer, be insulted and mocked, spending a certain time each day in prayer and upbuilding meditation, myself personally a penitent. Since I was who I was—yes, I do not deny it—in a certain sense I found a satisfaction in that life, in that inverted deception, a satisfaction in thinking that the intrigue succeeded so extraordinarily that the public and I came to say *du*[29] to each other, that I was in vogue proclaiming a gospel of worldliness, that even if I did not have the kind of esteem that can be obtained only by a completely different mode of life, yet secretly, and therefore all the more adored, I was the public's favorite, in everyone's good graces as tremendously interesting and pungent, although everyone no doubt considered himself better and more earnest and more honorable and more positive than I. This satisfaction, which was my secret, a satisfaction in which at times I was as if beside myself, could in other respects have been a dangerous temptation for me. That the world, the public, and the like would tempt me with its flattery, admiration, etc.—no, there I was certain. If I had capsized, it would have to have been on this reflection raised to the second power—an almost obsessed rapture over the thought of how the deception succeeded, which indescribably satisfied the secret resentment I had harbored since childhood, because long before I myself had ever seen it I had learned that lies and baseness and injustice ruled the world, which often led me to think of those words in *Either/Or*, "If you people only knew what it is you are laughing at,"[30] if you only knew with whom you are involved, who this *flâneur* is!

B

PERSONAL EXISTING IN RELATION TO THE
RELIGIOUS WRITING

In December 1845 I had completed the manuscript of *Concluding Postscript*[31] and had, as is my custom, delivered it lock, stock, and barrel to Luno,[32] for which the skeptical need not take my word, since this can be shown in Luno's records. This book constitutes the turning point in my entire work as an author, inasmuch as it poses the *issue*: becoming a Christian. Thereafter the transition to the second part is made, the series of exclusively religious books.

That my personal existing had to be conformed to this, or that I had to try to give my contemporaries another impression of my personal existing, I perceived at once. I also even had my eye on what had to be done when in a very convenient way something happened; a little circumstance, in which I saw a hint from Governance, assisted me in acting decisively in that direction.

But I am unable to develop this before I have tried in a few strokes to recall in the reader's recollection the state of things in Copenhagen at that time, a description that perhaps will now also show up better by comparison with the present state of war.[33] Gradually the not unremarkable circumstance developed that the whole population of Copenhagen, especially to the

XIII
550

degree that it was more ignorant and uncultured, became ironic and witty—it was irony and irony first and last. If the matter were not so serious, if I dared to regard it purely esthetically, I would not deny that it is the most ludicrous thing I have seen and that I actually believe one must travel far and still be very lucky to encounter anything so basically comic. The entire population of a city, first and foremost all the casual idlers on the highways and byways, down to schoolchildren and cobblers' apprentices, all the many legions of the only favored and privileged class in our day, those who amount to nothing, they become—*en masse* the entire population of a city, guilds, fraternities, tradespeople, people of station (in just about the same way as a middle-class citizen is accustomed to go to the carnival in Deer Park), they, with their families become—those thousands and thousands become (the one and only thing I would venture unconditionally to insist is impossible for them to become, especially *en masse* or in families)—they become "ironic" with the help of a newspaper,[34] which in turn, ironically enough, by means of an editorial staff of street-corner loafers,[35] usurpingly dominates the fashion, and the fashion that is stipulated is—the ironic. I believe it is impossible to think of anything more ludicrous. Irony presupposes a very specific intellectual culture, which is very rare in any generation—and this chaos of people consisted of ironists. Irony is unconditionally unsocial. Irony that is in the majority is *eo ipso* [precisely thereby] unconditionally not irony. Nothing is more certain, inasmuch as it is implicit in the concept itself. Irony essentially tends toward the presence of only one person, as is indicated in the Aristotelian view that the ironist does everything ἑαυτοῦ ἕνεκα [for his own sake][36]—and here an enormous public, arm in arm *in bona caritate* [good-naturedly], had become, damned if it hadn't, ironic.

But the matter was only all too serious. Even though the actual ringleader was indeed a man of not inconsiderable talent,[37] this irony, by passing into these thousands upon thousands, naturally became essentially nothing else than rabble-barbarism, which unfortunately is always popular. It was a demoralization that was all too terribly reminiscent of the punishment with which one of the ancient prophets in the name of the Lord threatens the Jews as the most dreadful of punishments: Boys shall judge you.[38] It was a demoralization that in relation to the proportions of the little country actually threatened a complete moral disintegration. To get an idea of the danger, one must see it close up, how even good-natured and worthy people become like totally different creatures as soon as they become the "crowd." One must see it close up, the spinelessness with which even otherwise honorable people say, "It is a disgrace; it is shocking to do or say anything like that"—and then themselves contribute their little bit to blanket the city and land in a snowstorm of blather and town gossip. One must see it close up, the callousness with which otherwise kind people act in the capacity of the public because their participation or nonparticipation seems to them a trifle—a trifle that with the contributions of the many becomes the monster. One must see how no attack is so feared as that of laughter, how even the person who courageously risked his life for a stranger would not be far from betraying his father and mother if the danger was laughter, because more than any other this attack isolates the one attacked and at no point does it offer the support of pathos, while light-mindedness and curiosity and sensuality grin and the nervous cowardice that itself shivers before such an attack incessantly shouts, "It is nothing," and the cowardice that despicably ransoms itself from an attack by bribery or by putting on a good face to the one concerned says, "It is nothing," and sympathy says, "It is nothing." How terrible it is when blather and grinning threaten to become "public opinion" in a little country. Denmark was about to be absorbed into Copenhagen, and Copenhagen was just at the point of becoming a market town. To do this is easy enough, especially with the help of the press; and once it is done, perhaps a generation is needed in order to recover from it.

But enough about this. It was of importance to me to alter my personal existing in accordance with my transition to setting forth the religious issues. I had to have a supporting existence-form corresponding to that kind of work as an author. As stated, it was in the month of December, and it was desirable to have everything in order by the time *Concluding Postscript* was to be published. So the step was taken,[39] still in the month of De-

XIII
552

cember. Given my familiarity with such situations, I readily perceived that two words[40] to that instrument of irony, which in one sense, that is, if I had not been the person I was, had up until now not without cunning venerated and immortalized me,[41] would be sufficient to turn my whole life situation around altogether dialectically in order to get that whole incalculable public of ironists to take aim at me, so I would become the object of everyone's irony—alas, I, the master of irony.[42]

So the order was then given. Lest capital be made of it as a newly invented and very stimulating form of irony, a considerable dose of the ethical was added by my requesting to be abused by that nauseating instrument of nauseating irony. That incalculable monster of ironists has naturally regarded me as lunatic. The individuals who saw more deeply into the matter probably did not without a shudder see me make this leap, or they thought it beneath my dignity to concern myself with something like that (because they had only a worldly understanding of dignity and did not consider what is divinely understood by it), whereas I would have found it beneath my dignity to have lived contemporaneously, without having acted decisively, with such a demoralization, satisfied with the cheap virtue of conducting myself like "the others"—that is, shirking action as much as possible while such a disproportionate journalistic contemptibility was surely bringing people to the grave, violated and infuriated, if not always the ones attacked, then certainly their wives, children, relatives, and close friends, was defilingly intruding into everything, even into the most intimate relationships of private life, even into school secrets, even into the sanctuary of the Church, was spewing out lies, slander, insolence, and juvenile jokes—all in the service of corrupt passion and wretched avarice, and responsible for all this were "street-corner loafers," the ones responsible under the press law! I realized that in order to serve my idea this was the right thing to do, and I did not vacillate. The consequences of that,[43] for which certainly no one at that time envied me, I therefore historically claim as my legitimate possession, the perspective value of which my eye easily discovers.

I had now figured out that the situation was dialectically right for using indirect communication again. Although I was devoting myself exclusively to religious writing, I dared to count on these daily drenchings of rabble-barbarism as negatively supporting, on their having an adequate cooling effect so that the religious communication would not become much too direct or would not much too directly gain adherents for me. The reader could not directly relate himself to me, because I now had in place, instead of the incognito of the esthetic, the danger of laughter and grins, which scare away most people. Even those whom it would not scare away would be disturbed by the next, the thought that I myself had voluntarily exposed myself to all this, had plunged myself into this, a kind of insanity. Ah, yes, surely that was just what the contemporaries thought of that Roman who made his immortal leap to save his country,[44] a kind of insanity—ah, yes, and once again, ah, yes, since dialectically it was exactly Christian self-denial—and I, the poor master of irony, became the sorry object of the laughter of a highly cultured public.

The costume was right. Every religious author is *eo ipso* polemical, because the world is not so good that the religious can be assumed to have triumphed or to be in the majority. A triumphant religious author who is *in vogue* is *eo ipso* not a *religious* author. The essentially religious author is always polemical and in addition suffers under the opposition or endures the opposition that corresponds to what in his time must be regarded as the specific evil. If it is kings and emperors, popes and bishops, and power that are the evil, then he must be recognizable by his being the object of their attacks. If it is the crowd—and blather, the public—and the brutish grinning that are the evil, then he must also be recognizable by his being the object of that kind of attack and persecution. And if the essentially religious author has just one syllogism that he uses as the jack, the miraculous syllogism, when asked whereby he demonstrates he is right and that what he says is true, he answers, "I demonstrate it by this, that I am persecuted; it is truth, and I demonstrate it by this, that I am laughed to scorn." That is, he does not demonstrate the truth or the justice of his cause by the honor, esteem, etc. he enjoys—just the opposite, because the essentially religious person is always polemical. Any religious author or speaker or teacher who shirks, who is not present where the danger is and where the evil has its haunt, is a deceiver, and this will also become manifest.

It holds for everyone that when he comes to death's door and it is opened for him he must discard all pomp and glory and wealth and worldly esteem and starred medals and emblems of honor—whether bestowed on him by kings and emperors or by the crowd and the public—discard them as totally irrelevant and superfluous. An exception is made only for anyone who has been a religious author, teacher, speaker, etc. in his lifetime and has been that on his own responsibility and at his own risk. If he is found to be in possession of any such thing, he is not allowed to discard it—no, it is packed up in a bundle and handed to him; he is compelled to keep it or to carry the bundle in the same way as a thief is himself compelled to carry stolen goods. And with this bundle he must enter the place where he shall be judged. After all, he was a religious teacher; so he will be judged by the authentic religious teachers, all those who as long as they lived were insulted, persecuted, laughed to scorn, mocked, spat upon. Ah, if it is terrible for the sensate human being to stand here on earth laughed to scorn, mocked, insulted, how much more terrible to stand in eternity with this bundle under one's arm or arrayed with—decorations.

The costume was right. In a grinning age (as was the one of which I speak, and in this regard it is at least my opinion that "the war" has been good fortune for Denmark), the religious author must for heaven's sake see to it that he more than anyone else becomes laughed to scorn. If the evil is coming from the crowd, then the contemporary religious author must for heaven's sake see to it that he becomes the object of its persecution and in this regard receives the first treatment. And my entire view of the crowd, which even the more perceptive at that time perhaps found somewhat exaggerated, now in 1848,[45] assisted by the gesticulations of existence (these are more powerful and in comparison with the single individual's thin voice are like the raging of the elements), now the objection probably is that I have not exaggerated enough. And that category *the single individual*, which was regarded as eccentric and the invention of eccentricity, which it indeed was, for was not the person who in one sense was its inventor, Socrates, at the time called ἀτοπώτατος (the most eccentric of men)[46]—I would not trade having brought it forth decisively at the time, I would not trade it for a kingdom. If the crowd is the evil, if it is chaos that threatens, there is rescue in one thing only, in becoming the single individual, in the rescuing thought: that single individual.

One triumph I have experienced, only one, but it satisfies me so completely that as a thinker I ask unconditionally nothing more in the world. The all too overwhelming world-historical events of the past few months have brought into the world the confused spokesmen of newborn, romantic, obviously confused thoughts and on the other hand have either silenced everything that hitherto had in various ways been the spokesman or placed it in the embarrassing position of having to obtain brand-new clothes in the greatest haste, and every system has been broken up. With such passion as if there were a gap of a generation, the past was broken from the present in the course of a few months. During this crisis I sat and read proof pages of a book[47] that accordingly had been written earlier. Not one word was added or deleted. It was the view that I, "the odd thinker," had already enunciated for several years. If one reads it, one will get the impression that the book was written after the crisis. A world-historical crisis such as that, which ranks so high that not even the disintegration of the ancient world was so imposing, is the absolute *tentamen rigorosum* [rigorous examination] for anyone who *was* an author. I experienced the triumph of not needing to modify or change one iota—indeed, what I had written before, if it were read now, would be much, much better understood than when it was written.

Just one more thing. When someday my lover comes, he will readily see that when I was regarded as being the ironic one the irony by no means consisted in what a highly cultured public thought it did—and of course my lover cannot possibly be so fatuous that he assumes that a public can be the judge of irony, which is just as impossible as being the single individual *en masse*. He will see that the irony consisted in just this, that in this esthetic author and under this *Erscheinung* [appearance] of worldliness the

religious author concealed himself, a religious author who at that
XIII
556
very time and for his own upbuilding perhaps consumed as much
religiousness as a whole household ordinarily does. Furthermore,
my lover will see that irony was again present in connection with
the next part, and precisely in that which the highly cultured
public regarded as madness. For the essential ironist there is nothing else to do in an ironic age (that great epitome of fools) but to
turn the whole relation around and himself become the object of
the irony of everyone. My lover will see how it all tallied at every
single point, how my existence-relations turned around in altogether accurate correspondence to the change in my writing. If
I had not had an eye or the courage for that and had changed the
writing but not my existence-relations, then the relation would
have become undialectical and confused.

XIII
557

    That I have needed and how I have continuously needed
God's assistance day after day, year after year—in order to turn
my mind to that, in order to be able to state it accurately, I do
not need the help of memory or recollection, or of journals and
diaries, or to compare these with one another—I am reliving it
again so vividly, so presently, at this moment. When it was a

XIII
558

matter of boldness, enthusiasm, zeal, almost to the border of
madness, what was this pen not able to present! And now when
I am to speak about my relationship to God, about what is repeated every day in my prayer, which gives thanks for the indescribable things he has done for me, so infinitely more than I
ever had expected; about what has taught me to marvel, to marvel over God, his love, and over what a human being's weakness
is capable of with his help; about what has taught me both to long
for eternity and not to fear to find it tedious, since that is the very

---

demand of the times," that it was submitted to the lenient judgment of a highly
esteemed public, *moreover*, that it was owing to this same highly esteemed public, to the approval and support and acclamation of my contemporaries, that it
prospered. Quite the contrary, fearing and loving God, I had to take care vig-
ilantly that the truth would be expressed that it was solely and only God's help,
that I owe neither the public nor my contemporaries anything but the wrong it
has done to me, to the truth, to the epigram of awakening, that at a time when
everything was general assemblies and associations and the setting up and setting
down and setting aside of committees, while nothing really happened, that at
that time a frail and solitary human being was granted the ability and energy to
work on a scale that was bound to foster the notion that it was the work of more
than one committee—in short, it was religiously my duty that my existing and
my existing as an author express the truth, which I had daily perceived and
ascertained—that there is a God.
    Perhaps the reader will now become aware of why I have even found it
necessary in the finite sense to work against my own efforts, simply in order that
the responsibility would fall completely upon me. Entirely alone, completely
alone, I had to be at every moment; yes, I was obliged to eliminate assistance lest
my responsibility become too light. Just one friend and collaborator, then the
responsibility becomes a fraction, not to mention if one gets the help of a whole
generation. But the point for me in the service of the truth was that if I went
astray, if I became presumptuous, if it were untrue, Governance would then
have to bear down on me absolutely, and that, facing the possibility of this
examination, which hovered over me at all times, I had to keep myself awake,
responsive, obedient.[49]

CHAPTER III

Governance's Part in My Authorship

In a certain sense, it has not been my preference or inclination to write what I have written up to this point. There is something painful about having to speak so much about oneself. Would to God I had dared to be silent even longer,[48] indeed, to die in silence about what has silently engaged me day and night as my work and my task. But, God be praised, now I breathe, now I really feel impelled to speak; now I have arrived at what is an indescribable bliss for me to think and speak about. This, my God-relationship, is in many ways the happy love of my unhappy and troubled life. And even though this love story (if I dare to call it that) has the essential mark of the true love story, that only one can completely understand it, and to only one does a person have absolute joy in telling it, to the beloved, therefore here the one by whom one is loved*—it nevertheless is enjoyable to speak of it to others also.

*Perhaps the reader will now become aware of how, humanly speaking, what has been the misfortune of all my writing, what has had the effect of coming to stand more as a superfluity than to intervene actively, is that, humanly speaking, it is too religious or the author's existence too religious, so that the author *qua* author has been thoroughly weak and therefore has absolutely needed God. If the author had been less weak, therefore humanly stronger (therefore less religious), he would have summarily taken over the authorship as his own. He probably would have secured for himself some confidants and friends, would have confided his aims to others in advance, sought their advice, called on them for help. And these, who can be compared to godparents, would in turn have appealed to others, and the authorship would have had an influence at the moment, would have been active at the moment—instead of being a superfluity, which in a finite sense God himself is, more than everything and everybody.

Perhaps the reader will now become aware of why day in and day out I have worked so hard and so sacrificially to keep the untruth from coming forth, the untruth that nevertheless, as it always does, would have secured for me money, honor, esteem, approval, etc., the untruth that what I had to say was "the

XIII
557

situation I need in order to do nothing other than to thank him—now when I am going to speak of this, a poet impatience awakens in my soul. More determined than that king who shouted, "My kingdom for a horse,"[50] and blessedly determined as he was not, I would give everything, my life included, to find—something that is more blessed for thought to find than for the lover to find the beloved—*the expression*,[51] in order then to die with this expression on my lips. See, it is offered, thoughts as enchanting as those fruits in that fabulous garden,[52] so rich, so warm, so fervent, expressions so soothing to the feeling of gratitude in me, so cooling to the hot longing—it seems to me that if I had a winged pen, indeed, ten of them, I still would be unable to keep up with the abundance offered to me. But then when I pick up my pen, for a time I cannot—just as one speaks of not being able to move a foot—move my pen; in that state not a line about this relationship is put down on paper. I seem to hear a voice that says to me: Obtuse fellow, what does he think he is; does he not know that obedience is dearer to God than the fat of rams?[53] Do the whole thing as a work assignment. Then I become completely calm; then there is time to write every letter, almost meticulously, with my slower pen. And if that poet passion awakens in me again for a moment, I seem to hear a voice speak to me as a teacher speaks to a boy: Now, just hold the pen properly and write each letter exactly. Then I can do it, then I dare not do anything else, then I write each word, each line, almost unaware of the next word and the next line. Then, when I read it through later, I find an entirely different satisfaction in it. Even though some glowing expressions perhaps did elude me, what has been produced is something else—it is not the work of the poet passion or of the thinker passion, but of devotion to God, and for me a divine worship. XIII
559

But what I at this moment am reliving or have relived has been continually experienced during all my work as an author. "The poet" is said to call upon the muse in order to get ideas. This has actually never been the case with me; my individuality debars me from even understanding it. But on the other hand, I have needed God every day to defend myself against the abundance of

thoughts. Indeed, give a person a creative talent like that, and
then such frail health, and he surely will learn to pray. At every
moment I have been and still am able to perform the feat of
sitting down and writing incessantly day and night and yet another day and night, because there is wealth enough. But if I did
that, I would collapse. Ah, just the slightest dietary indiscretion,
and I am in mortal danger. Then when I learn obedience, do the
work as a firm work assignment, hold the pen properly and write
each letter carefully, then I can do it. Thus, time and time again,
I have had more joy from my relationship of obedience to God
than from the thoughts I produced. —This obviously signifies, as
is easily seen, that I do not have an immediate God-relationship
to appeal to, nor do I dare to say that it is God who directly
contributes the thoughts to me, but that my relationship to God
is a relationship of reflection, inwardness in reflection, since reflection is the predominant quality of my individuality; this is also
why in praying my strength is in giving thanks.

Thus throughout all my work as an author I have incessantly
needed God's assistance in order to be able to do it as a simple
work assignment for which specific hours are allotted each day,
beyond which it was not permitted to work, and when this happened on rare occasions, I had to pay dearly for it. Nothing re-
sembles my conduct less than that outburst of genius and then a
tumultuous breaking off. I have basically lived like a scribe in his
office. From the very beginning I have been as if under arrest and
at every moment sensed that it was not I who played the master
but that it was someone else who was the master, sensed it with
fear and trembling when he let me perceive his omnipotence and
my nothingness, sensed it with indescribable bliss when I related
myself to him and the work in unconditional obedience. The
dialectical consists in this, that as a precautionary measure whatever extraordinariness was granted to me was granted in such an
elasticity that if I would not obey it would slay me. It was like a
father's saying to his child, "You have permission to receive it all
at once, it is yours, but if you refuse to obey and to use it as I want
you to use it—well, I will not punish you by taking it away—no,
take it, it will crush you." Without God I am too strong for

XIII
560

myself, and in perhaps the most agonizing way of all I am shattered. After becoming an author, I actually have never once experienced what I hear others lament over—the lack of thoughts or that they would not present themselves. If that were to happen to me, I very likely would almost be happy that I at last really had a day off. But I have frequently experienced and at all times have been horribly aware of a terrible torment that is akin to starving in the midst of abundance, to being overwhelmed by wealth—if I do not immediately learn obedience, let God help me, and produce in the same way, as calmly and unobtrusively as one does a work assignment.

But during my whole work as an author, I have continually, day after day over the years, needed God's assistance in another sense also, because he has been my one and only confidant, and only in trust to his co-knowledge have I dared to venture what I have ventured and been able to endure what I have endured; and I have found blessedness in it: to become very literally alone in the enormous world, alone, since wherever I was, whether in public or in private, I was always in disguise, consequently alone, became no more alone in the solitude of the night, alone, not in the forests of America with their horrors and dangers but alone in what changes even the most frightful *actuality* into refreshment and alleviation, alone in the company of the most dreadful *possibilities*, alone, with human language practically against me, alone in torments that have taught me more than one new note to that text about the thorn in the flesh,[54] alone in decisions where one could have needed friends, if possible a whole generation, to hold on to one, alone in dialectical tensions that—without God—would drive insane anyone with my imagination, alone in anxieties unto death, alone in a meaninglessness of existence without being able, even if I wanted it, to make myself understandable to a single person—what am I saying, "make myself understandable to a single person"—no, there were times when *that* was not lacking, so it could not be said "only *that* was lacking," times when I could not even make myself understandable to myself. When I now consider that years went by in this manner, I shudder; if for one single moment my eyes see incorrectly,

XIII
561

I collapse. But if I see correctly, then I trustingly rest in confidence in God's co-knowledge, then the blessedness is there again.

And now for the particulars, it would be futile if I were to try to tell how I have perceived God's assistance in this. For example, it has been inexplicable to me (what has so often happened to me) that when I did something and could not possibly say why or it did not occur to me to ask why, when I as a very specific person followed the prompting of my natural impulses, that this, which for me had a purely personal meaning bordering on the accidental, that this then turned out to have a totally different, a purely ideal meaning when seen later within my work as an author; that much of what I had done purely personally was strangely enough precisely what I should do *qua* author. It has been inexplicable to me how very often seemingly quite accidental little circumstances in my life, which then in turn admittedly became something very considerable through my imagination, brought me into a specific state, and I did not understand myself, became depressed—and see—then out of this developed a mood, the very mood I should use in the work with which I was engaged at the time, and at just the right place. There has not been the slightest delay in the writing; what was to be used has always been at hand the very moment it was to be used. In one sense all the writing has had an unbroken evenness, as if I had done nothing other than to copy each day a specific part of a printed book.

———————

But in this accounting I must in an even more precise sense bring out Governance's part in the authorship. If, for example, I were to go ahead and say that I had had an overview of the whole dialectical structure from the very beginning of the whole work as an author or that at every moment I had in advance exhausted in reflection, step by step, the possibilities in such a way that reflection did not teach me something later, at times something else, that what I had done was surely the right thing but that nevertheless only now did I myself properly understand it—if I were to do that, it would be a denial and an unfairness to God. No, in honesty I must say: I cannot understand the whole simply because I can understand the whole down to the slightest detail; but what I cannot understand is that I can now understand it and yet by no means dare to say that I understood it so accurately at the beginning—and yet I certainly am the one who has done it and with reflection has taken every step. In garrulous talk this could be explained easily by saying, as some have also said about me without having any idea of the totality of my authorship, that I was a genius of reflection. But just because I acknowledge the correctness of attributing reflection to me—I truly am too reflective not to see that this compounding of reflection and genius explains nothing, because insofar as someone has genius, he does not have reflection, and vice versa, since reflection is the very negation of immediacy.

XIII
562

If I were now to state as categorically definitely as possible Governance's part in the whole work as an author, I know of no expression more descriptive or more decisive than this: It is Governance that has brought me up, and the upbringing is reflected in the writing process. To that extent, then, what was developed earlier, that all the esthetic writing is a deception, proves to be in one sense not entirely true, since this expression concedes a little too much along the line of consciousness. Yet it is not entirely untrue, because I have been conscious during the upbringing, and from the beginning. The process is this: a poetic and philosophic nature is set aside in order to become a Christian. But the unusual thing is that the movement begins concurrently and therefore is a conscious process; one gets to see how it happens; the other does not commence after a separation of some years from the first. Thus the esthetic writing is surely a deception, yet in another sense a necessary emptying. The religious is decisively present already from the first moment, has decisive predominance, but for a little while waits patiently so that the poet is allowed to talk himself out, yet watching with Argus eyes lest the poet trick it and it all becomes a poet.*

---

*This idea, that it is "the poet" whom one must move away from, finds its expression as early as *Either/Or,* even though, understood in the totality of my

XIII
563
I think that the significance my work as an author has for the age appears best from this point of view. If in a word I were to express my judgment of the age, I would say: It lacks religious upbringing. To become and be a Christian has become a banality. The esthetic plainly has the upper hand. By going further than to be a Christian (which everyone supposedly is), we have reverted to or have passed into a sophisticated esthetic and intellectual paganism with an admixture of Christianity. The task that is to be assigned to most people in Christendom is—away from "the poet" or from relating oneself to or having one's life in what the poet recites, away from speculative thought, from having one's life imaginatively (which is also impossible) in speculating (instead of existing) to becoming a Christian. The first movement is the total significance of the esthetic writing in the totality of my work as an author; the second movement is that of *Concluding Postscript*, which, by drawing in or editing all the esthetic writing to its advantage in order to throw light on its issue, the issue of *becoming a Christian*, itself makes the same movement in another sphere: away from speculative thought, away from the system etc., to becoming a Christian. The movement is **back**, and even though it is all done *without authority*, there is still something in the tone that is reminiscent of a policeman when he says to a crowd: Move back! This is indeed why more than one of the pseudonymous writers calls himself a policeman, a street inspector.[56]

And now I, the author, in my judgment what relation then do I have to the age? Am I perhaps "the apostle"?[57] Abominable! I have never given occasion for such an idea; I am a poor, lowly human being. Am I then the teacher, the one who does the upbringing? No, not that either. I am the one who himself has been brought up, or the one whose authorship describes what it
XIII
564 means to be brought up to become a Christian; just as the up-

---

XIII
563
entire work as an author, it of course holds true that one must move away from or back from "the poet" in a far deeper sense than the second part of *Either/Or* could explain. That this is the case in *Either/Or* is already noted in *Concluding Postscript*, p. 188, lines 21 ff.[55] The transition made in *Either/Or* is really from a poet existence to existing ethically.

bringing and accordingly as the upbringing puts pressure on me, I in turn put pressure on the age, but teacher I am not—only a fellow-pupil.

———————

In order to elucidate further the part of Governance in the authorship, it becomes necessary to explain, insofar as I have the explanation at my disposal, how I happened to become an author.

About my *vita ante acta* [earlier life] (that is, from childhood until I became an author), I cannot give details here, however remarkable it is for me how from my earliest childhood and step by step in my whole development I was predisposed to becoming precisely the kind of author I became. For the sake of what follows, I must, however, give a few lines, something I do with shyness, as an individual presumably always does when he must speak purely personally about himself.

From childhood on I have been in the grip of an enormous depression, the depth of which finds its only true manifestation in the equally enormous proficiency granted me to hide it under a seeming cheerfulness and zest for life. My only joy from almost as far back as I can remember was that no one could discover how unhappy I felt; this circumstance (the equally great magnitude of my depression and of my dissimulative art) does indeed signify that I was assigned to myself and the God-relationship. —As a child, I was rigorously and earnestly brought up in Christianity, insanely brought up, humanly speaking—already in earliest childhood I had overstrained myself under the impression that the depressed old man, who had laid it upon me, was himself sinking under—a child attired, how insane, as a depressed old man. Frightful!

No wonder, then, that there were times when Christianity seemed to me the most inhuman cruelty, although I never, even when I was furthest away from it, gave up my veneration for it and was firmly resolved, especially if I did not personally choose to become a Christian, never to initiate anyone into the difficulties that I knew and that I never either read or heard discussed.

But I have never broken with Christianity or given it up; to attack it has never entered my mind. No, from the time it was possible to speak of the application of my powers, I had firmly resolved to employ everything to defend it, or in any case to present it in its true form, because, through my upbringing, I very early was already able to ascertain how seldom Christianity is presented in its true form, how those who defend it most often betray it, and how rarely the attackers actually hit it, although they often, which is still my view, superbly hit established Christendom, which certainly might rather be called the caricature of true Christianity or an enormous quantity of misunderstanding, illusion, etc. sprinkled with a sparse little dash of true Christianity.

Thus I did in a way love Christianity—to me it was the venerable—to be sure, it had made me extremely unhappy, humanly speaking. It was closely linked to my relationship with my father, the person I have most deeply loved—and what does this mean? Part of it is precisely that this is the person who has made one unhappy—but out of love. His fault consisted not in a lack of love but in mistaking a child for an old man. To love the person who makes one happy is, in terms of reflection, a deficient definition of love; to love the person who out of malice made one unhappy is a virtue; but to love the person who out of love, accordingly through a misunderstanding but out of love, made one unhappy—as far as I know, this has hitherto never really been delineated but is indeed normative reflection's formula for loving.

So I went out into life, favored in every way with regard to mental capacity and outward circumstances; everything was done and continued to be done to develop my mind and spirit as richly as possible. Confidently—yet with a decided sympathy and predilection for what it is to suffer or for what in one way or another is oppressed and suffering—I can in a certain sense say that I went forth into life with an almost rashly proud air. I have never at any moment in my life been deserted by the faith: one can do what one wills—except one thing, otherwise unconditionally everything—except one thing, lift the depression in whose power I was. It has never at any time occurred to me (to others this will probably seem a delusion, but for me it has truly been so, just as truly as what I say next, which to others will probably again seem a delusion) that someone was living who was or someone would be born a contemporary who would become my superior—in my innermost being I was myself the most wretched of all. It never occurred to me at any time that I would not be victorious, even if I would have attempted something utterly rash—except in one thing, otherwise unconditionally in everything, but not in one thing—to lift this depression, the suffering of which I have been completely free scarcely one whole day. At the same time, however, together with this it must be understood that I was initiated very early into the thought that to be victorious is to be victorious in the infinite sense, which in the finite sense is to suffer. So this again is in agreement with depression's understanding in my innermost being that I actually was good for nothing (in the finite sense). XIII 566

What reconciled me to my fate and to my suffering was that I, alas, the so unhappy, so agonizing captive, had received this boundless freedom in being able to deceive, that I had and was given permission to be unconditionally alone with the pain—of course this was still enough to make all the rest of my capability not very pleasant for me. —When this is presupposed (such a pain and such a concealment), how the turn is made depends on an individuality's difference, whether this solitary, inner anguish daimonically finds its expression and its satisfaction in hating humankind and cursing God, or just the opposite. The latter was the case with me. As far back as I can remember, I was convinced of one thing—that for me there was no comfort or help to be sought in others. Replete with the much that otherwise was granted me, as a human being longing for death, *qua* spirit desiring the longest possible life, I, who sadly loved people, wanted to be helpful to them, to find comfort for them, above all clarity in thought, *in specie* [in particular] about Christianity. Very far back in my recollection goes the thought that in each generation there are two or three who become sacrificed for the others, are used to find out in frightful sufferings what is beneficial for others. That is how I sadly understood myself, that I was designated for this.

So I went out into life—initiated into every possible enjoyment of life yet never actually enjoying it, but instead, and this
was my pleasure related to the pain of my depression, striving to
produce the appearance that I was enjoying it—in association
with all possible people, but it never occurred to me that I had a
confidant in any one of them, and it certainly never occurred to
any one of them that he was my confidant. That is, I had to
become and did become an observer, as an observer and as spirit
was extraordinarily enriched with experiences by this life, came
to see very close at hand that epitome of desires, passions, moods,
feelings, etc., and had practice in entering into and coming out
of a person and also in imitating him. My imagination and my
dialectic continually had plenty of material to work on and
plenty of time, free of all activity, to be idle. For long periods I
have done nothing but practice dialectical exercises with an admixture of imagination, testing my mind and spirit as one tunes
an instrument—but *I* was not really living. I was tossed about in
life, tested in very much and in almost the greatest variety of
things, unfortunately also in mistakes—alas, and also on the road
of perdition. Then in my twenty-fifth year, I—myself an enig-
matically developed extraordinary possibility, the meaning and
destiny of which, despite my superb reflection, which possibly
understood everything, I did not understand—understood one
thing, that my life was most properly used in doing penance. But
I had not really lived, except in the category of mind and spirit;
a human being I had not been, child and youth least of all.

XIII
567

Then my father died.[58] In a mitigation of ideality, the powerful religious impression of childhood acquired a renewed power
over me. Indeed, I had also grown so much older that I was
better suited to my upbringing; the trouble with it was simply
that it really would not be to my benefit until I became forty
years old. My misfortune, more or less from birth and completed
by my upbringing, was not to be fully human. But to be a
child—and the other children laugh, tease, or do whatever they
ordinarily do; and to be a young man—and the other young
men fall in love, dance, or do whatever they ordinarily do—and
then, although one is a child and youth, to be mind and spirit:
what frightful torment, even more frightful if with the aid of the

imagination one knows how to perform the feat of making it appear as if one were the youngest of all. But this misfortune is already eased when one is forty years old, and in eternity it does not exist.

I have had no immediacy, and therefore, understood in a purely and simply human sense, I have not lived. I began at once with reflection, did not accumulate a little reflection in later life, but I actually am reflection from first to last. In the two ages of immediacy (childhood and youth), I, deft (as reflection always is), aided myself, had to aid myself, with something rather counterfeited, and I, myself not yet clear about what had been granted to me, suffered the pain of not being like the others, something I at that time would of course have given everything to be able to be for just a brief time. A spirit can superbly tolerate not being like others; indeed, this is specifically the negative qualification of spirit. But childhood and youth relate to the qualifications of the species, the human race, and for that very reason it is the greatest agony at that time to be unlike the others, or as with me, strangely turned the wrong way, to happen to begin where few in each generation end. Most people, who only live out the elements of the psychical-physical synthesis, never arrive at the qualification: spirit. But, on the other hand, I now have my life ahead of me in an altogether different sense. Nothing is more unfamiliar and foreign to me than this sad longing for childhood and youth. I thank my God that it is over and done with, and now I feel happier with each day I grow older, yet blessed only through the thought of eternity, because temporality is not and never will be the element of spirit but in one sense is its suffering.

An observer will see how everything was set dialectically in motion: I had a thorn in the flesh, intellectual endowments (especially imagination and dialectic), and education in abundance, an enormous development as an observer, a truly rare Christian upbringing, an altogether unique dialectical relation to Christianity. From childhood I was trained in obedience, absolute obedience, was equipped with an almost reckless faith in being capable of everything, except one thing—to become a free bird, even if it were for just one single whole day, or to slip out of the chains of depression in which another power held me—finally,

XIII
568

I myself was a penitent. As I now see it, it seems as if from the very first moment another power had been watching this and said as the fisherman says of the fish: Just let it run; it is still too soon to pull it in. Strangely enough—and this goes far back in my recollection without my being able in any way to say when I began or how such a thing occurred to me—I continually, that is, every day, prayed to God to give me the zeal and patience for the work he himself would assign to me.

In this way I became an author.

———————

Prior to the real beginning of my work as an author, there was an event, or rather a fact[59]; an event most likely would not have been enough; it was a fact—I myself had to be an acting agent. I cannot give further particulars about that fact, its nature, how frightfully complex it was dialectically even though in another sense quite simple, and where the collision actually lay, but only ask the reader not to think of revelations and the like, since with me everything is dialectical. I will, however, present the result of the fact insofar as it serves to throw light on the authorship. It was a double fact. However much I have lived in another sense, I had really leaped over, humanly speaking, childhood and youth. This _{presumably} presumably had to be retrieved (that no doubt was the view of Governance)—instead of having been young, I became a poet, which is youth a second time. I became a poet, but with my religiously oriented background, indeed, with my definite religiousness, the same fact became for me a religious awakening also. So in the most decisive sense I came to understand myself in the religious, in the religiousness to which I had, however, related myself as to a possibility. The fact made me a poet. If I had not been the one I was, and the event on the other hand the one it was, and I acted as I did act—that would have been the end of it; I would have remained a poet and then after many years perhaps would have come into a relation to the religious. But just because I was as religiously developed as I was, the fact gripped me far more deeply and in religious impatience annihilated in a

XIII
569

certain sense what I had become, a poet—annihilated it, or in any case I began concurrently, at the very same time, in two places, yet in such a way that to be a poet was actually no concern of mine, was what I had become through something else; on the other hand, the religious awakening did not occur through myself but occurred in conformity with myself, that is, in a deeper sense I did not recognize myself in being a poet but did indeed recognize myself in the religious awakening.

Here the reader readily perceives the explanation for the duplexity of the whole authorship, except that this duplexity was also assimilated in the author's consciousness. What was to be done? Well, the poetic element had to be emptied out—for me there was no other possibility. But the entire esthetic production was taken into custody by the religious; the religious put up with this emptying out of the poetic but continually pressed on, as if it would say, "Aren't you soon finished with that?"* While the

---

*Now one perhaps realizes what I earlier saw to be the trouble, humanly speaking, with the entire work as an author: it is too imposing; it does not fit into any moment of actuality, partly because of the enormous speed with which it was done, and partly because it covered such a crucial development as from the esthetic to the religious, the Christian. This was concealed in connection with *Either/Or* as the first work; no criterion had yet been established, nor was the duplexity in place. *Either/Or* was considered to be the fruit of many years of work.[60] This illusion helped, and many other things also helped *Either/Or*. Therefore, that is, with the help of this illusion, the public could see the great diligence that had been expended with regard to the style—and yet *Either/Or* literally was written in the shortest time and in it perhaps the least diligence was expended on the style. But of course the public could also see that the first part of *Either/Or* was written perhaps several years before the second part; just the opposite, however, was the case—the second part was written first. So it was with *Either/Or*. But then when the illusion was made impossible and the criterion established, there was no other way to look at it than to regard it as a botched piece of work not worth any attention—naturally, a work on which I took five years ordinarily ought to take fifteen. —Now perhaps people will also understand and agree with me that I wished to have no reviews[61] because I did not dare to hope for any substantial review. In such a little country, how did I dare to count on a contemporary who would have the qualifications and also the time to assess such deliberately cunning writing—and direct communication I did not dare to impart to anyone, since I had understood silence religiously as my duty. Or I wonder if it actually occurred to anyone for a single

XIII
570

XIII
570

poet-productions were being written, the author was living in decisive religious categories.*

In a certain sense, it was not at all my idea to become a religious author. My idea was to empty myself of the poetic as quickly as possible—and then out to a rural parish.[62] By this chart I steered. I felt alien to the whole poet-production, but I could not do otherwise. As I stated, originally it was not my intention to become a religious *author*. What I had thought of as a way to express emphatically that I had been religious and that the pseudonymous was foreign to me was the sudden transition: promptly to take to the country as a rural pastor.

However, in me the need to write was so great that I could not do otherwise. I let *Two Upbuilding Discourses*[63] be published, and I came to an understanding with Governance. Time for poet-production was granted, but continually in the custody of the religious, which kept its eye on me as if it would say, "Aren't you

XIII
571

soon finished with that?" And I understood myself in satisfying the religious by becoming a religious author.

Now Governance really had me shackled; perhaps like a dubious character I have been kept on a very restricted regimen. I am accustomed to living in such a way that at most I believe I have only one year left and at times, not rarely, when things are tightened up, I live on a one-week, yes, a one-day prospect. Governance had curbed me in every respect. As for the esthetic production, I could not leave it understood in such a way that it ended with my having my life in the esthetic. Even if the religious had not been in the background, that "thorn in the flesh" would still have kept me from it. As for the religious authorship, Governance had shackled me so that I did not arrogate anything to myself, since I understood myself to be in a great debt.

---

moment, when he saw *Either/Or*, that its author was a religious person, or that he himself, if he were to follow my work as an author, would in two or three years speedily find himself right in the middle of the most decisive Christian writings.

*Here one will see the significance of the *pseudonyms*, why I had to be pseudonymous in connection with the esthetic production, because I had my own life in altogether different categories and from the very beginning understood this writing as something temporary, a deception, a necessary emptying out.

And now I come to a term descriptive of me, the author, a term I am accustomed to use about myself when I am speaking with myself, a term that relates to the inverse movement of all the writing (that I did not begin by saying where I wanted to go), which is connected to my capacity as an observer, also to my awareness of being one who himself needs upbringing—that in the spheres of the intellectual and the religious, and with my sights on the concept *to exist* and then on the concept *Christendom*, I am like a spy in a higher service, the service of the idea. I have nothing new to proclaim, I am without authority; myself hidden in a deception, I do not proceed directly but indirectly-cunningly; I am no saint—in short, I am like a spy who in spying, in being informed about malpractices and illusions and suspicious matters, in exercising surveillance, is himself under the strictest surveillance. See, the police also use such people. For that purpose they do not choose only people whose lives have always been most upright; what is wanted is only experienced, sly, scheming, sagacious people who can sniff out everything, above all pick up the trail and expose. Thus the police have nothing against having such a person under their thumb by means of his *vita ante acta* [earlier life] in order precisely thereby to be able to force him unconditionally to put up with everything, to obey, and to make no fuss on his own behalf. It is the same with Governance, but there is this infinite difference between Governance and the municipal police—that Governance, who is compassionate love, precisely out of love uses such a person, rescues and brings him up, while he uses all his sagacity, which in this way is sanctified and consecrated. But in need of upbringing himself, he realizes that he is duty-bound in the most unconditional obedience. It is entirely certain that God can unconditionally require everything from every human being, that he must unconditionally put up with everything; but it is also entirely certain that consciousness of earlier errors contributes significantly to speed and ability in this respect.*

XIII
572

*If someone were to say (what I would call a penetrating remark), "If this is so, if the view that you are like a spy is true, then the entire work as an author is indeed a kind of misanthropic treason, a crime against being a human being"—I would answer: Ah, yes, the crime is namely this—that I have *Chris-

But it certainly is obvious that Christendom has gone astray in reflection and sagacity. Immediate pathos, yes, even if one were to sacrifice one's life in immediate pathos, does not help. There is far too much reflection and sagacity available not to be able to wipe out his significance. In this age, even for a martyr to be of benefit, he must have reflection in order to implicate the age in such a way that it actually gets caught when it puts him to death—and that then the awakening can follow.

This is how I understand myself in my work as an author: it makes manifest the illusion of Christendom and provides a vision of what it is to become a Christian. Whether there is such a high level of religiousness that all the esthetic writing before it can be regarded not as a necessary emptying out, not as a holy deception, but as something that must be repented—that I do not know. I have never understood it in that way, and it will hardly occur to anyone before my saying it now. But since everything with me is reflection, this thought has of course not escaped me either. I can imagine the objection made out of a scrupulous and

---

tianly loved God. I have not with the smallest fraction of the capacities granted me striven to express (what perhaps is loving people) that the world is good, loves the true, wills the good, that the demand of the times is the truth, that the human race is the true or presumably even God, and therefore the task (Goethean and Hegelian) is to satisfy the age. On the contrary, I have tried to express that the world, if it is not evil, is mediocre, that "the demand of the times" is always foolishness and fatuousness, that in the eyes of the world the truth is a ludicrous exaggeration or an eccentric superfluity, that the good must suffer. I have tried to express that to apply the category "human race" to what it means to be a human being, especially as a term for the highest, is a misunderstanding and paganism, because the human race, humankind, is different from an "animalkind" not only by the advantages of race but by this *humanness*, that every individual in the human race (not just an outstanding individual, but every individual) is more than the race. This has its basis in the God-relationship (and this is Christianity, whose category *the single individual* is so strangely laughed to scorn by an esteemed Christian age), because to relate oneself to God is far superior to relating oneself to the race or through the race to God. This I have striven to express. I have not orated or thundered, have not lectured, but have disclosed that it is the case with the age and the contemporaries also in our time that with regard to the good and the true things are deplorable and confused. I have tried to make this manifest with all the craftiness and subtlety at my disposal. In contrast to the view and the life that merely humanly and with

pusillanimous conception of duty to speak the truth, a conception that leads, consistently, to being totally silent for fear of saying something untrue and, since silence can also be an untruth, leads, consistently, to: Do it or don't do it, be silent or speak— both are equally wrong.[64] But anxiety bordering on madness is not to be regarded as a higher form of religiousness. The teleological suspension related to the communication of truth (temporarily suppressing something precisely in order that the true can become more true) is a plain duty to the truth and is part and parcel of a person's responsibility to God for the reflection granted to him.

Familiar as I was with the inner suffering involved in becoming a Christian and rigorously brought up in it, I almost missed the other side of the matter. Here Governance assisted and assisted in such a way that the outcome of what I did truly benefited me and my cause, so that, to compare intellectual endowment to a stringed instrument, I not only remained in tune but gained an extra string on my instrument—the fruit of being

XIII
574

---

human self-complacency loves being human and betrays God, in contrast to that I have committed the crime of loving God and striving in every way, but indirectly, *qua* spy, to get this treason made manifest. On the assumption that I had always had my capacities freely at my disposal (and that it had not been the case that another power was able at every moment to force me if I would not voluntarily), then from the very beginning I could have converted all my writing into the interest of the times; I would have had it in my power (if this betrayal would not otherwise have been punished in such a way that I would have been annihilated) to become what the times demanded and thus, Goethean and Hegelian, would have become one more demonstration that the world is good, that the human race is the truth and the present generation the court of authority, the public the inventor and judge of truth etc., since by this treason I would have managed to make an exceptional success in the world etc. Instead, I became (indeed, was constrained to become) a spy. There is nothing meritorious in this. I truly do not rely on this with regard to my salvation. But I do still take a childish delight in having served in this way, although in relation to God I offer this my entire work more shamefacedly and bashfully than a child who gives its parents a gift the parents have given the child. Oh, but what parents would be so cruel as to take the gift from the child and say, "Why, this is ours!" instead of smiling at the child and going along with its idea that it is a gift—so also with God; he is not that cruel when someone brings him as a gift—his own.

XIII
573

brought up more fully in what it is to be a Christian. Since at that decisive moment I altered my existence-relations on the occasion of *Concluding Postscript*, I have had the opportunity to experience what one can never really believe without having experienced it, this Christian scale: that love is hated.

Truly, I have always been anything but exclusive; myself of humble descent, I have loved the common man or what is called the simple class—this I know I have done. I sadly found my joy in that—and yet they are the very ones who were incited to attack me and made to think that I was exclusive. If I had actually been exclusive, this never would have happened to me. See, this is precisely the Christian scale, and sufficient to enable me to throw light on the essentially Christian from this side. The complaint that could be made about my mode of living, if the purely human and not Christianity is to be the judge, can be stated only as follows: that I have not asserted myself enough, have not been exclusive, that humanly speaking I have with levity (from the Christian point of view, God-fearingly) jested about worldly honor and esteem, that by impairing, if possible, all my worldly esteem I have also contributed to impairing worldly esteem in general. As stated before, I would find it quite all right if the exclusive and esteemed, in consideration thereof, would have been somewhat inimical to me, and I appreciate all the more that the exact opposite is and has been the case. But that I, because I have lived as I have lived, have been exposed to the common man's hatred because I have not been exclusive enough—that I have therefore been attacked, not by the distinguished but by the common man—this is lunacy—and the Christian scale.

XIII
575   Thus my entire work as an author revolves around: becoming a Christian in Christendom. And the expression for Governance's part in the authorship is this: that the author is himself the one who in this way has been brought up, but with a consciousness of it from the very beginning.

"But what have you done here!" I hear someone say. "Do you not see what you have lost in the eyes of the world by this information and attestation?" Indeed, I do see it very well. By doing this, I lose what from a Christian point of view must be regarded as a loss in being possessed: every worldly form of the interesting. I lose the interesting, to proclaim the seductive subtlety of pleasure and the enjoyment of life, the joyful gospel of the most sophisticated enjoyment of life, and mockery's overweening pride. I lose the interesting, to be an interesting possibility, whether it was not just possible that the one who maintained the ethical with equal enthusiasm and warmth, whether it was not just possible that he was the very opposite in *either* one way *or* another, since, interestingly enough, it is impossible to say for sure which he is. I lose the interesting, to be a riddle, whether this defense of Christianity carried to the extreme was not the most subtly devised form of an attack. This interesting I lose; in its place is substituted what is anything but interesting, *direct communication*, that the issue was and is: becoming a Christian. I have lost the interesting in the eyes of the crowd, in the eyes of the world—if, that is, I get off that lightly, if it does not become furious that someone has dared to be cunning in this way.

True enough, in one sense things are going backward for me (Christianly understood, forward). I began as an author with a tremendous force, to be secretly regarded almost as a villain—but naturally for that very reason charming and, especially as such, tremendously interesting and pungent. This was necessary in order to get "the crowd" of Christians along somewhat. Even if XIII one were a saint, to begin with that means *eo ipso* to surrender 577 everything, since in an age of reflection, in which we live, people are promptly defensive, and not even his death is of benefit. No, in reflection everything must be done inversely. That is how I began. At the time, I was at my highest point in relation to the multitude of people, and—since we are living in Christendom, where all are Christians—I was also at my highest point in relation to the multitude of Christians, the enormous multitude of Christians, all the novel readers male and female, the esthetes, the beautiful souls, who all are also Christians.

That was the beginning. Gradually, as I moved ahead and that public of Christians became aware, or came to suspect—indeed, that certainly is backward enough—came to suspect that I might not be so downright bad, the public dropped off more and more, and little by little I began to fall into the boring categories of the good—while I, who walked alongside in the upbuilding discourses, saw with joy that "that single individual, whom I with joy and gratitude call *my* reader," became more than one, a somewhat more numerous category, but certainly not any public. And there when I acted with a little Christian decisiveness, did what I am conscious of having done as a true good deed for little Denmark, something that will unconditionally give me joy at my hour of death, when as a sacrifice I hurled myself against the uprising of rabble-barbarism—then I was regarded by the public as lunatic and eccentric, was judged to be almost a criminal—but of course there was not the slightest trace of villainy or scoundrelism in what I did.[65] —How it does all fall together! I do not think that more can be demanded of a spy.

And now, now I am not at all interesting any longer. That what it means to become a Christian should *actually* be the fundamental idea in the whole authorship—how boring! And all this about "The Seducer's Diary,"* this tremendously intriguing book! Well, that also belongs. If someone in a purely esthetic sense were to ask me my opinion of the esthetic writing, I will

*It is psychologically worthy of note and perhaps also deserves to be perpetuated that a person whose name I will grant a place here in order to carry him along with me, that Herr P. L. Møller[66] quite correctly regarded "The Seducer's Diary" as central to the whole authorship. This reminds me so vividly of the epigraph for *Stages on Life's Way,* the very work that he, with "The Diary of a Seducer" as his point of view, fell upon or fell over—which epigraph I therefore once reminded him of in a little rebuff to him,[67] but which perhaps may fittingly be repeated here again since it appropriately and epigrammatically preserves the memory of Herr P. L Møller's esthetic and critical profit from my authorship: *Solche Werke sind Spiegel: wenn ein Affe hineinguckt, kann kein Apostel heraussehen.* [Such works are mirrors: when an ape looks in, no apostle can look out.]

XIII 578

XIII 578

not conceal that I know very well what is achieved there but add that for me the esthetic value of the achievement itself signifies in a deeper sense how infinitely important is the decision to become a Christian. In immediacy to become a Christian is very *direct*, but the criterion for the truth and inwardness of the reflective expression with regard to becoming a Christian is precisely how valuable that is which is discarded in reflection. One does not become a Christian through reflection, but in reflection to become a Christian means that there is something else to discard. A person does not reflect himself into being a Christian but out of something else in order to become a Christian, especially when the situation is Christendom, where one must reflect oneself out of the appearance of being a Christian. The nature of the something else determines how deep, how significant the movement of reflection is. The reflection-qualification is specifically this: that one comes from a distance, and from what distance one comes to become a Christian. The reflection-qualification is the difficulty, which is greater in proportion to the value and significance of what is left behind.

This is how I think that I have served the cause of Christianity, while I myself was being brought up in the process. The one who was regarded with amazement as nearly the most clever (and this was achieved by *Either/Or*), the one who was readily granted position as "the interesting" (and this was achieved by *Either/Or*)—he was the very one who was duty-bound [*forpligtet*[68]] in the service of Christianity, who had dedicated* himself to it from the first moment when he began that pseudonymous work as an author; he was the very one who struggled within himself and as

XIII
579

---

*The dedication, inasmuch as it goes back in time even further, was: Even if I never managed to become a Christian, I would before God employ all my time and all my diligence at least to get it made clear what Christianity is and where the confusion in Christendom has its basis, a task for which I had basically prepared myself from my earliest youth. Humanly speaking, that was certainly a noble resolve. But Christianity is too great a power to want as a matter of course to use a person's noble resolve (which was no doubt almost the expression of the relation to my father); therefore it or Governance took the liberty of arranging the rest of my life in such a way that there could be no misunderstanding—which indeed there never was from the beginning—as to whether it was I who needed Christianity or Christianity that needed me.

an author in order to set forth this simple matter: becoming a Christian. The movement is not from the simple to the interesting, but from the interesting to the simple—becoming a Christian—where *Concluding Postscript* is located, *the turning point* in the whole work as an author, which poses "the issue" and then itself in turn, by means of indirect fencing and Socratic dialectic, mortally wounds "the system"—from behind, fighting against the system and speculative thought, lest *the way* be from the simple to the system and speculative thought instead of from the system and speculative thought back to the simple, becoming a Christian, therefore fighting and cutting through in order to find the way back. Consequently, here it is not a former esthete who later turns away from the world, but it is one who had decisively turned away from the world and the wisdom of the world. He must indeed be said to have had from the beginning quite extraordinary qualifications for becoming a Christian, but these were still all dialectical. Moreover, at this moment he feels no need to go further than to become a Christian. With his conception of the task and his consciousness of being far from perfection, he feels only the need to go further in becoming a Christian.

If the well-disposed reader has read this little book attentively, he knows what I am as an author.* This is how I portray myself. If it should so happen that my contemporaries refuse to understand me—well, this is how I belong to history, where I know I shall find my place and which place it will be. Humble before God, I also know—and I know, too, that precisely here it is my duty not to suppress this but to say it, since if pride and haughtiness, which arrogate something to themselves, are an abomination to God, then cowardly fear of people, which in mendacious modesty disparages itself, is just as much so—I also know who I was, humanly speaking (*historice* [in a historical sense], because it is in God's power every day, even today, to change this), that the extraordinary (verging on genius) was granted to me.

With the present little book, which thus also belongs to a bygone time, I bring to an end the entire earlier work as an author,

---

*That I myself have a more detailed purely personal interpretation of my own person is naturally quite as it should be.

and then as the author (not as an author, but as the author) I go forward into the future. What the immediate future will be, I do not know; how what comes after that, the historical, will turn out—that I know. But whatever I know pertaining to this would not comfort me if I were not, although humble and also penitent, yet in faith and confidence, on my way to the future closest at hand and at every moment equally close: eternity. Suppose, if I live longer, that time deprives me of everything, suppose posterity makes full compensation—what harm or what benefit is there actually in this for me anyway—the former does not harm me if I just take care to be an absentee, and the latter will not benefit me since I will have indeed become an absentee.

CONCLUSION[69]

I have nothing more to say, but in conclusion I will allow someone else to speak, my poet, who, when he comes, will usher me to the place among those who have suffered for an idea and will say:

"The martyrdom this author suffered can be described quite briefly in this way: He suffered being a genius in a market town.[70] The criterion he applied with regard to capabilities, diligence, disinterestedness, sacrifice, absoluteness of thought categories, etc. was much too high for the average of his contemporaries, jacked up the price all too unreasonably, and pressed down their price all too unreasonably. It almost made it seem as if the market town and the majority there did not have *absolutum dominium* [absolute rule], but that there was a God. So they at first mutually entertained one another for a time; they loquaciously discussed and discussed why he, after all, should have received these extraordinary capabilities, why he, after all, should be independent and thus able to be so industrious, and why be that anyway—they loquaciously discussed this so long (while they also took offense at one or another eccentricity [*Særhed*] in his mode of living, which actually was not eccentric, but no doubt was very particularly [*særligen*] calculated to serve his life's purpose)—until the *summa summarum* [sum of sums] became: It is his pride; everything can be explained by his pride. Thereupon they went further, from loquacious discussion to action. Since it is his pride,

XIII
580

they said, then any hidden opposition, any brazenness toward him and mistreatment of him, is not only permissible, no, it is a duty to God—indeed, it is his pride that must be punished. O you inestimable market town, how priceless you are when you put on your dressing gown[71] and become sanctimonious, when abandoning yourself to every nauseating inclination of envy, coarseness, and rabble barbarism also becomes the expression for doing obeisance to God. But, now, what about 'his pride'? Was his pride due to the great capabilities? That would be like reproaching the yellow bunting, saying that wearing all its gold ornaments is its pride or is out of pride. Or was it his diligence etc.? If a very strictly brought up child worked together with others in the class, would it not be strange to say that his diligence etc. were pride, even if it was the case that the others could not keep up with him? But such instances rarely occur, because the child is promoted to a new class. But unfortunately the person who in many ways is ready to be promoted to eternity's class—there is only one class, temporality's, where he perhaps must remain for a long time.

"This was the martyrdom. But this is why I, his poet, also see the epigram, the satire, not the particular things that he wrote but what his whole life was. I see that now—when all the many 'real' people, with whom he by no means could compare favorably, especially when 'legs' are supposed to provide the criterion,[72] not for what it is to be cattle (*animal*) but for what it is to be a human being, now when their legs like his have turned to dust in the grave and he has arrived in eternity, where, parenthetically speaking, 'legs' do not determine the outcome, neither their thinness nor their thickness, where, parenthetically speaking, he, praise God, is forever freed from the company of the brutish—I see that all these real people furnish an essential appurtenance, a chorus, a priceless market-town chorus, which took its stand on what it understood, his trousers, which became 'the demand of the times,' or even more precious, a chorus that wanted to ironize—the ironist. When I merely think of it, I can laugh loudly. But it comforts him in eternity that he has suffered this, that he voluntarily exposed himself to it, that he did not support his cause with any illusion, did not hide behind any illusion, but by suffering with God-fearing sagacity saved up for eternity: the recollection of surmounted sufferings, that he had remained faithful to himself and to his first love, the love with which he has loved only what has suffered in the world. Even though humble, he will not sneakily approach those glorious ones, not sneakily as if his life on earth had expressed that their lives must have been either an accident or an untruth or an immaturity, since by serving the truth he had won great honor and esteem, had everywhere met spirit and understanding, unlike those glorious ones, who almost everywhere met brutishness and misunderstanding.

XIII
582

"Yet also here in the world he found what he sought: 'that single individual'; if no one else was that, he himself was and became that more and more. It was the cause of Christianity that he served; from childhood his life was wonderfully fitted for that. Thus he completed the task of reflection—to cast Christianity, becoming a Christian, wholly and fully into reflection. The purity of his heart was to will only one thing.[73] What in his lifetime was his contemporaries' complaint against him—that he refused to scale down, to give in—became posterity's eulogy on him— that he did not scale down, did not give in. But the imposing undertaking did not beguile him; while he *qua* author dialectically maintained supervision over the whole, he Christianly understood that for him the whole undertaking meant that he himself was being brought up in Christianity. The dialectical structure he completed, the parts of which are previous separate works, he could not attribute to any human being, even less would he attribute it to himself. If he should have attributed it to anyone, it would have been to Governance, to whom it was indeed attributed day after day, year after year, by the author, who historically died of a mortal disease but poetically died of a longing for eternity in order unceasingly to do nothing else than to thank God."[74]

Supplement

"THE SINGLE INDIVIDUAL"

TWO "NOTES" CONCERNING MY
WORK AS AN AUTHOR

by S. Kierkegaard[75]

In these times everything is politics. The viewpoint of the religious is worlds (*toto caelo* [a whole heaven]) apart from this, just as the starting point and ultimate goal are also worlds (*toto caelo*) apart, since the political begins on earth in order to remain on earth, while the religious, taking its beginning from above, wants to transfigure and then to lift the earthly to heaven.

An impatient politician who hastily glances at these pages will certainly find only little for his upbuilding—so be it. If, however, he would kindly be a little patient, I am convinced that he, too, will become aware, even in the brief suggestions communicated on these pages, that the religious is the transfigured rendition of what a politician, provided he actually loves being a human being and loves humankind, has thought in his most blissful moment, even if he will find the religious too lofty and too ideal to be practical.

This cannot disturb the religious person, who certainly knows that Christianity is and is called the practical religion but also knows that *the prototype* and the relative prototypes normatively formed accordingly, each one separately, managed by their many years of exertion, work, and disinterestedness to become nothing in the world, laughed to scorn, insulted, etc.— which then to a politician must seem the peak of impracticality, whereas even a pagan and none other than antiquity's "practical philosopher"[76] was with heart and soul an avowed fervent lover of *this* impracticality.

But although "impractical," yet the religious is eternity's transfigured rendition of the most beautiful dream of politics. No politics has been able, no politics is able, no worldliness has been able, no worldliness is able to think through or to actualize to the ultimate consequences this idea: human-equality, human-likeness [*Menneske-Lighed*].[77] To achieve perfect equality in the medium of *world-likeness* [*Verds-Lighed*], that is, in the medium that by nature is dissimilarity, and to achieve it in a *world-like* [*verds-ligt*], that is, differentiating way, is eternally impossible, as one can see by the categories. If perfect equality, likeness, should be achieved, then *worldliness* would have to be completely eradicated, and when perfect equality, likeness, is achieved, *worldliness* [*Verdslighed*] ceases to be. But is it not, then, like an obsession, that *worldliness* has gotten the idea of wanting to force perfect equality, likeness, and to force it in a worldly way—in worldliness, world-likeness! Ultimately only the essentially religious can with the help of eternity effect human equality [*Menneske-Lighed*], the godly, the essential, the not-worldly, the true, the only possible human equality; and this is also why—be it said to its glorification—the essentially religious is the true humanity [*Menneskelighed*].

Yet just one word more, if I may. What the times *demand*—yes, who could ever finish figuring that out, now that worldliness has caught fire by spontaneous combustion caused and occasioned by the worldly friction of worldliness against worldliness. On the other hand, what the times in the deepest sense *need* can be totally and completely expressed in one single word—the times need: eternity. The misfortune of our age is precisely that it has become merely *time* by itself, temporality, which impatiently wants to hear nothing about eternity and subsequently, well-intentioned or furious, even wants to make the eternal utterly superfluous by means of a contrived imitation, which will never in all eternity succeed, because the more we think we are able to or harden our hearts to be able to dispense with the eternal, all the more do we stand basically in need of just that.

S. K.

For the Dedication to "That Single Individual"*

1846

Dear Reader! Please accept this dedication. It is offered, as it were, blindly, but therefore in all honesty, untroubled by any other consideration. I do not know who you are; I do not know where you are; I do not know your name. Yet you are my hope, my joy, my pride, and covertly my honor.

It comforts me that you now have this opportunity, that which I have honestly aimed at during my work and in my work. If it were feasible that reading what I write came to be common worldly practice or at least pretending to have read it in hopes thereby of getting ahead in the world, this would not be the opportune time, because then on the contrary misunderstanding would have triumphed, and it would also have beguiled me if I had not striven to prevent anything like that from happening.

———————

This is in me partly a possible change, which I myself desire, attributed to mood of soul and mind, which does not make a claim to be more and consequently makes anything but a claim, rather an admission; it is partly a thoroughly- and well-considered view of *the Life*, of *the Truth*, of *the Way*.[79]

XIII
592

———————

*This piece, which has been reworked and considerably expanded, was written for and intended to accompany the dedication to "that single individual" that is found in *Upbuilding Discourses in Various Spirits*. Copenhagen, Spring 1847.

There is a view of life that holds that truth is where the crowd is, that truth itself needs to have the crowd on its side.* There is another view of life that holds that wherever the crowd is, untruth is, so that even if—to carry the matter to its ultimate for a moment—all individuals who, separately, secretly possessed the truth were to come together in a crowd (in such a way, however, that "the crowd" acquired any *deciding*, voting, noisy, loud significance), untruth would promptly be present there.**

"The crowd" is untruth. What Paul says is eternally, divinely, Christianly valid: "Only one reaches the goal,"[80] not by way of comparison, since in a comparison "the others" are of course included. This means that everyone can be this one; God will help him in that—but only one reaches the goal. This in turn means that everyone should be careful about becoming involved with "the others," essentially should speak only with God and with himself—since only one reaches the goal. This in turn means that humankind has kinship with or that to be a human being is to have kinship with the divine.

XIII
593

The worldly, temporal, busy, sociable-friendly version is: "How unreasonable that only one would reach the goal. After all, it is much more probable that several jointly reach the goal; and if we become many, then it becomes much more certain and also easier for each one individually." To be sure, it is much *more probable*, and it is also true with regard to all earthly and material goals; and it becomes the one and only truth if it is allowed to dominate, because then this view abolishes both God and eter-

---

*Yet it is perhaps most appropriate to mention once and for all something that is self-evident and something I certainly have never denied—namely, that with regard to all temporal, earthly, worldly goals, the crowd can have its validity, even its validity as the decisive factor, that is, as the authority. But I am not speaking about such matters, no more than I occupy myself with such things. I am speaking about the ethical, the ethical-religious, about *the truth*, and I say that from the ethical-religious point of view the crowd is untruth if it is supposed to be valid as the authority for what *truth* is.

**Yet it is perhaps most appropriate to mention, although it seems to me almost superfluous, that it naturally could not occur to me to object, for example, to the preaching or the proclaiming of *the truth*, if it were to an assembly of hundreds of thousands. No, but even if it is an assembly of only ten people—and if a vote is to be taken, that is, if the assembly is supposed to be the authority, if the crowd is to determine the issue—then untruth *is* there.

nity and *humankind's* kinship with the divine, abolishes it or changes it into fable and substitutes the modern view (incidentally the old paganism)—namely, that to be a human being is to belong as a specimen to a race endowed with understanding. Then the race, the species, is higher than the individual or then there are only specimens, not individuals.

But eternity, which, quiet as the nocturnal sky, arches high over temporality, and God in heaven, who from the blessedness of this sublime serenity, without the least tremor of dizziness, surveys these countless millions and recognizes each and every individual—and he, the great examiner, says, "Only one reaches the goal." This means that everyone can and everyone should become this one, but only one reaches the goal.

Thus where there is a crowd or where decisive importance is attributed to the fact that there is a crowd, there is no working *there*, no living there, no striving there for the highest goal but only for some earthly goal, because there can be working for the eternal, decisively, only where there is one, and to become this one, which all can be, is to be willing to let God help—"the crowd" is untruth.

A crowd—not this crowd or that, the contemporary crowd or a deceased crowd, a crowd of commoners or of the elite, of rich or poor, etc., but a crowd understood in the concept*—is untruth, since a crowd either makes for impenitence and irresponsibility altogether, or for the single individual it at least weakens responsibility by reducing the responsibility to a fraction. See, there was no individual soldier who dared to lay hands on Caius Marius;[81] that was the truth. But just three or four women conscious of or with the idea of being a crowd and hoping that no one could definitely say who it was or who it was who started—they had the courage to do it—what untruth! In the first place,

XIII
594

---

*Therefore the reader will recall that here by "crowd," "the crowd," is understood a purely formal conceptual qualification and not what is usually understood by "the crowd" when it presumably is also a qualification, inasmuch as human egotism irreligiously divides humankind into "the crowd" and the elite etc. Good Lord, how would the religious mentality ever dream up such an inhuman inequality! No, "crowd" is number, the numerical; a number of aristocrats, millionaires, important dignitaries, etc.—as soon as the numerical is operative, it is "crowd," "the crowd."

the untruth is this, that it is "the crowd" that does what either *only the single individual* in the crowd does or in any case *each individual* does. A crowd is an abstraction, which does not have hands; but every individual ordinarily has two hands; so when he, an individual, lays his two hands on Caius Marius, then they are that individual's two hands, certainly not those of his neighbors, even less of the crowd, which has no hands. In the second place, the untruth is that the crowd had the "courage" to do it, since not even the most cowardly of all the individuals was ever as cowardly as the crowd always is. Each individual who escapes [*flygte*] into the crowd and thus cowardly avoids [*flye*] being the single individual (who either has the courage to lay hands upon Caius Marius or at least has the courage to admit that he does not have it) contributes his portion of cowardliness to the "cowardliness" that is: a crowd.

Take the supreme example, think of Christ—and the whole human race, all the people who were born and ever will be born. But the situation is one of particularity—as an individual alone with him in a solitary place, as an individual to go up to him and to spit on him—the human being never was born and never will be who would have the courage or brazenness to do it; that is the truth. But then they became a crowd; then they had the courage for it—frightful untruth!

The crowd is untruth. Therefore no one basically has more contempt for what it is to be a human being than those who make a profession of standing at the head of a crowd. Suppose that someone, a single human being, comes up to such a person; well, what does he care about him? That is much too little; he haughtily sends him away—there must be hundreds at least. If there are thousands, then he bows and scrapes to the crowd— what untruth! No, if it is a single human being, then one is to express the truth by respecting what it is to be a human being; and if it perhaps is, as we cruelly say, a wretched indigent, then this is what one should do—one should invite him into the best room and, if one has several voices, use the kindest and friendliest—that is the truth. On the other hand, if it is a gathering of thousands or more and *truth* is to be a matter of voting, then this is what one should do: one should devoutly—if one does not prefer to pray silently the petition in the Lord's Prayer: Deliver us from evil—one should devoutly declare that ethically and religiously the crowd as the authority is untruth, whereas it is eternally true that everyone can be the one. That is the truth.

The crowd is untruth. Therefore Christ was crucified, because he, even though he directed his words to all, would not have anything to do with the crowd, because he in no way wanted a crowd for support, because in that regard he unconditionally thrust away, would not form a party, did not allow balloting, but wanted to be what he was, the truth, which relates itself to the single individual.

This is why everyone who in truth wants to serve the truth is *eo ipso* in some way a martyr. If it were possible that an individual in the womb could resolve in truth to will to serve *the truth*, then that individual, whatever the martyrdom turns out to be, is *eo ipso* a martyr even in the womb. To win a crowd is not such a great art; all that is needed for that is some talent, a certain dose of untruth, and a little familiarity with human passions. But no truth-witness—alas, and every person, you and I, should be that—dares to become involved with a crowd. The devout work of the truth-witness—who of course has nothing to do with politics and does his utmost to see to it that he is not confused with a politician—is to become involved with everyone if possible, but always individually, is to speak with each one individually, on the highways and byways—in order to split up a crowd or to speak to a crowd, not in order to form a crowd but in order that one or two individuals might go home from the gathering and become the single individual. But when "the crowd" is treated as the authority in relation to *the truth* and its judgment as the judgment, the truth-witness shuns the crowd more than the young virtuous girl shuns a low dance hall. And those who address "the crowd" as the authority, he regards as tools of untruth. To repeat again, whatever may at times have complete, at times partial, legitimacy in politics and similar areas becomes untruth when it is carried over into the realms of the intellectual, the spiritual, and the religious. For the sake of what is perhaps excessive circumspection, just one more thing: by *truth* I always understand *eternal truth*. But politics etc. has nothing to do with

XIII
596

eternal truth. A politics that in the sense of *eternal truth* was in earnest about carrying *eternal truth* into actuality would to the highest degree immediately show itself to be the most "unpolitical" that can be imagined.

The crowd is untruth. And I could weep; in any case I can learn to long for eternity when I think of the wretchedness of our age, even merely in comparison with the worst of antiquity, when I think that the daily press and anonymity make it even more deranged with the help of "the public," which then is actually the abstraction that claims to be the authority with regard to *truth,* since assemblies that make this claim presumably do not take place. That with the help of the press an anonym can say what he pleases day after day (also with regard to the intellectual, the ethical, and the religious), the slightest part of which he perhaps would not in the remotest way have the courage to say personally in a situation of individuality, can *instantaneously* address thousands upon thousands, can get thousands upon thousands to repeat what was said every time he opens his, well, it can hardly be called a mouth, opens his craw—and nobody has responsibility; that it is not, as in ancient times, even the relatively unrepentant crowd that is the all-powerful, but the absolutely unrepentant crowd—nobody, an anonym the author, an anonym the public, at times even anonymous subscribers—consequently, nobody! Nobody! Good heavens, and then nations even call themselves Christian nations!

Do not say that *truth,* again by means of the press, can then run down the lies and the errors. O you who talk that way, ask yourself: Do you dare to maintain that people taken in a crowd are just as quick to grasp for truth, which is not always palatable—as for untruth, which is always delectably prepared—to say nothing of when, to boot, the truth is bound up with a confession that one has let oneself be deceived! Or do you dare simply to assert that *truth* can just as quickly be understood as untruth, which requires no previous acquaintance, no schooling, no discipline, no abstinence, no self-denial, no honest self-concern, no tedious hard work! No, *truth,* which indeed abhors this untruth that has but one aim and aspiration, to disseminate, is not so quick and agile. In the first place it cannot work by means of the fantastical, which is untruth; its communicator is only an individual. In the second place, its communication relates itself to the single individual, since this view of life, the single individual, is precisely the truth. The truth can neither be communicated nor be received without being, as it were, under the eyes of God, without the help of God, without God's being a participant, the middle term, since God is the truth. Therefore it can be communicated by and received only by *the single individual,* who as a matter of fact could be every person who is living. The only category is that of truth in contrast to the abstract, the fantastical, the impersonal, "the crowd"—"the public"—which excludes God as the middle term (because the *personal* God cannot be the middle term in an *impersonal* relationship), thereby also excludes the truth, because God is the truth and its middle term.

To honor every individual human being, unconditionally every human being, this is the truth and is to fear God and to love *the neighbor,* but ethically-religiously to recognize "the crowd" as the authority with regard to *the truth* is to deny God and cannot possibly be loving *the neighbor. The neighbor* is the absolutely true expression for human equality. If everyone in truth loved the neighbor as himself, then perfect human equality would be achieved unconditionally. Everyone who in truth loves the neighbor expresses human equality unconditionally; everyone who, even if he confesses, as I do, that his striving is weak and imperfect, is still aware that the task is to love the neighbor; he is also aware of what human equality is. But I have never read in Holy Scripture this commandment: You shall love the crowd, to say nothing of: ethically-religiously you are to recognize the crowd as the authority with regard to *the truth.* But to love the neighbor is, of course, self-denial; to love the crowd or pretend to love it, to make it the authority for *the truth,* is the way to acquire tangible power, the way to all kinds of temporal and worldly advantage—it is also untruth, since the crowd is untruth.[82]

———

But the person who acknowledges this view, which is rarely enunciated (because it more frequently happens that a man believes the crowd is in untruth, but if it, the crowd, will only *en masse* accept his opinion, then everything is all right), himself confesses that he is the weak and powerless one; moreover, how would one individual be able to stand against the many, who have the power! And he could not wish to get the crowd on his side in order to push through the view that the crowd as the authority, ethically-religiously, is untruth; that would surely be ridiculing himself. But if this view is from the beginning an admission of weakness and powerlessness and thus perhaps seems rather uninviting and is therefore perhaps seldom heard, it then has the good point of being equable—it insults no one, not one single person; it makes no distinction, not of one single person.

XIII
598

To be sure, a crowd is formed of individuals; consequently each one has the power to remain what he is—an individual. No one, no one, is excluded from being an individual, except the one who excludes himself by becoming many. On the contrary, to become a crowd, to collect a crowd around oneself, is the differentiation of life. Even the most well-intentioned person who speaks about this can easily insult an individual. But then once again the crowd has power, influence, status, and domination—it is indeed the differentiation of life that, dominating, disregards the single individual as the weak and powerless, temporally and in a worldly way disregards the eternal truth: the single individual.

Note: The reader will recall that this piece (the beginning of which is marked by a mood from that moment when I voluntarily exposed myself to the crudity of literary rabble-barbarism) was originally written in 1846, although later reworked and considerably expanded. Since that time existence, almighty as it is, has shed a light also upon the thesis that the crowd as the authority, ethically-religiously, is untruth. Truly, this serves me well. Just as I myself have been aided thereby to understand myself more confidently, I also no doubt will already be understood in quite another way than at that time when my weak and solitary voice was heard as a ludicrous exaggeration, whereas now it is scarcely heard because of the loud voice of existence that is speaking about the same thing.

A Word on the Relation of My Work as an Author to "the Single Individual"*

A triviality, as is known, leads a disdained and disregarded life—then in turn it has its revenge. At the base of a misunderstanding, especially if it is vehement and malicious, there naturally is a triviality—otherwise it of course would not be a misunderstanding but an essential disagreement. What constitutes a misunderstanding is that what the one regards as significant the other regards as insignificant, yet in such a way that basically it is a triviality that comes between them, and that in the misunderstanding the disagreeing parties have not first taken the time to understand each other. *At the base* of all *actual disagreement*, there is an understanding; the *baselessness* of *misunderstanding* is that the preliminary understanding is lacking, without which both agreement and disagreement are a misunderstanding. A misunderstanding, therefore, can be removed and become agreement and understanding, but it can also be removed and become actual disagreement. That two people are actually in disagreement is no misunderstanding—they are actually in disagreement simply because they do understand each other.

I surely am not far wrong when I assume that what has caused and is causing the disagreement between quite a few of my contemporaries and myself with regard to my work as an author is in part this: that single individual. Undoubtedly quite a few people would read my books if it were not for this, and certainly the crowd would leave me alone entirely if it were not for this.

Now, if this matter of *that single individual* were a triviality to me, I could, of course, drop it—indeed, do it with pleasure, and shame on me if I was not willing to do it most courteously. But

*This article was written in 1847 but was later reworked and expanded.

this is by no means the case. To me, not personally but as a thinker, this matter of the single individual is the most decisive. Thus there remains only the possibility of removing the misunderstanding—if I could succeed in making it obvious to the individuals that it truly is no triviality. In that case the disagreement would indeed be removed. What is disturbing is, namely, that it is regarded as a triviality—and that I then want to make such a big fuss about a triviality. Consequently, one of two alternatives: either the others are right, that it is a triviality and I ought to give it up, or that it is, as I understand it, something very essential. Then there is indeed no reason to take exception to my making such a big fuss—about the essential; there is, however, good reason to dwell a little on it earnestly and thoughtfully. What ought not to be neglected on my side has not been neglected. At one time (in a little article by Frater Taciturnus* in *Fædrelandet*[84]) I carried the issue as close to eccentricity as possible—certainly not out of eccentricity. On the contrary, I was very well aware of what I was doing, that I was acting responsibly, aware of my responsibility, that not to do it would have been irresponsible. I did it (and precisely in a newspaper, and precisely in a newspaper article that made contact with town gossip from start to finish), because to me it was very important to provoke attention upon this point, which is achieved neither by ten books that develop the doctrine of the single individual nor by ten lectures on the subject, but in these days is achieved simply and solely by getting the laughter aimed at oneself,** by making people somewhat angry, and then by getting them mockingly to reproach one again and again and continually for that—precisely for that which one wants inculcated and, if possible, brought to the knowledge of all. This is unconditionally the surest kind of tutor-

*By the way, please remember that it was a pseudonymous writer and that in connection with a polemical article I had the added difficulty of making it a poetical response—consequently in the character of the pseudonym.

**Between laughter, properly understood, and me there is a secret, happy understanding. I am—properly understood—a friend and lover of laughter; in one sense, that is, seriously speaking, I was no doubt the best and truest friend and lover of laughter at the very moment when all the others, all those thousands upon thousands, became ironic and I, ironically enough, became the only one who had no understanding of irony.[85]

ing. But anyone who is to effect something must know his age—and then have the courage to risk the danger of using the surest means.

[86]These I have used, although the dialectic of *the single individual* has continually been made equivocal in its double movement. In every one of the pseudonymous books, the subject of the single individual appears in some way, but there the single individual is predominantly the single individual esthetically, defined in the eminent sense, the outstanding individual, etc. In every one of my upbuilding books, the subject of *the single individual* appears, and as officially as possible, but there the single individual is someone every human being is or can be. In other words, the point of departure of the pseudonymous writers is the difference between person and person with regard to intelligence, culture, etc.; the point of departure of the upbuilding discourses is in the upbuilding, that is, in the universally human. But this doubleness is precisely the dialectic of *the single individual. The single individual* can mean the most unique of all, and *the single individual* can mean everyone. Now if one desires to stimulate attention dialectically, one will always use the category *the single individual* in a double stroke. The pride in the one thought incites a few; the humility in the other thought repels others, but the confusion in this doubleness dialectically provokes attention, and, as stated, this doubleness is precisely the idea of *the single individual.* I believe, however, that for the most part people have taken notice of the *individual* of the pseudonymous writers and have promptly associated me with the pseudonymous writers—hence all the talk about my pride and arrogance, by which judgment one actually manages only to inform on oneself.

So the subject of that single individual has been inculcated almost to the point of becoming a byword—and I, poor fellow, have had to put up with the laughter. If I had tearfully pleaded and beseeched everyone for heaven's sake to pay attention to this idea, which is eternity's, practically no one would have paid any attention to it.

Now since it has been inculcated, I shall make an attempt, and in it do my best, to try to remove at least part of the misunderstanding, which, however, can actually exist only for those who have not made themselves familiar with the writings in a deeper sense—and it could occur only to a stripling to want to preclude all misunderstanding entirely when one intends to undertake something. One must beware of misunderstanding—that is, one must beware of wanting to prevent it entirely. There is nothing that so easily gets out of hand and so easily becomes misunderstood as misunderstanding; even if one were to attempt to do nothing whatever except to preclude misunderstanding—well, he very likely would become misunderstood more than ever.

XIII
602

---

[87]That from the beginning I have had more than one reader, I do of course realize. "Denmark is a little country." Its people, who have a language of their own, are not numerous; the literary setting is so small that there is not or for a long time there has not been even a literary journal, but literature was reduced (*in absurdum*) to the attention that the daily newspapers, wholesale merchant Nathanson in particular, according to his own words, "bestow upon it."[88] As an author I have worked unusually hard and unusually fast. In the service of the truth, I have continually used part of my energy and ingenuity not to prevent the circulation of the books but to prevent their being circulated misunderstood—commensurate with that, I am even widely read. I am well aware of this, and, knowing it, I am not unappreciative and perhaps have shown my appreciation more honestly and sincerely by never misusing this as a means to attract buyers or readers. Therefore, that from my side there would be any hindrance to wanting to have my more popular books read and understood by everyone, if possible, is something that only foolishness and spite could have hit upon[89] and only envy could utilize in order to confuse the confused even more, which succeeds easily and occurs by itself, and in order, if possible, to make the right-minded, the better people, the more insightful, indignant toward me, which does not occur by itself and which, praise God, failed far beyond my expectations, inasmuch as the very opposite happened, truly an upbuilding joy to me.

Every more earnest person who has an eye for the condition of these times will readily perceive how important it is to oppose

XIII
603

boldly an immoral confusion that philosophically and socially wants to demoralize *the single individuals* by means of *humanity* or fantastic social categories, to oppose it, basically and observing all consistency, under the weight of an enormous responsibility but also unto every true ultimate—a confusion that wants to teach an ungodly contempt for what is the first condition of all religiousness: to be an individual human being. This confusion can be opposed, if possible, only by getting hold of people individually—but every human being is indeed an individual human being! Every more earnest person who knows what upbuilding is, everyone, whatever else he or she is, high or low, wise or simple, male or female, anyone who has ever felt built up and felt God as very present, will certainly agree with me unconditionally that it is impossible to build up or to be built up *en masse*, even more impossible than to "fall in love *en quatre* [in fours]" or *en masse*—upbuilding, even more decisively than erotic love, pertains to the single individual. The single individual, not the single individual in the sense of the outstanding and the especially gifted, but the individual in the sense in which every human being, unconditionally every human being, can be and should be an individual, should place his honor—but will also truly find his salvation—in being an individual. Every individual of the many who have read my upbuilding books, and for upbuilding, everyone whom I as an upbuilding author may have influenced—if he privately and honestly asks himself (and he owes this to himself, the one judging, and perhaps even also to me, who frequently enough have had to bear the brunt in those places where it is not exactly wisdom that judges) the question whether I deceived him with this talk about the single individual, whether I deceived him by exposing myself* for a time, for the sake of this idea (so

---

*That it was also for other reasons in addition to the reason cited here, I shall not develop here, not even this, that it was also, if possible, to make my contemporaries aware of a literary immorality all too appalling and engulfing in proportion to the little country that I, as an emergency volunteer [*sig Devoverende*] ventured [*vovede*] for a time to become—alas, the poor Magister of irony!—the sacrifice to that laughter, yet something that in one respect filled my soul with sadness (but then irony and sadness are, after all, really one and the same), since the one called the common man in the nation has scarcely had many in Copenhagen who Christianly have loved him more sincerely than I have—but of course I have been neither a journalist nor an agitator.

I could get *that* tightened up properly and, if possible, make *him* properly aware of it), to the laughter of the many and to whatever uses envy could make of this laughter—will certainly rather confess, if not to me, which is not required, then to himself, that what ails him is simply that he still has not really become the single individual, which I myself do not pretend to be, although I have struggled, but as yet have not grasped it, and am struggling, but as one who does not forget that according to the supreme criterion *the single individual* is beyond a human being's powers.

---

⁹⁰*The single individual* is the category through which, in a religious sense, the age, history, the human race must go. And the one who stood at Thermopylae was not so secure as I, who have stood, in order at least to bring about an awareness of it, at this narrow pass, *the single individual*. His particular task was to keep the hordes from pressing through the narrow pass; if they pressed through, he would have lost. My task at least exposes me far less to the danger of being trampled down, since it was as a lowly servant (but, as I have said from the beginning and repeat again and again, *without authority*) to prompt, if possible, to invite, to induce the many to press through this narrow pass, *the single individual*, through which, please note, no one presses except by becoming the single individual; the opposite is indeed a categorical impossibility. —And yet, yes, if I were to request an inscription on my grave, I request none other than *that single individual*; Even if it is not understood now,* it surely will be.

With the category *the single individual*, the pseudonymous writers took aim at the system** in a day when everything here at home was system and system; now the system is scarcely men-

*The reader will recall that this was written in 1847. The world upheavals in 1848 have forced the understanding considerably closer.

**Everyone who is at all dialectical will see that it is impossible to attack "the system" from a point within the system. But outside there is only one indubitably seminal point: the single individual, ethically and religiously, existentially accentuated.

tioned anymore,* at least not as the shibboleth and as the demand of the times. With the category *the single individual*, I marked the beginning of the writing bearing my signature; it remains as a uniformly repeated formula—therefore this matter of the single individual is not a later invention of mine, but my first. —My possible ethical significance is unconditionally linked to the category *the single individual*. If this was the right category, if all was in order with this category, if I perceived correctly here, understood correctly that this was my task, even though by no means pleasant or appreciated, to bring about awareness of it, if this was bestowed on me, although involving inner sufferings such as probably are seldom experienced, although involving external sacrifices such as a person is not every day found willing to make—then I stand and my writings with me.

This category, having used this category, moreover so decisively and personally, determines the outcome ethically. Without this category and without the use of it that has been made, the reduplication of the entire work as an author would be missing. Just because the books said, presented, developed, and expressed all that they expressed, and perhaps with imagination, dialectic, psychological insight, and other such qualities—from this it would by no means follow summarily that the author had understood, and had understood how to express altogether decisively with a single phrase, also to express in action, that he had understood his age and was himself aware: **that it was an age of disintegration.****⁹¹

This is why the author does not call himself a *truth-witness*—no, oh no, far from it! By such a term is not actually understood everyone who says something true. Thank you, no; then we would have truth-witnesses enough. No, in a truth-witness the personal existing must be seen ethically in relation to what was said, whether the personal existing expresses what was said—a consideration that, it is entirely right to say, the systematizing and the didacticizing and the characterlessness of the age have most wrongly abolished. The author's life has indeed fairly accu-

*And now in 1848!
**For an interpretation of the present age, see, for example, *A Literary Review* by S. K., Copenhagen 1846, the last section.⁹²

rately expressed what was ethically accentuated: to be the single
individual; he has associated with countless people, but he has
always stood alone, in his striving also striving to be allowed to
stand alone, while in the surrounding world almost everything
was the setting up, down, and aside of committees. For the sake
of his category, he has also made more than one sacrifice, exposed himself to one and another danger—and, note well, to
precisely the kind of danger that categorically corresponds to
the single individual—exposed himself to "the crowd" and "the
public."

But even if there was no other hindrance, he has not been
obliged to work for a living. That alone is enough, is a preferential position that ethically places him down in a lower class. But
in addition he has also had too much imagination and much too
much of the poet to dare to be called a truth-witness in the
stricter sense. He himself has been far from having an overview
of everything from the beginning; so he has only successively
become aware of having apprehended correctly. He has so often
had occasion to take to heart Lessing's felicitously expressed wise
advice, "*Lasz uns nicht weise seyn wollen, wo wir nichts als glücklich
gewesen* [Let us not pretend to be wise when we have only been
lucky],"[93] or has had occasion to be reminded of the duty to give
God what is God's.[94] He has had too much to do with the ethical
to be a poet, and in that regard recalls the esthete's first and later
repeated words in *Either/Or** concerning not wanting to be a
poet and the ethicist's** stressing this as right, because a person
should move from being a poet and into the existential, the ethical;† but he is still too much of a poet to be a truth-witness. He

---

*See *Either/Or*, I, p.1, first Diapsalm; see also p. 23, "In vain do I resist. My
foot slips. My life nevertheless remains a poet-existence" etc.[95]

**See *Either/Or*, II, p. 217; see *Concluding Postscript*, p. 188.[96]

†This movement from "the poet" to religious existing is basically the movement in the entire work as an author regarded in its totality. See *Works of Love*
(II A, B[97]) concerning the use again made there of "the poet" as the *terminus a
quo* [point from which] for Christian religious existing. As for the movement,
which is described in a series of books, *from* the philosophical, the systematic, to
the simple, that is, the existential, this movement, only in another situation, is
essentially the same as from the poet to religious existing.

is a *confinium* [border territory] in between, which is, however, properly related categorically to the future of history.

The single individual is the category of spirit, of spiritual awakening, as diametrically opposite to politics as possible. Earthly reward, power, honor, etc. are not involved in its proper application. Even when it is used in the interest of the established order, inwardness does not interest the world; and when it is used cataclysmically, it still does not interest the world, because to make sacrifices, to be sacrificed—which must indeed become the consequence of not seeking to become a power in the external world—does not interest the world.

---

[98] *The single individual*—from the Christian point of view, this is the decisive category, and it will also become decisive for the future of Christianity. The fundamental confusion, what could be called the fall of Christendom, is: year after year, decade after decade, century after century, to have insidiously wanted—almost half-unconscious of what it wanted to do and essentially unaware of what it did—to trick God out of his proprietary right to Christianity and has taken into its head the idea that the race, the human race, has itself invented or has itself at least as good as invented Christianity. As in the state, property falls to the state when it has been left for a certain number of years and no owner has claimed it, just so the human race, spoiled by knowing in a banal sense that Christianity does after all exist, has thought something like this, "It is a very long time since God has let anything be heard from him *qua* owner and master; so Christianity has fallen to us, whether we want either to abolish it totally or to modify it *ad libitum* [as desired] and treat it more or less as our possession and invention." This is treating Christianity—not as something that in the submission of *obedience under God's majesty* **shall** *be believed*, but as something that in order to be

accepted must seek with the help of "reasons" to satisfy "the times," "the public," "this distinguished assembly," etc. Every rebellion in science and scholarship: against discipline, every rebellion in society: against obedience, every rebellion in politics: against secular rule—is connected with and derived from this rebellion of the human race against God in regard to Christianity. This rebellion—the abuse of the category of "human race"—is not, incidentally, reminiscent of the rebellion of the Titans but is the rebellion of *reflection*, the insidious rebellion, continued from year to year, from generation to generation.

Reflection continually takes only a very little bit at a time, and of this very little bit we are always able to say, "After all, one can compromise on small things"—until reflection will have taken everything, something one would not become aware of because it happens little by little and "one can easily compromise on little things." Therefore people must become individuals in order to receive the Christianly pathos-filled impression of Christianity. The single individual, every individual, will surely guard against wanting to initiate a lawsuit against God regarding which of the two unconditionally and to the very last jot has the proprietary right to Christianity. God must again become the thoroughly decisive middle term, but *the single individual* corresponds to God as the middle term. If "the human race" is to be "the authority" or even the middle term, then Christianity is abolished, if in no other way, then by the *wrong, unchristian form* that is given to the *Christian* communication. Not even the most sagacious and most trusted spy of the police can vouch more confidently for the correctness of the content of his report than I, a poor private operator, a spy, *si placet* [if you please], will vouch for the correctness of this.

The single individual—with this category the cause of Christianity stands or falls, now that the world-development has gone as far as it has in reflection. Without this category pantheism would be unconditionally victorious. No doubt there will be those who know how to tighten this category dialectically in a completely different way—without having had the labor of bringing it forth—but the category *the single individual* is and remains the fixed point that can hold against pantheistic confusion, is and remains the weight that can be put on, except that those who are to work and operate with this category must be more and more   XIII dialectical accordingly as the confusion becomes greater and   609 greater.[99] One can promise to make a Christian of every individual one can get in under this category—insofar as one person can do this for another—and therefore, more correctly, one can assure him that he will become that. As *the single individual* he is alone, alone in the whole world, alone—face-to-face before God—then he will no doubt manage to obey. All doubt (which, noted *in parenthesi* [parenthetically], is nothing but disobedience to God if it is regarded ethically and a scholarly fuss is not superiorly made about it) ultimately has its haunt in temporality's illusion that there are quite a few of us, or all humanity as such, which as such can finally intimidate God, itself even be Christ. And pantheism is an acoustical illusion that confuses the *vox populi* [voice of the people] and the *vox dei* [voice of God], an optical illusion, a vaporous image formed out of the fog of temporality, a mirage formed by its reflexion, which claims to be the eternal. But the fact is that this category cannot be taught directly; it is a being-able [*Kunnen*], an art [*Kunst*], an ethical task and art, the practice of which at times may claim the lives of its practitioners. The self-willed race and the confused crowds regard the highest, divinely understood, as high treason against "the human race," "the crowd," "the public," etc.

---

[100] *The single individual*—this category has been used only once, its first time, in a decisively dialectical way, by Socrates,[101] in order to disintegrate paganism. In Christendom it will be used a second time in the very opposite way, to make people (the Christians) Christians. It is not the missionary's category with regard to the pagans to whom he proclaims Christianity, but it is the missionary's category within Christendom itself in order to introduce Christianity into Christendom. When he, *the missionary*, comes,

he will use this category. If the age is waiting for a hero, it surely waits in vain; instead there will more likely come one who in divine weakness will teach people obedience—by means of their slaying him in impious rebellion, him, the one obedient to God, who would still use this category on an even much greater scale, but also with *authority*. But nothing further on this; grateful to Governance, I continue both in the one sense and in the other, in my obviously and in every respect infinitely subordinate role—*to make aware* of this category.[102]

XIII
610

POSTSCRIPT

What is said here is said of something past, something done, as the reader surely will have noted just from the tenses that are used; and the category is: to make aware, which I repeat in order to do my utmost until the very end to prevent misunderstanding.

(1849)

March 1855

On reading through these two pieces now, I want to add the following.

Jesus Christ, to name the supreme example, truth itself, certainly had followers; and, to name a human example, Socrates had followers.

If, then, I seem in one sense to force the ideality of the single individual even higher, how do I understand this? I understand it partly as an imperfection in me and partly as connected with the special nature of my task. I understand it as my imperfection, because, as I have frequently said, my entire work as an author has also been my own development, in which I myself have ever more deeply concentrated on my idea, my task. But as long as this was my situation, I was not matured enough to be able to draw individuals closer to me, even if I had wanted to. —I understand this as connected with the special nature of my task. My task is to work against a given wrong propagation (therefore not a task of propagating something) along the line of what could be called smoke-abatement, but in that case it is important to keep watch with great circumspection over the extent to which one becomes involved with individuals, lest the smoke-abatement in turn become a false propagation. It is not my task, and "in Christendom" it cannot truly be the task to create more nominal Christians or to contribute to strengthening millions in the notion that they are Christians. No, the task is precisely to shed light upon this scoundrel trick that to the benefit of the princes of the Church, of the pastors, of mediocrity—under the name of Christian fervor and zeal (how sophisticated!)—has procured these millions. It is a matter of shedding light upon and of shining light through this scoundrel trick and of getting it made clear that "in Christendom" Christian fervor and zeal will be precisely the thankless (and here, too, is the mark of the essentially Christian, just as profit is the mark of worldliness) task of relieving Christianity of some of those battalions of Christians.

Just one word more. Christ certainly had followers, and, to take a human example, Socrates also had followers; but neither Christ nor Socrates had followers in the sense that the thesis as I have presented it would become false—ethically, ethically-religiously, the crowd is untruth, the untruth of wanting to exert influence by means of the crowd, the numerical, of wanting to make the numerical the authority for what truth is.

ARMED NEUTRALITY

*OR MY POSITION AS A CHRISTIAN AUTHOR
IN CHRISTENDOM*

Armed Neutrality[1]

OR MY POSITION AS A CHRISTIAN
AUTHOR IN CHRISTENDOM

By this phrase "armed neutrality," especially as I explain it more
and more precisely, I think I am able to characterize the position
I intend to take and have taken in throwing light on Christianity
or what Christianity is or, more accurately, what is involved in
being a Christian. Naturally, this cannot mean that I want to
leave undecided whether I am myself a Christian, aspire to it,
fight for it, pray about it, and trust to God that I am that. What
I have wanted and want to *prevent* is that the emphasis would in
any way be that I am a Christian to an extraordinary degree, a
distinguished kind of Christian. This I have wanted and want to
prevent. But what I have wanted and want to *achieve* through my
work, what I also regard as the most important, is first of all to
make clear what is involved in being a Christian, to present the
picture of a Christian in all its ideal, that is, true form, worked out
to every true limit, submitting myself even before any other to be
judged by this picture, whatever the judgment is, or more accurately, precisely this judgment--that I do not resemble this picture. In addition, because the task of producing this ideal picture
is a work in which emphasis falls upon differential qualifications
for being able to do this, especially since it is to be done in relation to the manifold confusions of modern times,[2] I have chosen
for purpose of designation the words: *neutrality* and *armed*.

I do not think that without exaggeration one can say that Christianity in our time has been completely abolished. No, Christianity still exists and in its truth, but as a *teaching*, as *doctrine*. What
has been abolished and forgotten (and this can be said without
exaggeration), however, is being a Christian, what it means to be

a Christian; or what has been lost, what seems to exist no longer, is the ideal picture of being a Christian.

That this is so can be perceived readily in the nature of the confusion. (1) Christendom is an established order. This is confusing, because it is really impossible to be a Christian under this form, since an established order as the true arena for religiousness gives all Christian qualifications an unchristian, conciliatory perspective within the temporal, whereas instead the true Christian perspective for every Christian qualification is polemical within or away from finitude toward the eternal. Piety at rest is Jewish piety;[3] a militant piety (engaged at two points, first in oneself with oneself in order to become a Christian, and then with the world's opposition and persecution because one is a Christian[4]) is Christianity or being a Christian. (2) Every decisive qualification in being a Christian is according to a dialectic or is on the other side of a dialectic. The confusion is that, with the help of the scientific-scholarly annulment of the dialectical element, this has been completely forgotten. In this way, instead of presumably going further than original Christianity, we have thrown all Christianity back into the esthetic. To be, to exist (the particular) is implicit in the dialectical element; what speculative thought calls unity is first achieved in eternity, only momentarily in temporality. By unceremoniously permitting the dialectical element to be annulled this way in existence, the existence of the single individual, all the navigation marks, if I may use the expression, with regard to being a Christian have been abolished. It is possible that the present Christendom is the most perfect form of Christianity that has ever been seen; it is also possible that it is thoroughgoing worldliness.[5] (3) The medium for being a Christian has been shifted from existence and the ethical to the intellectual, the metaphysical, the imaginational; a more or less theatrical relationship has been introduced between thinking Christianity and being a Christian—and in this way has abolished being a Christian.

X[5]
B 107
290

Therefore what first and foremost must be brought into prominence again is the ideal picture of a Christian, so that it can appear as a task, beckoning, and on the other side, so that it can crush with all its weight the presumptuousness of wanting to go further than being a Christian, something that can be explained only by the fact that what it means to be a Christian has been forgotten.

It is this ideal picture that I have tried to present and will try to present. The reader will kindly be patient and not rush at once to judge or estimate to what extent the particular also serves to throw light on this picture. From the very beginning my work has not been a rush job, has not been an impetuous amendment to the total confusion or a new patch on an old garment.[6] Be patient—and perhaps I do still have a kind of right to ask this, since even more patience is truly required to carry out the work—be patient, and then be attentive.

———————

Therefore, to present in every way—dialectical,[7] pathos-filled (in the various forms of pathos[8]), psychological, modernized by continual reference to modern Christendom and to the fallacies of a science and scholarship—the ideal picture [*Billede*] of being a Christian: this was and is the task. Jesus Christ, it is true, is himself the prototype [*Forbillede*] and will continue to be that, unchanged, until the end. But Christ is also much more than the prototype; he is the object of faith. In Holy Scripture he is presented chiefly as such, and this explains why he is presented more in being than in becoming, or actually is presented only in being, or why all the middle terms are lacking—something that everyone has indeed ascertained who, even though humbly and adoringly, has earnestly sought to order his own life according to his example. Furthermore, in the course of time, the essentially Christian, unchanged, has nevertheless been subject to modifications in relation to changes in the world. My view is certainly not that it is the essentially Christian that should be improved and perfected by new modifications—I am not that speculative. No, my view is that the essentially Christian, unchanged, at times may need by way of new modifications to secure itself against the new, the new nonsense that is now in vogue. Let me clarify this relation by reference to another circumstance. In the far, far distant past, in times more simple than these, it was of course also

X[5]
B 107
291

the custom to draw up legal documents, contracts, etc. But if we take such a contract from olden times and compare it with a contract of the same kind from 1848, we undeniably find the latter considerably modified. We must not, however, be in a hurry to say that this one is therefore better than the former; ironically it might turn out that it is still a question whether it would not have been better that all these modifications had not been necessary. But since those simple times there have been so many rogues and swindlers that modifications have become necessary. So also with the modifications that the essentially Christian, unchanged, undergoes in the course of time—they are of evil or on account of evil, but with good intentions. But as the essentially Christian is modified, what it is to be a Christian is also modified. By the ideal picture of a Christian, I understand in part a kind of human interpretation in relation to Christ as the prototype, a human interpretation that, although he is and remains the object of faith, contains all the middle terms pertaining to derivatives and casts everything into becoming—and the modifications are in part related to the confusions of the past and those of a given time.

But who, now, is to do this, who is to be the one who places this picture into the situation of actuality and holds it up? If someone comes rushing headlong and points to himself, saying, "I am the one, I am myself this ideal of a Christian"—then we have fanaticism and all its woeful consequences. God forbid that it should happen in this way! As far as I am concerned, I certainly think that this would be the greatest impossibility for me at any time. Nothing is more foreign to my soul and nothing is more foreign to my nature (the dialectical), nothing more impossible, than fanaticism and fury. If I were to be regarded as furious in any way, it would have to be if it were said—and it probably is said of me—that I have a furious composure, that is, a composure that could infuriate others. From the very beginning of my work as an author, there no doubt has been a very solitary person hidden here and there who, aware of what I have been able to present poetically, only waited for the moment when I had confused myself with a poetical presentation, had rushed forth, had made myself out to be the ideal, the awaited one, etc.—in order then

X⁵
B 107
292

to attach himself to me as a follower, an adherent etc.—and who therefore is infuriated by my composure, by which he is restrained, until finally, infuriated by my composure, he would wish me dead or far away, because I would stand in the way, so that out of a kind of respect for me he would not be able to make himself out to be what he would have preferred me to be. Thus in one way or the other I would be a hindrance to setting fanaticism in motion.

It certainly is of the utmost importance that the ideal picture of a Christian be held up in every generation, elucidated particularly in relation to the errors of the times, but the one who presents this picture must above all not make the mistake of identifying himself with it in order to pick up some adherents, must not let himself be idolized and then with earthly and worldly passion pass judgment upon Christendom. No, the relation must be kept purely ideal. The one who presents this picture must himself first and foremost humble himself under it, confess that he, even though he himself is struggling within himself to approach this picture, is very far from being that. He must confess that he actually relates himself only poetically or *qua* poet to the *presentation* of this picture, while he (which is his difference from the ordinary conception of a poet) in his own person relates himself Christianly to the *presented* picture, and that only as a poet is he ahead in presenting the picture.

x⁵
B 107
293

In this way no fanaticism develops; the poet or, more accurately, the poet-dialectician, does not make himself out to be the ideal and even less does he judge any single human being. But he holds up the ideal so that everyone, if he has a mind to, in quiet solitariness can compare his own life with the ideal. It is impossible for the presentation of the ideal not to be polemical to a certain degree, but it is not polemical against any particular person, is not finitely polemical against anything finite but is infinitely polemical only in order to throw light on the ideal; it has no proposal to make and does not lean toward any decision in the external, in the secular world.

This was and is my idea of a reformation, which, whether or not it succeeds and to whatever extent it succeeds or not, in any case will go ahead on its own and take place without general assemblies, synods, balloting—in short, without any profanation. During the few years I have been a writer, I dare say I have shown an unusually productive wealth; I do not feel it diminished but rather on the increase, but I have never had and do not have a single comma to offer to a general assembly or society of balloters. I have had much to say, I feel far from emptied; on the contrary, I feel that I still have much more to say, but I have never had and do not have anything, not an infinitesimal iota, that tempts in a worldly way by being something new. There is only one thing that in every direction can halt a vortex, and thus also only one thing that can halt the vortex or the dizziness in which—and this is precisely the kind and degree of dizziness— the ideal little by little and finally entirely diminishes and is lost, the dizziness that one person is certainly just as good a Christian as all the others and thus is a Christian simply by comparison around the whole circle; there is only one thing that can halt it—no general assembly, no balloting can do it, since they only foster the sickness—and this is that the single individual, instead of swooning into a comparison relation to "the others," relates himself to the ideal.[9] In that very moment he is halted forever— and even if he were to live a hundred years, he would never make a proposal in a general assembly.

In order to present this ideal as faithful, as true, as polemically true, and with as much true pathos as it is possible for me, I will use my every day, ask for no reward—because for me this work is another expression of the fact that, as stated, I myself am brought to a halt by the ideal, not as if I had grasped it, not as if I were that—ah, I am so far from being it that in a whole lifetime I very likely will not finish the task of rightly discovering and being able to present the ideal.

Humble before God, with my knowledge of what it indeed means in truth to be a Christian, and with my knowledge of myself, I by no means dare to maintain that I am a Christian in any remarkable sense or permit any accent of distinction to fall on my being a Christian. For example, I would not dare, particularly not in Christendom, to expose myself to becoming a martyr, persecuted, deprived of life, because I was a Christian. Do not pass premature judgment on what I am saying here but rather take time to understand it. Many people all too hastily give assurances that they are Christians to the degree that they are willing to die for it, whereas the difficulty possibly lies at an entirely different point than they suspect. Let me take an imaginary situation. With a sword hanging over my head, I am ordered to say whether or not I am a Christian. My answer would be: I trust to God that I am a Christian; I believe that out of grace he will accept me as a Christian, and so on. If they are not satisfied with the answer but say, "You must say either that you are a Christian or that you are not," then I would answer: No, that I will not do. If they persist—"Then we will put you to death because you will not answer as we demand"—my answer would be: Go ahead, I have nothing to object to that; according to my understanding I accept this martyrdom. By this I mean that I am not afraid of being put to death—although I by no means flaunt a willingness for it nor am I eager for it, and therefore I must ask the reader to recall that the discussion here is, of course, hypothetical. But what I do fear is what my death would come to signify through what I say about myself. In other words, I am not afraid of dying, but I do fear to say too much about myself. I do not cowardly flee from a martyrdom, but I must be aware of and be of one mind about how I can defend falling as a martyr.

The question of whether I am a Christian (and thus for every individual, whether he is a Christian) is entirely a God-relationship. When I (and thus always for the single individual) declare that I am Christian, I am really speaking with God, even if it is human beings who ask me and therefore it is human beings I am speaking with, and therefore I dare not speak differently from the way I would speak with God. That is, as soon as I (and thus always the single individual) speak about my being a Christian, God hears it. I cannot speak of my being a Christian according to a merely human standard or within the sphere of human comparison. But then before God, would I dare to say: I am—a Christian? No, I would not dare to do this—I least of all. But therefore neither would I dare to let the emphasis fall upon my being a

X⁵
B 107
295

Christian, so that I would be put to death because I was a Christian—for suppose God thought otherwise and I had forgotten respectful deference to God, in my expression about myself had forgotten to express that God is the judge. If I, then, were put to death because I, according to my own apodictic declaration, was a Christian, my life would be taken—but this would be the least important part of it; I would by no means be through with it, because suppose I would run into trouble in eternity, that it was arrogance on my part to have said apodictically, instead of hypothetically because of reverence for God, that I was a Christian. I do indeed face judgment; therefore on Judgment Day I shall have to repeat that I was put to death because I, according to my own statement, was a Christian. But if I will say it, then by this I will be saying to God that I was a Christian; this is certain enough, nothing is more certain, since I would be put to death because I was a Christian. But I would not dare say this to God under any circumstances. Face-to-face with God I would have to use a much humbler expression: I trust to God that in his mercy he will receive me as a Christian.

X⁵
B 107
296 Obviously it is not my idea or of *armed neutrality* to abolish martyrs or to make a martyrdom an impossibility; I only move it reflectively into inwardness. [*Deleted:* , since I do not let the martyr become so muddleheaded on the occasion of being executed that what he says about his God-relationship does not come out quite right but is rather garbled, presumably because he is so occupied with his imminent death, but I let him be occupied solely with his God-relationship and be like an absent-minded person in regard to his imminent death.] Generally it is disregarded that martyrdom is a category of freedom, that it is not "the others" who have the martyr in their power but he who has them in his. They can put him to death, to be sure, but from a spiritual point of view he can determine *where* he is to fall. It is impossible to force a person to declare something specific if it is against his will and he is willing to give his life for it. Thus people may say: We are going to put you to death because you will not say it—to this, however, he has nothing to object. This is the power or superiority that lies in the willingness to make a sacrifice; to the same degree to which a person is willing to make a

sacrifice, he has this superiority. Therefore it rests with the martyrs themselves to assign, so to speak, the place of the martyrdom. But to be the Christian in relation to other people, to be put to death because, according to one's own declaration, one is a Christian—this can so very easily be a satisfaction of human passion.

Let us imagine the martyrdom I have suggested. One will not say: I am a Christian, but: I trust to God to be a Christian, and the like. Thereupon he is told: Well, then you will be put to death because you will not answer the way we demand. To this he replies: All right. He is put to death. This is a martyrdom. Through death he departs and enters eternity—for judgment. Under judgment he trusts that God in his mercy will receive him as a Christian—he has not said too much about himself. —The more inwardness, the greater the fear and trembling before God. Externally oriented thinking is preoccupied with having the courage in relation to people to become a martyr; inwardly oriented thinking is preoccupied with having the courage in relation to God to be a martyr. This is martyrdom's proper fear and trembling. Many a pagan has also had the courage to be put to death for an idea, but the pagan did not have the fear and trembling of the God-relationship.

But the ideality with regard to being a Christian is a continual inward deepening. The more ideal the conception of being a Christian, the more inward it becomes—and indeed the more difficult. Being a Christian then undergoes a change that I will illustrate with a worldly analogy. Formerly there were in Greece wise men, σοφοί. Then came Pythagoras and with him the reflection-qualification, reduplication,[10] in connection with being a wise man; therefore he did not even venture to call himself a wise man but instead called himself a φιλόσοφος [friend or lover of wisdom, philosopher].[11] Was this a step backward or a step forward; or was it not because Pythagoras had more ideally apprehended what it would really mean, what would be required to call oneself a wise man; therefore there was wisdom in his not even having dared to call himself a wise man.

Now to my *armed neutrality*. Truly, it would not be impossible for me to come to experience martyrdom in some way, but truly,

X⁵
B 107
297

I also want the basis of it very accurately defined. I do not say of myself that I am a remarkable Christian; I think I would have failed in my task completely, would have misunderstood my individuality and all my qualifications entirely if I had exposed myself to any attack or any persecution along these lines. But I do maintain that I know with uncommon clarity and definiteness what Christianity is, what can be required of the Christian, what it means to be a Christian. To an unusual degree I have, I think, the qualifications to be able to present this. I also think it is my duty to do it, simply because it seems to be forgotten in Christendom, and obviously there is no likelihood that the present generation is qualified to provide upbringing in Christianity. I think it is my duty to Christianity, my duty to what has been passed on from the fathers and was also entrusted to me by a father, whose upbringing is in large part my efficacy. In this regard I am also frequently reminded of the teachers of my childhood and youth, the admired and unforgettable principal of the Borgerdyds School,[12] who wrote almost nothing about me in his report of me but wrote instead a eulogy on my father. I believe it is my clearly understood duty to do this, because a person so rigorously brought up in Christianity will soon be a great rarity.

X⁵
B 107
298

But to do this undauntedly in the service of the truth can easily expose me to the opposition of people, insofar as they generally take a dim view of jacking up the price or the requirement for being what they already think they are, the name of which they do not want to give up. Here is the place where I think I should not avoid any danger, even the most extreme; on the contrary, when a storm blows up in this direction, I understand my task to be precisely that of confronting the danger and remaining in it. It only must be clear that what I have fought for, and if I should fall, what I have fallen for, or if I come to suffer in some way, what I am suffering for—is not that I have maintained that I was the distinguished Christian, but that in the service of the truth I have championed what it means to be a Christian.

Armed Neutrality. If my relation were to pagans, I could not be neutral; then in opposition to them I would have to say that I am a Christian. But I am living in Christendom, among Christians, or among people who all say they are Christians. It is not now up to me, a human being, to judge others, particularly not in the role of one who knows human hearts, which here would have to be the case. If I were now to insist that I am a Christian, what would this mean in the situation? It would mean that I am a Christian in contrast to Christians—that is, that I am a Christian raised to the second power, the distinguished Christian. This is why I keep it neutral with regard to my being a Christian. On the other hand, this cannot possibly be a denial of Christianity, since I am living in Christendom and presumably am a Christian like all the others. Moreover, I also declare forthrightly that I am a Christian in the sense that others are, but not in contrast to them. This way I keep neutral, not in contrast to being a Christian but in contrast to being a Christian raised to the second power. Then I carry on my work presenting the ideal of a Christian. In order to do this, I must in turn have this neutrality. How would I dare to be so brazen as to occasion in the remotest way the repugnant notion that it was myself I spoke about, or how would I in all modesty be capable of saying anything at all if I did not in every way prevent [*in margin:* do the utmost, do everything in order in every way to prevent] the indecent, the repugnant notion that it was myself I spoke about.

The task, then, is to present the ideal of a Christian, and here I intend to do battle. If someone says to me, "What you say is untrue; you have a confused, false conception of what it is to be a Christian"—then I will answer: Enlighten me about it; then I will alter my conception; if not, of course not one iota. If whimpering says to me, "Give up this undertaking, revoke what you have done, spare us; this presentation becomes like a terror over us, it jacks up the price in such a way that we are brought to despair"—then I shall answer: No, not one iota; I, too, know the pain of it, but I neither dare nor am able to do otherwise. I pray to God that in this regard he will Christianly harden my heart and mind or make me Christianly tough enough not to dabble in human pity. If they threaten me so that out of the fear of people I would abandon my undertaking or with trembling hands would botch the picture, I pray to God, whatever danger comes in the form of bloody persecution or in the form of mockery,

X⁵
B 107
299

laughter, and ridicule, whether the suffering is physical pains or spiritual pains, that he will give me the strength not to deviate a hair's breadth from the understood truth.

This is my idea of the judgment that I think will fall upon Christendom—not that I or any single individual should judge others, but the ideal picture of what it is to be a Christian will judge me and everyone who permits himself to be judged. In a finite sense the ideal picture infringes upon no one; it has the infinite distance of the ideal from all busy earthly judgment and condemnation of this one and that one or of these particular actual persons; when the ideal is used in this way, it is already debased.

But it is completely accidental that I am the one who has the task of presenting this picture; yet someone must do it. I certainly will not thereby win honor and esteem or other earthly advantage. If the work is done creditably, the reward will be an analogy to the honorarium of the true Christian in the world, only in a somewhat mitigated form, and only without my coming to suffer because I am a Christian but in the capacity of a poet, a thinker, etc. The mitigated form is, of course, evidence of my imperfection, evidence that I am not the true Christian. Far be it from me, that childish talk, to demonstrate on the basis of my gaining earthly advantage that I will the true and the good. No, the evidence that one or whether one actually wills the good and the true is, Christianly, always the opposite. That I nevertheless do enjoy some esteem in the world demonstrates, regrettably, only how imperfect I still am; and that I perhaps will get through life somehow, tested only in a mitigated kind of martyrdom, is evidence, of course, that I have not pursued it to perfection.

Finally, if some impetuous pate, who in regard to himself knows at once whether or not he is a Christian, finds it remarkable that the person who was capable of presenting this picture and consequently uninterruptedly occupied himself with such thoughts would not in regard to himself know definitely whether he is a Christian, then I would answer: That I have not said, but I have said that to say about oneself that one is a Christian means to speak with God, and that therefore a human being must speak with fear and trembling. After having said this, for the sake of that

X⁵
B 107
300

impetuous pate (who in speaking of himself perhaps calls himself one of those more profound natures who feels a deep need for positiveness, somewhat like those who in relation to falling in love look upon themselves as more profound natures who are not satisfied with falling in love but feel a deep need—for external certainty) I shall then add, *in usum Delphini*,[13] an example of a remarkable kind of slowness along a somewhat similar line. People with impetuous pates naturally know at once and very definitely that they are human beings. Now, I dare say I am right in maintaining that not many have lived who knew human nature as well as Socrates did, who in addition knew himself. And the *summa summarum* [sum of sums] of his knowledge in his seventieth year was that he did not definitely know whether he was a human being.[14] How can this be explained? I wonder if this was not because he had employed his time first and foremost in thinking about what it means to be a human being? This is done very quickly by impetuous pates, because they leap over this question, assume that they know it—and then in all impetuousness there appears that remarkable being (who could give a slower person much to think about and would almost seem to have to make even the impetuous one a little slower himself)—a human being who knows definitely that he is a human being but does not know definitely what it means to be a human being. Surely it has been the same with thousands of Christians: they have known definitely that they were Christians but did not know definitely what it means to be a Christian. And yet, yet it is still perhaps possible, by continuous diligence over a number of years, to pursue this to the point of **knowing** *definitely* what it means to be a Christian; whether one oneself is that cannot be **known**, and not with *definiteness either*—it must be believed, and in faith there is always fear and trembling.

x⁵
B 107
301

SUPPLEMENT

KEY TO REFERENCES

Marginal references alongside the text of *On My Work as an Author* and *The Point of View for My Work as an Author* are to volume and page [XIII 500] in *Søren Kierkegaards samlede Værker*, I-XIV, edited by A. B. Drachmann, J. L. Heiberg, and H. O. Lange (1 ed., Copenhagen: Gyldendal, 1901–06). The same marginal references are used in Sören Kierkegaard, *Gesammelte Werke*, *Abt.* 1–36 (Düsseldorf, Cologne: Diederichs Verlag, 1952–69).

References to Kierkegaard's works in English are to this edition, *Kierkegaard's Writings* [*KW*], I-XXVI (Princeton: Princeton University Press, 1978–). Specific references to *Writings* are given by English title and the standard Danish pagination referred to above [*Either/Or*, I, p. 120, *KW* III (*SV* I 100)].

Marginal references alongside the text of Kierkegaard's *Armed Neutrality* [X⁵ B 107 300] and other references to the *Papirer* [*Pap.* I A 100; note the differentiating letter A, B, or C, used only in references to the *Papirer*] are to *Søren Kierkegaards Papirer*, I-XI³, edited by P. A. Heiberg, V. Kuhr, and E. Torsting (1 ed., Copenhagen: Gyldendal, 1909–48), and 2 ed., photo-offset with two supplemental volumes, XII-XIII, edited by Niels Thulstrup (Copenhagen: Gyldendal, 1968–70), and with index, XIV-XVI (1975–78), edited by Niels Jørgen Cappelørn. References to the *Papirer* in English [*JP* II 500] are to the volume and serial entry number in *Søren Kierkegaard's Journals and Papers*, I-VI, edited and translated (and occasionally amended in the Supplement) by Howard V. Hong and Edna H. Hong, assisted by Gregor Malantschuk, and with index, VII, edited by Nathaniel Hong and Charles Barker (Bloomington: Indiana University Press, 1967–78).

References to correspondence are to the serial numbers in *Breve og Aktstykker vedrørende Søren Kierkegaard*, I-II, edited by Niels Thulstrup (Copenhagen: Munksgaard, 1953–54), and to the corresponding serial numbers in *Kierkegaard: Letters and Docu-*

ments, translated by Henrik Rosenmeier, *Kierkegaard's Writings,* XXV [*Letters,* Letter 100, *KW* XXV].

References to books in Kierkegaard's own library [*ASKB* 100] are based on the serial numbering system of *Auktionsprotokol over Søren Kierkegaards Bogsamling* [Auction-catalog of Søren Kierkegaard's Book-collection], edited by H. P. Rohde (Copenhagen: Royal Library, 1967).

In the Supplement, references to page and lines in the text are given as: 100:1–10.

In the notes, internal references to the present volume are given as: p. 100.

Three spaced periods indicate an omission by the editors; five spaced periods indicate a hiatus or fragmentariness in the text.

Om min Forfatter-Virksomhed.

Af

S. Kierkegaard.

Kjøbenhavn.

Forlagt af Universitetsboghandler C. A. Reitzel.

Trykt hos Kgl. Hofbogtrykker Bianco Luno.

1851.

On My Work as an Author.

By

S. Kierkegaard.

Copenhagen.

Published by University Bookseller C. A. Reitzel.

Printed by Royal Printer Bianco Luno.

1851.

Synspunktet for min Forfatter-Virksomhed.

En ligefrem Meddelelse,

Rapport til Historien

af

S. Kierkegaard.

Kjøbenhavn.

C. A. Reitzels Forlag.

1859.

The Point of View for My Work as an Author.

A Direct Communication,

Report to History

by

S. Kierkegaard.

[emblem]

Copenhagen.

C. A. Reitzel's Publishing House.

1859.

SELECTED ENTRIES FROM
KIERKEGAARD'S JOURNALS AND PAPERS
PERTAINING TO *ON MY WORK AS AN AUTHOR*
AND *THE POINT OF VIEW FOR MY WORK
AS AN AUTHOR*

See 105–12:

See 105–12:

To the Dedication

VII¹
A 176
112

"That Single Individual"

in the occasional discourse[1] the following piece
should really have been added.

Dear Reader,
Please accept this dedication. It is offered, as it were, blindly,
but therefore in all honesty, untroubled by any other consideration. I do not know who you are; I do not know where you are;
I do not know your name—I do not even know if you exist or
if you perhaps did exist and are no more, or whether your time
is still coming. Yet you are my hope, my joy, my pride, in the
uncertainty my honor—because if I knew you personally with a
worldly certainty, this would be my shame, my guilt—and my
honor would be lost.

It comforts me, dear reader, that you have this opportunity,
the opportunity for which I know I have honestly worked. If it
were feasible, that reading what I write came to be common
practice, or at least pretending to have read it in hopes of getting
ahead in the world, this would not be the opportune time for *my*
reader, because then the misunderstanding would have triumphed—yes, it would have beguiled me to dishonesty if with
all my powers I had not prevented anything like that from happening—on the contrary, by doing everything to prevent it I
have acted honestly. No, if reading what I write becomes a dubi-

VII¹
A 176
113

ous good (—and if with all the powers granted me I contribute
to that, I am acting honestly), or still better, if it becomes foolish
and ludicrous to read my writings, or even better, if it becomes
a contemptible matter so that no one dares to acknowledge it,
that is the opportune time for *my* reader; then he seeks stillness,
then he does not read for my sake or for the world's sake—but
for his own sake, then he reads in such a way that he does not
seek my acquaintance but avoids it—and then he is *my* reader.

I have often imagined myself in a pastor's place. If the crowds
storm to hear him, if the great arch of the church cannot contain
the great throngs and people even stand outside listening to
him—well, honor and praise to one so gifted that his feelings are
gripped, that he can talk as one inspired, inspired by the sight of
the crowds, because where the crowd is there must be truth,
inspired by the thought that there has to be a little for some,
because there are a lot of people, and a lot of people with a little
truth is surely truth—to me this would be impossible! But suppose it was a Sunday afternoon, the weather was gloomy and
miserable, the winter storm emptied the streets, everyone who
had a warm apartment let God wait in the church until better
weather—if there were sitting in the empty church a couple of
poor women who had no heat in the apartment and could just as
well freeze in the church, indeed, I could talk both them and
myself warm!

I have often imagined myself beside a grave. If all the people
of honor and distinction were assembled there, if solemnity per-
vaded the whole great throng—well, honor and praise to one so
gifted that he could add to the solemnity by being prompted to
be the interpreter of the throng, to be the expression for the truth
of sorrow—I could not do it! But if it was a poor hearse and it was
accompanied by no one but a poor old woman, the widow of the
dead man, who had never before experienced having her husband go away without taking her along—if she were to ask me,
on my honor I would give a funeral oration as well as anyone.

VII¹
A 176
114

I have often imagined myself in the decision of death. If there
was alarm in the camp, much running in to inquire about me—I
believe I could not die, my old irascible disposition would once
more awaken and I would have to go out once again and con-

tend with people. But if I lie secluded and alone, I hope to God I may die peacefully and blessedly.

There is a view of life that holds that truth is where the crowd is, that truth itself needs to have the crowd on its side. There is another view of life that holds that wherever the crowd is, untruth is, so that even if all individuals who, separately, secretly possessed truth were to come together in a crowd (in such a way, however, that the crowd acquired any deciding, voting, noisy, loud significance), untruth would promptly be present there. But the person who recognizes this latter view as his own (which is rarely enunciated because it more frequently happens that a person believes the crowd lives in untruth, but if it only accepts his opinion everything is all right) confesses that he himself is the weak and powerless one; moreover, how could one individual be able to stand against the crowd, which has the power! And he would not possibly wish to have the crowd on his side—that would be ridiculing himself. But if this latter view is an admission of weakness and powerlessness and thus perhaps seems somewhat uninviting, it at least has the good point of being equable—it insults no one, not one single person; it makes no distinction, not of one single person.

To be sure, the crowd is formed by individuals, but each one must retain the power to remain what he is—an individual. No one, no one, not one is excluded from being an individual except the person who excludes himself—by becoming many. On the contrary, to become part of the crowd, to gather the crowd around oneself, is what makes for distinctions in life. Even the most well-intentioned person talking about this can easily insult an individual. But then once again the crowd has power, influence, status, and domination—this is also a distinction in life that, dominating, disregards the individual as weak and powerless.

—*JP* V 5948 (*Pap.* VII[1] A 176) *n.d.*, 1846

The most thankless existence is and continues to be that of an author who writes for authors. Authors can be divided into two types: those who write for readers and, the genuine authors, those who write for authors. The reading public cannot understand the latter type but regard such writers as crazy and almost scorn them—meanwhile the second-class authors plunder their writings and create a great sensation with what they have stolen and distorted. These second-class authors generally become the worst enemies of the others—it is, of course, important to them that no one finds out about the true relationship.—*JP* I 160 (*Pap.* VIII¹ A 53) *n.d.*, 1847

VIII¹
A 482
213

"The Single Individual [Den Enkelte]"
A Hint

The single individual is the category through which, in a religious sense, the age, history, the human race must go. And the one who stood and fell at Thermopylae was not as secure as I am who stand at this narrow pass, *the single individual.* His particular task was to keep the hordes from pressing through that narrow pass; if they pressed through, he had lost. My task is easier, at least at first sight, and exposes me far less to the danger of being trampled down, since it is, as a lowly servant, to help, if possible, the hordes press through this narrow pass, *the single individual,* through which, please note, no one in all eternity presses except by becoming *the single individual.* And yet, yes, if I were to request an inscription on my grave, I request none other than *that single individual*—even if it is not understood now, it surely will be. With the category *the single individual,* I took a polemical aim at the system in the day when everything here at home was system and system—now the system is never mentioned anymore. My possible historical significance is linked to this category. Perhaps my writings will be quickly forgotten, as many another writer's. But if this was the right category, if all was in order with this category, if I perceived correctly here, understood correctly that this was my task, even though by no means pleasant, comfortable, or appreciated, if this was granted to me, although involving inner sufferings such as probably you seldom experienced, although involving external sacrifices such as a person is not every day willing to make—then I stand and my writings with me.

VIII¹
A 482
214

The single individual—with this category the cause of Christianity stands or falls, now that the world-development has gone as far as it has in reflection. Without this category, pantheism would be unconditionally victorious. No doubt there will be those who know how to tighten this category dialectically in a completely different way (without having had the labor of bringing it forth), but the category *the single individual* is and continues to be the anchor that can hold against pantheistic confusion, is and continues to be the medicine that can make people sober, is and continues to be the weight that can be put on, except that those who are to work with this category (at the lever or in applying the weights) must be more and more dialectical accordingly as the confusion becomes greater and greater. I promise to make a Christian of every individual I can get in under this category, or, since one human being certainly cannot do this for another, I assure him that he will become that. As *the single individual* he is alone, alone in the whole world, alone—face-to-face before God—then he will no doubt manage to obey. All doubt has its ultimate haunt in temporality's illusion that there are quite a few of us, or all humanity as such, which as such can finally intimidate God (as "the people" intimidate the king and "the public," the councilman) and even be Christ. Pantheism is an optical illusion, a vaporous image formed out of the fog of temporality or a mirage formed by its reflexion, which claims to be the eternal. But the fact is that this category cannot be taught directly; to use it is an art, an ethical task and an art, an art of which the practice is always dangerous and at times may claim the lives of its practitioners. The self-willed race and the confused crowds regard the highest, divinely understood, as high treason against "the human race," "the crowd," "the public," etc.

The single individual—this category has been used only once before (its first time) in a decisively dialectical way, by Socrates in order to disintegrate paganism. In Christendom it will be used a second time in the very opposite way, to make people (the Christians) Christians. It is not the missionary's category with regard to the pagans to whom he proclaims Christianity, but it is the missionary's category within Christendom itself, for the

VIII¹
A 482
215

inward deepening of being and becoming a Christian. When he, the missionary, comes, he will use this category. If the age is waiting for a hero, it waits in vain; instead there will more likely come one who in divine weakness will teach people obedience—by means of their slaying him in impious rebellion, him, the one obedient to God.—*JP* II 2004 (*Pap.* VIII¹ A 482) *n.d.*, 1847

From draft of "A Defense":

The difficulty for me in writing a defense [*Apologie*]—for it is as Socrates says in the *Apology*:² my accusers are invisible—gossip, rumors.

The difficulty lies also in the circumstances themselves, that in Copenhagen there are two stages, and one must act on both. Copenhagen is not large enough to have two stages that are kept separate. These two stages are not like two churches in which one pastor preaches. No, they are related inversely—what pleases one completely displeases the other. Under such conditions, of which I had been aware earlier, the only right thing is to steer by the stars.

I have now lived this way as an author for five to six years— and have been silent, but chatter about me has never been silent. —Copenhagen [*Kjøbenhavn*] a market town [*Kjøbstad*]—one's clothes are attacked—if a foreigner saw it he would be amazed, and even more when he perceived that Copenhagen is actually in the process of becoming a market town out of zeal for imitating a big city.—*Pap.* VIII² B 179:1 *n.d.*, 1847

In margin of Pap. VIII² B 179:1:

Off and on I have said to myself half ironically and half with pathos: Basically your life is wasted; you have actually become somebody or are regarded as that in Denmark, and in Denmark one lives happily only when one is nobody.

This is to be used preferably at the end.
—*Pap.* VIII² B 179:2 *n.d.*, 1847

From draft of "A Defense":

Until now I have been silent, but gradually the invisible attacks have actually attacked also the idea that I serve, and in this
regard I must now present a defense that I request be read with
the good will customarily shown by everyone who has respect
for his own judgment.—*Pap.* VIII² B 179:3 *n.d.*, 1847

In margin of Pap. VIII² B 179:3:

What is done with me is not suited for eliciting a defense, but
now when the attacks on me will distort the idea that I, humble
before God, am proud to have the honor to serve—then I must
not be too proud to explain the correct nature of the matter.
—*Pap.* VIII² B 179:4 *n.d.*, 1847

From draft of "A Defense":

With regard to stage A (the public, the common man, etc.):
in what sense I have spoken of that single individual,
not in the sense of haughtiness but of humbleness.
—*Pap.* VIII² B 179:5 *n.d.*, 1847

From draft of "A Defense":

With regard to stage B (the aristocrats)
a defense of my public life in contrast to their coterie.
My walking the streets so much is explained here as
vanity, propensity for display. The falsity of this.
—*Pap.* VIII² B 179:6 *n.d.*, 1847

From draft of "A Defense":

It has always been my intention to end my strenuous work as
an author with a quiet, forgotten remoteness in a rural parsonage
in order to sorrow over my sins and over whatever offenses I may
have committed personally. That is why I have so completely

isolated myself in literature. —Now I assume that it is my calling to remain in the place assigned to me and to use the powers granted me to fill the place assigned to me instead of for penance.
—*Pap.* VIII² B 179:10 *n.d.*, 1847

From draft of "A Defense":

VIII²
B 180
282

Preface

It is my request that everyone will read this little defense [*Apologie*] with the readiness to listen that is so desirable, with the slowness to judge that is so amiable, with the good will and good nature that dwell inwardly within every human being, even in a person who in a spell knows only the passions of indignation but does not know himself. This is my request, and I make this request for my own sake, but it pertains also to the one whom I address, because to judge hastily, frivolously, badly in judging another is worst for him himself, and although appeals for circumspection are ordinarily made to people in very many ways when one warns them against deceivers and seducers and the world and people, let us not forget how important it is to say to the single individual—watch out for yourself.—*Pap.* VIII² B 180 *n.d.*, 1847

VIII²
B 180
283

Addition to Pap. VIII² B 180:

Preface

This defense [*Apologie*] is written in such a way that everyone can understand it. I do not therefore require that everyone shall read it, but since I write it for the sake of peace and in order to ameliorate, there also seems to be a certain fairness in my request that—inasmuch as so many who have had neither the time nor desire to read my books have had the time and desire to hear and read all possible misunderstandings, slander, and attacks with regard to me—they will show such respect for themselves that for once they would listen to the much-talked-about one speak. In relation to the particular individuals who in the service of literary contemptibility seek to make everything deranged, just as I will never know how to make peace and to be pleased to be ridiculed by them, so on the other hand, in relation to the many people with whom it has never occurred to me to have conflict, I will do everything my cause needs to maintain a good and well-disposed understanding.—*Pap.* VIII² B 181 *n.d.*, 1847

Invitation

VIII²
B 186
292

The undersigned plans to give a little series of lectures on the organizing theme throughout my entire work as an author[3] and its relation to the modern period illuminated by references to the past.

As auditors I have in mind particularly theological graduates or even more advanced students. I assume that the auditors will be well acquainted with the works beforehand, and others are requested not to consider this invitation. I would also say in advance that these lectures will in no sense be an enjoyment but rather hard work, and therefore I do not entice anyone. This work will have times when, in the understanding of the moment and of impatience, it is plainly boring, which in my opinion is inseparable from all deeper understanding, and therefore I warn everyone against participating. If I succeed in being understood, the auditor will have the benefit that his life will have been made VIII²
B 186
293 considerably more difficult than ever, and for this reason I urge no one to accept this invitation.

As soon as ten have signed up, I will begin; the limit is twenty, inasmuch as I wish to have such a relation to the auditors that the lectures might be, if necessary, made colloquies.

The fee is five rix-dollars, registration with the undersigned.
—*JP* V 6094 (*Pap.* VIII² B 186) *n.d.*, 1847–48

Invitation

VIII²
B 188
295

Gratified to learn that my upbuilding writings, addressed to the single individual, are still read by many individuals, I have considered obliging these my readers, and perhaps gaining more individuals as readers, by publishing such works in the future in smaller sections on a subscription basis.[4] The possible advantages are, first, that the books will be read better if they are read in smaller sections; second, that a certain calmness of understanding may enter into the relation between author and reader, so that a beginning need not be made each time; and finally, that the publication can properly take place quietly and unnoticed, avoiding all irrelevant attention.

From July 1 of this year I plan, then, to publish under the more general title

Upbuilding Reading

a section of six, at most eight sheets [*Ark*] every three months.
. . .

VIII²
B 188
296   S. Kierkegaard

January 1848.

at the end of the year, the common title page, the table of contents, a list of the subscribers.
—*JP* V 6095 (*Pap.* VIII² B 188) January 1848

A word on my work as an author
with regard to "that single individual."
and
an accompanying word to my
issued invitation to subscription.

When someone who, like me, has continually and so decisively written only for "the single individual" issues a subscription plan, this might seem a contradiction to some who have misunderstood my earlier work. I will therefore do my part and try to remove at least a part of the misunderstanding—to want totally to prevent all misunderstanding when one intends to undertake something could certainly occur only to a youth.—*Pap.* VIII² B 196 *n.d.*, 1848

Originally I had thought to end my work as an author with *Concluding Unscientific Postscript*, to withdraw to the country, and in quiet unobtrusiveness to sorrow over my sins. The fear and trembling in my soul about being a Christian, my penitence, seemed to me to be sufficient suffering. I had almost forgotten that being a Christian is and should be a thing of scorn in the world, as he was, my Lord and Master, who was spat upon: then Governance came to my assistance again. I became aware of that and now stay in my place. God in heaven, who has reason to be disgusted with me because I am a sinner, has nevertheless not rejected what I, humanly speaking, honestly intended. Yet before God even my best deed is still miserable.—*JP* VI 6157 (*Pap.* IX A 54) *n.d.*, 1848

. . . . . Thus in a certain sense I began my activity as an author with a *falsum* [deception] or with a *pia fraus* [pious fraud]. The situation is that in so-called established Christendom people are so fixed in the fancy that they are Christians that if they are to be made aware at all many an art will have to be employed. If someone who otherwise does not have a reputation of being an author begins right off as a Christian author, he will not get a hearing from his contemporaries. They are immediately on their guard, saying, "That's not for us" etc.

I began as an estheticist—and then, although approaching the religious with perhaps uncustomary alacrity, I denied being a Christian etc.

This is the way I present myself as an author to my contemporaries—and in any case this is the way I belong to history. My thought is that here I am permitted and am able to speak of myself only as an author. I do not believe that my personality, my personal life, and what I consider my shortcomings are of any concern to the public. I am an author, and who I am and what my endowments are I know well enough. I have submitted to everything that could serve my cause.

I ask the more competent ones in particular to be slow to judge the capabilities and a use of capabilities that is not seen every day—I ask this especially of the more competent, for there is no use in requesting this of fools. But as a rule every more competent person has respect for himself and for his judgment— and for just this reason I request him to judge carefully.

IX A 171 82

IX A 171 83

It is Christianity that I have presented and still want to present;
to this every hour of my day has been and is directed.—*JP* VI
6205 (*Pap.* IX A 171) *n.d.*, 1848

In margin of Pap. IX A 171:

It was important for me to learn to know the age. Perhaps the
age found it quite easy to form a picture of this author: that intellectually he was an exceptionally gifted person, dedicated to
pleasure and wallowing in a life of luxury. Ah, it was mistaken.
It never dreamed that the author of *Either/Or* had said good-bye
to the world long before, that he spent much of the day in fear
and trembling reading devotional books, in prayer and supplica-
tion. Least of all did it think that he was and is conscious of
himself as a penitent from the very first line he wrote.—*JP* VI
6206 (*Pap.* IX A 172) *n.d.*, 1848

IX
A 213
110

I cannot repeat often enough what I so frequently have said: I
am a poet, but a very special kind, for I am by nature dialectical,
and as a rule dialectic is precisely what is alien to the poet. Assigned from childhood to a life of torment that perhaps few can
even conceive of, plunged into the deepest despondency, and
from this despondency again into despair, I came to understand
myself by writing. It was the ethical that inspired me—alas, me,
who was painfully prevented from realizing it fully because I was
unhappily set outside the universally human. If I had been able
to achieve it, I no doubt would have become terribly proud.
Thus in turn I related to Christianity. It was my plan as soon as
Either/Or was published to seek a call to a rural parish and sorrow

IX
A 213
111

over my sins. I could not suppress my creativity, I followed it—
naturally it moved into the religious. Then I understood that my
task was to do penance by serving the truth in such a way that it
virtually became burdensome, humanly speaking, a thankless
labor of sacrificing everything. That is how I serve Christianity—
in all my wretchedness happy in the thought of the indescribable
good God has done for me, far beyond my expectations.

The situation calls for Christianity to be presented once again
without scaling down and accommodation, and since the situa-

tion is in Christendom: indirectly.[*] I must be kept out of it: the awakening will be all the greater. Men love direct communication because it makes for comfortableness, and communicators love it because it makes life less strenuous, since they always get a few to join them and thus escape the strain of solitariness.

Thus do I live, convinced that God will place the stamp of Governance on my efforts—as soon as I am dead, not before—this is all connected with penitence and the magnitude of the plan. I live in this faith and hope to God to die in it. If he wants it otherwise, he will surely take care of that himself; I do not dare do otherwise.—*JP* VI 6227 (*Pap.* IX A 213) *n.d.,* 1848

[*]*In margin:* but not as one who enthusiastically proclaims Christianity but as a dialectician is able to do it, by Socratically starving the life out of all the illusions in which Christendom has run aground. It is not that Christianity is not proclaimed, but it is Christendom that has become sheer expertise in transforming it into illusion and thus evading it.—*JP* VI 6228 (*Pap.* IX A 214) *n.d.,* 1848

The world has become all too sagacious. The person who intends to work for the religious must work undercover—otherwise he is not of much use. If someone passes himself off as religious, the world has a thousand evasions and illusions with which they protect themselves against him and get rid of him. The struggle now is no longer as in the old days against wild passions, against which direct action is appropriate. No, Christendom has run aground in sagacity. In order to get rid of it, there must be a person who is more than a match for them in sagacity.

Even if it pleases God to select a person as his instrument, that person's whole strategy must be entirely different from that in former times. The person who is to be used in this way must possess what the age prides itself on, but to its own misfortune. But he must not misuse his sagacity to be of assistance into a new sagacity; with the aid of sagacity, he must effect a return to simplicity.

This is how I understand myself, except that I do not dare to

IX
A 215
111

IX
A 215
112

call myself an instrument of God in a special sense, because, just as everything in me is dialectical, so also my relation to God. On the other hand, it is my blessed conviction that every human being is essentially equally near to God.

But simply because everything in my existence is combined in this way, I can actually not be effective until after my death.

—*Pap.* IX A 215 *n.d.*, 1848

IX
A 216
112
Yes, it had to be this way. I have not become a religious author; I was that: simultaneously with *Either/Or* appeared two upbuilding discourses—now after two years of writing only religious books there appears a little article about an actress.[5]

Now there is a moment, a point of rest; by this step I have learned to know myself and very concretely.

So the publication must proceed (that is, of course I have more, I have finished what is to be used: (1) A Cycle of Ethical-
IX
A 216
113
Religious Essays, (2) The Sickness unto Death, (3) Come Here, All You . . . . .), if I do not happen to die beforehand. My health is very poor, and the thought of dying has gotten the upper hand with me as I use this half year to sorrow for my sins and work further in the presentation of Christianity. Perhaps it is a despondent thought, perhaps also because I have become disinclined to make the finite decisions involved in publication—in any case I have now been prodded by it.

The next publication will be very decisive for my outer life. I always have held on to the remote possibility of seeking a pastoral call if worst comes to worst financially. When I publish the last books, this may well be denied me even if I were to seek it; so the problem will not be as before, if I do dare to undertake it, but rather that it will not even be given to me. . . .—*JP* VI 6229 (*Pap.* IX A 216) *n.d.*, 1848

IX
A 218
115
It was a good thing that I published that little article[6] and came under tension. If I had not published it, I would have gone on living in a certain ambiguity about the future use of indirect communication.

Now it is clear to me that henceforth it will be indefensible to use it.

The awakening effect is rooted in God's having given me power to live as a riddle—but not any longer, lest the awakening effect end in being confusing.

The thing to do now is to take over unambiguously the maieutic structure of the past, to step forth definitely and directly in character, as one who has wanted and wants to serve the cause of Christianity.

If I had not published that little article, indirect communication would have continued to hover vaguely before me as a possibility and I would not have had the idea that I dare not use it.

I would not dare to say of myself that I have had a clear panorama of the whole plan of production from the outset; I must rather say, as I have continually acknowledged, that I myself have been brought up and developed in the process of my work, that personally I have become committed more and more to Christianity than I was. Nevertheless this remains fixed, that I began with the deepest religious impression, alas, yes, I who when I began bore the tremendous responsibility for the life of another human being and understood it as God's punishment upon me.—*JP* VI 6231 (*Pap.* IX A 218) *n.d.*, 1848

IX
A 218
116

Now add the thought of death to the publication of that little article![7] If I were dead without that: indeed, anyone could publish my posthumous papers, and in any case R. Nielsen[8] would be there. But that illusion that I did not become religious until I was older and perhaps by reason of accidental circumstances would still have been possible. But now the dialectical breaks are so clear: *Either/Or* and *Two Upbuilding Discourses, Concluding Postscript*, the upbuilding writings of two years,[9] and then a little esthetic treatise.—*Pap.* IX A 228 *n.d.*, 1848

N.B.   N.B.

IX
A 234
131

Yes, so it stands: therefore a direct explanation of my authorship and what I want *in toto.*

In relation to the decisively Christian, one cannot bear the responsibility in the middle term of one's human reflection.

And just as what I on the whole have tended toward is the

restitution of the simple, this is such an essential component that the one who brings it to this cannot himself in turn use the maieutic arts; in one sense this is even a contradiction.

The point about what one *in toto* wants is that it stands direct and clear; it is another matter (something not to be avoided by the person who after all has superiority of reflection) that one can use it in the particular, but within the direct attesting to what one *in toto* wants. In relation to the essentially Christian, it is also dangerous to hold it in suspension if one does not oneself positively feel bound to Christianity; however much one served the cause of Christianity, this is an unchristian way to go about it, even if for a time usable and relatively justified precisely because Christendom has become paganism.

To remain ambiguous about what one wants *in toto* oneself is the real maieutic.[10] But it is also the daimonic, because it makes a human being the middle term between God and other human beings.

Direct communication, a witness once and for all, is decisive for preventing the maieutic. The maieutic is not to be cryptic in this or that particular but is to be cryptic concerning the whole—for example, to be cryptic about whether one is a Christian oneself.

Then the difficulty arises again, so that it does not appear as if one had an immediate relation to God. In that case a relationship of reflection is something far more humble.

Yet all this in which I have really become involved, I owe to the publication of that little article.[11] Without it I would neither have realized so clearly the change that must be made, nor would I have been able to set it forth so decisively. If I had taken such a step earlier, it would have been too much in continuity with the earlier works and would have been neither the one nor the other.—*Pap.* IX A 234 *n.d.*, 1848

In margin of Pap. IX A 234:

The maieutic actually hides the fact that God is the one who moves the whole thing. But on the other hand, in contrast, since this witnessing has become a triviality just as everything else in

Christendom has become that, the maieutic could have its significance.—*Pap.* IX A 235 *n.d.*, 1848

N.B.   N.B.

IX
A 248
139

It has generally been thought that reflection is the natural enemy of Christianity and would destroy it. With God's help I hope to show that God-fearing reflection can retie knots that a shallow, superficial reflection has diddled with so long. The divine authority of the Bible and everything related to it has been abolished; it looks as if one final unit of reflection is expected to finish the whole thing. But look, reflection is on the way to do a counterservice, to reset the coil springs in the essentially Christian so that it can stand its ground—against reflection. Of course Christianity remains the same, altered in no way; not an iota is changed. But the battle becomes a different one; up until now it has been between reflection and the immediate, simple Christianity—now it becomes a battle between reflection and simplicity armed with reflection.

There is sense in this, I believe. The task is not to comprehend Christianity but to comprehend that one cannot comprehend it. This is the holy cause of faith, and reflection is therefore sanctified by being used in this way.

Oh, the more I think of what has been granted to me, the more I need an eternity in which to thank God.[12]—*JP* III 3704 (*Pap.* IX A 248) *n.d.*, 1848

IX
A 248
140

Now I see my way to writing a short and as earnest as possible explanation of my previous authorship, which is necessary before a transition to the next. And why do I see my way to doing it now? Simply because I am now clear about the relation between direct communication and decisive Christianity. For this very reason I now am able to illuminate and interpret indirect communication. Earlier I had been continually unclear. One must always be over and beyond what one wants to interpret. Previously I had been uncertain about the whole thing, because I was not myself clear and basically maintained the connection with

IX
A 265
151

indirect communication. This relation would have altogether ruined the entire presentation.—*JP* VI 6248 (*Pap.* IX A 265) *n.d.*, 1848

Inscription on a Grave
The daily press is the state's disaster, "the crowd" the world's evil.

"That Single Individual"
—*JP* II 2154 (*Pap.* IX A 282) *n.d.*, 1848

On this point I am brought to a halt. If I open myself to others, then, *ipso facto*, my life is less strenuous. Humanly speaking (that is, in the sense of human self-love), people have a right to demand this of me, but in relation to God do I have the right? I can see with half an eye that, far out as I myself am, I gain no one; my opening myself will mean that I get dragged down. On the other hand, my progress is certain destruction. But is there, then, not an absolute? Here it is again. The moment I lay my life out in relativities, I am understood, and in a deeper sense my cause is lost—humanly speaking, it is then won.

The only true way of expressing that there is an absolute is to become its martyr or a martyr to it. It is this way even in relation to absolute erotic love.

The human race is so far from the ideal that in a few generations there is occasionally one who more or less expresses that there is an absolute, and he is then trampled upon by the generation.—*JP* VI 6253 (*Pap.* IX A 285) *n.d.*, 1848

IX
A 288
161 This is how I actually am treated in Copenhagen. I am regarded as a kind of Englishman, a half-mad eccentric, with whom we jolly well all, society people and street urchins, think to have their fun. My literary activity, that enormous productivity, so intense that it seems to me that it must move stones, IX
A 288
162 single portions of which not one of my contemporaries is able to compete with, to say nothing of its totality, that literary activity is regarded as a kind of hobby *ad modum* [in the manner of] fish-

ing and such. Those who are able to produce something themselves envy me and are silent—the others understand nothing. I
do not receive the support of one single word in the form of
reviews and the like. Minor prophets plunder me in silly lectures
at meetings and the like but do not mention my name. No, that
is unnecessary.

Consequently that hobby is regarded as a lark. The game is
really to see if they can drive me crazy—that would be great
sport—or get me to decamp, that would be great sport.

Behind all this is a tremendous impression of what I am, of the
extraordinariness granted to me, but the envy of a market town
fosters the desire that my having such advantages be, if possible,
a greater torment than being the most wretched of all; and everything is left up to the capriciousness of the market town.

In a somewhat more lenient version, the situation is this. I am
supposed to be a genius, but such an introverted genius that I can
see and hear nothing. All this sport is something the market town
is supposed to share in common (society people in common with
the commoners and they with the street urchins), something that
consequently is nothing.

Well, so be it! When I was a child, I was taught that they spat
upon Christ.[13] Now, I am a poor insignificant man and a sinner
and no doubt will get off more leniently. This, you see, is the
Christian syllogism, not the preacher-nonsense that says: Be a
good, loving, and altruistic person and people will love you—for
Christ, who was love, was loved by people.

Generally speaking, there no doubt will be no one in eternity
who will be judged as severely as those professional pastors. From
the point of view of eternity, they are what public prostitutes are
in temporality.—*JP* VI 6254 (*Pap.* IX A 288) *n.d.*, 1848

I am still very exhausted, but I have also almost reached the
goal. The work *The Point of View for My Work as an Author* is now
as good as finished. Relying upon what I have done in existential
action in the past to justify my productivity, in the recent period
I have been only a writer. My mind and spirit are strong enough,
but regrettably all too strong for my body. In one sense it is my

mind and spirit that help me to endure such poor health; in another sense it is my mind and spirit that overwhelm my body.
—*JP* VI 6258 (*Pap.* IX A 293) *n.d.*, 1848

See 124:9:

IX
A 298
167

From a supplement (4) to "The Point of View for My Work
as an Author" that was not used.[14]

IX
A 298
168

My heart has expanded, not as if it ever had been constricted
in my breast, but the inner intensity that has been my life and that
I believed would be my death has gotten a breathing spell, the
dialectical bond has been broken, I dare to speak directly.

I love my native land—it is true that I have not gone to war—
but I believe I have served it in another way, and I believe I am
right in thinking that Denmark must seek its strength in the spirit
and the mind. I am proud of my mother tongue, whose secrets
I know, the mother tongue that I treat more lovingly than a
flutist his instrument.

I honestly know that I have loved every person; no matter
how many have been my enemies, I have had no enemy. As I
remarked in the book,[15] I have never known thoughts and ideas
not to present themselves. But I have known something else. If,
on my way home after a walk, during which I would meditate
and gather ideas, overwhelmed with ideas ready to be written
down and in a sense so weak that I could scarcely walk (one who
has had anything to do with ideas knows what this means)—then
if a poor man on the way spoke to me and in my enthusiasm over
the ideas I had no time to speak with him—when I got home all
the ideas would be gone, and I would sink into the most dreadful
spiritual trial at the thought that God could do to me what I had
done to that man. But if I took time to talk with the poor man
and listened to him, things never went that way. When I arrived
at home everything was there and ready. All assurances are disdained these days—and yet the best assurance that an individual
loves people is and will be that God is as close as life to him,
which is the case with me and almost every moment.—*JP* VI
6259 (*Pap.* IX A 298) *n.d.*, 1848

When I sold the house,[16] I considered putting an end to writ-
ing, traveling for two years abroad, and then coming home and
becoming a pastor. I had, in fact, made about 2,200 rix-dollars on
the place.

But then it dawned on me: But why do you want to travel
abroad? To interrupt your work and get some recreation. But
you know from experience that you are never so productive as
when you are abroad in the extreme isolation in which you live
there, so when you return from your travels in two years you will
have a staggering amount of manuscripts.

So I rented rooms,[17] an apartment that had tempted me in a
very curious way for a long time and that I frequently had told
myself was the only one I could like.

This plan to travel for two years was no doubt just a whim.
The fact is that I had a complete book[18] ready to publish, and,
as I said, by going abroad I would open the sluice gates of my
productivity.

But it was the thought of traveling for two years that prompted
me to take the cash I got from the sale of the house, which in
general I had decided to leave alone, and to buy government
bonds—the most stupid thing I ever did and which I probably
should regard as a lesson, because I have now lost about 700
rix-dollars on them. [*In margin:* For the rest of the cash I later
bought shares, on which I perhaps have not lost anything.]

So I rented that apartment, printed *Christian Discourses,* and sat
in the middle of the proofreading when the whole confusion
started—Anders[19] was taken from me: and it was fortunate that
I had the apartment.

I moved in. In one sense I suffered greatly because the apart-
ment proved to be unsuitable. But on the other hand here, too,
Governance came to my assistance and turned my mistake into
a good. If anything helps me to be less productive and diminish
my momentum and in general limit me, it is finite anxieties and
inconveniences.

In that residence, however, I have written some of the best
things I have written;[20] but in this connection I have had constant
occasion to practice pianissimo the idea of halting my produc-

tivity or in any case to pay more attention to my livelihood. It would never have happened abroad, where, far from all distractions, suffering slightly from a little depression, I would have plunged into the most enormous productivity.

Last summer I drew R. Nielsen[21] a little closer to me; that means that I reduce my writing and yet do little to limit my endeavor.

If I could travel without becoming productive, travel and travel for some time, it perhaps would be a good thing. But a prolonged sojourn in one place makes me more productive than ever. I have been much better off learning a little by not having Anders and other such conveniences that perhaps encourage the writing too much.

I wanted to travel for two years, because among other things I was also sick and tired of this whole mess[22] in Copenhagen. But it does not help. I am well suited to seeing things like this through, if only I stay patiently where I am.

But the economic situation in these confused times has been a drain on me in various ways. It is no doubt good that I became thoroughly aware of it in time. It also helps burn out whatever selfishness there is in me and my work—for my position as author is in fact becoming serious enough.—*JP* VI 6268 (*Pap.* IX A 375) *n.d.*, 1848

N. B.

Perhaps it would be best to publish all the last four books ("The Sickness unto Death," "Come Here," "Blessed Is He Who Is Not Offended," "Armed Neutrality") in one volume under the title

Collected Works of Completion [*Fuldendelse*] [*]

with "The Sickness unto Death" as Part I. The second part would be called "An Attempt to Introduce Christianity into Christendom" and below: Poetic—Without Authority. "Come Here" and "Blessed Is He Who Is Not Offended" would be entered as subdivisions. Perhaps there could also be a third part,[23] which I am now writing,** but in that case Discourse No. 1 would be a kind of introduction that is not counted.

And then it should be concluded.

[*]*In margin:* Perhaps rather: "Collected Works of Consummation [*Fuldbringelse*]" and the volume should be quarto.

**"From on High He Will Draw All to Himself." The three: "Come Here," "Blessed Is He Who Is Not Offended," and "From on High," would then have a separate title page: An Attempt to Introduce Christianity into Christendom, but at the bottom of the page: A Poetic Attempt—Without Authority.

—*JP* VI 6271 (*Pap.* IX A 390) *n.d.*, 1848

Through my writings I hope to achieve the following: to leave behind me so accurate a characterization of Christianity and its relationships in the world that an enthusiastic, noble-minded young person will be able to find in it a map of relationships as accurate as any topographical map from the most famous institutes. I have not had the help of such an author. The old Church Fathers lacked one aspect: they did not know the world.—*JP* VI 6283 (*Pap.* IX A 448) *n.d.*, 1848

IX
A 448
258

I will hardly be able to carry out the whole project. It is too much for one man. Precisely because it centered upon reflecting Christianity out of an enormous sophistication, culture, out of scholarly-scientific confusion, etc., I myself would have to be in possession of all that culture, be sensitive in one sense as a poet, pure intellect as a thinker. But for the next part there must be physical strength and another kind of rigorous upbringing: to be able to live on little, not to need many creature comforts, to be able to apply some of one's mind to this self-discipline.

X¹
A 39
25

Take a strong, healthy child and train him in this kind of self-mastery. In a few well-spent years, he will have mastered my whole movement of thought; he will not need a tenth of my mental concentration and effort, nor the kind of talents I have had and which were particularly necessary for the first attack. But he will be the man who is needed: tough, rigorous, and yet adequately armed dialectically.

But I do indeed dare say that the work I have done was Herculean. For this I have had the decisive qualifications, wonderfully

X¹
A 39
26

good fortune, and blessing, but I do not have the qualifications for the next part. I would have to become a child again and above all, not a child of old age,[24] for such children often are physically weak; I would have to have better physical health and much less imagination and dialectic.—*JP* VI 6308 (*Pap.* X¹ A 39) *n.d.*, 1849

X¹
A 74
58

. . . I have another concern regarding *The Point of View for My Work as an Author*: that in some way I would have said too much about myself, or whether in some way God would want me to be silent about something. On the first point I have emphasized as decisively as possible in "A Cycle of Ethical-Religious Essays"[25]

X¹
A 74
59

that I am without authority; furthermore it is stated in the book that I am a penitent, that my entire work as an author is my own upbringing, that I am *like* a spy in a higher service. Finally, in "Armed Neutrality," every misunderstanding, as if I were an apostle, has been forestalled as decisively as possible. . . . —*JP* VI 6325 (*Pap.* X¹ A 74) *n.d.*, 1849

X¹
A 78
62

N.B.   **N.B.**
N.B.

"The Point of View for My Work as an Author" must not be published, no, no!

(1) And this is the deciding factor (never mind all those ideas I had about endangering my future and my bread and butter): I cannot tell the full truth about myself. Even in the very first manuscript (which I wrote without any thought at all of publishing), I was unable to stress the primary factor: that I am a penitent, and that this explains me at the deepest level. But when I took the manuscript out with the thought of publishing it, I was obliged to make a few small changes, because in spite of every-

X¹
A 78
63

thing the accent was too strong for it to be published. But I can and will speak about the extraordinary gifts entrusted to me only if it can sound just as strong (as it does in my inner being when I consider the matter myself) about sin and guilt. Not to do so would be taking the extraordinary in vain.

(2) I cannot quite say that my work as an author is a sacrifice. It is true I have been unspeakably unhappy ever since I was a child, but I nevertheless acknowledge that the solution God found of letting me become an author has been a rich, rich pleasure to me. I may be sacrificed, but my work as an author is not a sacrifice; it is, in fact, what I unconditionally prefer to continue to be.

Thus I cannot tell the full truth here, either, since I cannot speak this way in print about my torment and wretchedness— then the pleasure becomes really predominant.

But perhaps I have had my head somewhat in the clouds and possibly could have deceived myself about the extent to which, if it came to that, I would really prefer being slain to being obliged to seek a quieter, more tranquil activity.

(3) Once I have articulated the extraordinary about myself, even with all the guardedness I have used, then I will be stuck with it, and it will be a torment and a fearful responsibility to go on living if I am solemnly looked upon with pathos as someone extraordinary.

(4) The fact that I cannot give the full truth in portraying myself signifies that essentially I am a poet—and here I shall remain.

<hr>

But the situation is this: the past year (when I wrote that piece) was a hard one for me; I have suffered greatly. The mistreatment by rabble-barbarism has interfered somewhat with my incognito and tended to force me to be direct instead of dialectical as I have always been, to force me out beyond myself. My incognito was to be a sort of nobody, eccentric, odd-looking, with thin legs, an idler, and all that. All this was of my own free will. Now the rabble have been trained to stare at me inhumanly and mimic me, day after day, with the result that I have become tired of my incognito. So I was in danger of making a complete turnabout.

X[1]
A 78
64

This must not happen, and I thank God that it was precluded and that I did not go ahead and publish "The Point of View for My Work as an Author" (indeed, there always was something in me that opposed it).

The book itself is true and in my opinion masterly. But a book like that can be published only after my death. If my sin and guilt, my intrinsic misery, the fact that I am a penitent are stressed a bit more strongly, then it will be a true picture. But I must be careful about the idea of dying, lest I go and do something with the thought of dying in half a year and then live to be eighty-two. No, one finishes a book like that, puts it away in a drawer, sealed and marked: To be opened after my death.

And now suppose, speaking quite humanly, that I ventured too little, that I could have ventured a bit further. In that case the good Lord, God in heaven who is love, my Father in heaven, who forgives me my sins for the sake of Christ, he surely will forgive me this as well. After all, he is not a cruel master, not a jealous lover, but the loving Father. To him I dare to say: I do not presume to venture more, I have a fear of becoming false, of being brash toward you. I would rather stick with my incognito and let everyone think what he pleases about me than solemnly become somebody, an extraordinary. There is no one to whom I can make myself completely understood, because that which is crucial in my possible extraordinariness is that I cannot, after all, speak of my sin and guilt.

So God surely will turn it all into good for me.

Moreover, what I have written can very well be used—if I do indeed continue to be an author—but then I must assign it to a poet, a pseudonym.

For example—

by

the poet Johannes de Silentio

edited

by

S. Kierkegaard.

But this is the best evidence that "The Point of View for My Work as an Author" cannot be published. It must be made into something by a third party: A Possible Explanation of Magister Kierkegaard's Authorship, that is, so it is no longer the same book at all. For the point of it was my personal story.

And then I must go abroad in the spring.

But it was due to God's solicitude that I was flushed out of this indolent productivity, producing and producing (and in one sense superbly), but I never took the trouble to think about publishing, partly because I was hoping for death.—*JP* VI 6327 (*Pap.* X^1 A 78) *n.d.*, 1849

X^1
A 78
66

N.B.   N.B.
N.B.

X^1
A 79
66

It was indeed an act of Governance that I did not publish "The Point of View for My Work as an Author" at this time. And what melancholy impatience! It was written historically after a whole intermediate series of writings, which must be published first if there is to be any question at all of publishing it while I am alive.

On the whole, it is becoming more and more clear to me that when existence itself undertakes to preach for awakening as it is doing now, I do not dare to jack it up even more in that direction; something extraordinary like that has not been entrusted to me and scarcely can be entrusted to any human being. In a soft, refined, overcultured time, I was and ought to be for awakening. At present I ought to come closer to the established order.

[*In margin:* It is true that the religious, the essentially Christian, shows itself at its very firmest in such disturbed times; instead of remaining mild, it jacks up the price still more. That is the case with Christ, as I have shown elsewhere. But I neither dare nor have the strength to venture that far; it would be presumptuous, personally destructive, and would add to the confusion.]

From the very beginning I have had in mind the idea of ceasing to be an author; I have frequently said that the place was still vacant: an author who knew when to stop. Indeed, I actually

X^1
A 79
67

thought of quitting as early as with the publication of *Either/Or*. But I have never been closer to stopping than with the publication of *Christian Discourses*. I had sold the house and received two thousand for it. I was very tempted to use it for traveling. But I am no good at traveling and in all likelihood would just become productive, as I usually am most of all when traveling. So I stayed home, had the full torment of the confused times, lost money on the bonds I bought, etc.[26] During all this I continued to be productive (and have written what I would not have achieved without these afflictions and a certain melancholy) but became more and more accustomed to being delayed.

Now the second edition of *Either/Or* is coming out, but "A Cycle of Ethical-Religious Essays" will correspond precisely to that, and the publication will correspond to the direction I must take. What I have ready will stay there. It is gold but must be used with great circumspection.—*Pap.* X[1] A 79 *n.d.*, 1849

[*In margin:* N.B.]
Incidentally, the "supplements"[27] to "The Point of View" could very well be published, and separately. They will then be read considerably. In fact, I now will and should get more involved in the times.—*JP* VI 6329 (*Pap.* X[1] A 84) *n.d.*, 1849

And then perhaps, as stated frequently, all the writings that lie finished (the most valuable I have produced[28]) can also be used, but, for God's sake, in such a way as to guarantee that they are kept poetic, as poetic awakening.—*JP* VI 6337 (*Pap.* X[1] A 95) *n.d.*, 1849

From preface to no. 5 (on Adler) of the proposed "Cycle of Ethical-Religious Essays":

X[6]
B 40
48

What lay at the root of the crisis will then become apparent, that it is the opposite of the Reformation—then everything appeared to be a religious movement and proved to be political—now everything appears to be politics but will turn out to be a religious movement. And when this becomes apparent, then (whether or not this is considered necessary in time) it will also become apparent that what is needed is *pastors*. *There* is where the battle will be; if there is to be a genuine victory, it must come about through pastors. Neither soldiers nor police nor diplomats nor the political planners are capable of it. *Pastors* are what will be needed: pastors who, possessing the desirable scientific-scholarly education, yet in contrast to the scientific game of counting, are practiced in what could be called spiritual guerrilla skirmishing, in doing battle not so much with scientific-scholarly attacks and problems as with the human passions; pastors who are able to split up "the crowd" and turn it into individuals; pastors who would not set up too great study-requirements and would want anything but to dominate; pastors who, if possible, are power-fully eloquent but are no less powerful in keeping silent and enduring without complaining; pastors who, if possible, know the human heart but are no less learned in refraining from judg-ing and denouncing; pastors who know how to use authority through the art of making sacrifices; pastors who are brought up and educated and prepared to obey and to suffer, so they would be able to mitigate, admonish, build up, move, but also to con-strain—not with force, anything but—no, constrain by their own obedience, and above all patiently to suffer all the rudeness of the sick without being disturbed, no more than the physician is disturbed by the patient's abusive language and kicks during the operation. For the generation is sick, spiritually, sick unto death. But just as a patient, when he himself is supposed to point to the area where he suffers, frequently points to an utterly wrong place, so also with the generation. It believes—yes, it is both laughable and lamentable—it believes, as is said, that a new ad-ministration will help. But as a matter of fact it is the eternal that is needed. Some stronger evidence is needed than socialism's be-lief* that God is the evil, and so it indeed says itself, since the daimonic always contains the truth in reverse. It is eternity that is needed, and the physician must—even if in another sense yet as once was the custom in the past—prescribe: the pastor.

This is my view or conception of the age, the view of an insignificant man who has something of the poet in him but otherwise is a philosopher, but—yes, how often I have repeated

X⁶
B 40
49

what to me is so important and crucial, my first declaration about myself—"without authority."

In margin: *that frightful sigh (from hell) uttered by socialism: God is the evil; just get rid of him and we will get relief. Thus it says what it needs itself.—*JP* VI 6256 (*Pap.* X⁶ B 40) *n.d.*, 1849

From draft of the proposed "Cycle of Ethical-Religious Essays":

X⁶
B 41
49

"*Christian*" *pastors* are what will be needed, also with regard to one of the greatest of all dangers, which is far closer than one possibly can believe—namely, that when the crisis spreads and turns into a religious movement (and the strength in *communism*

X⁶
B 41
50

obviously is the same ingredient daimonically potential in religiousness, even Christian religiousness), then, like mushrooms after a rain, daimonically tainted characters will appear who soon will presumptuously make themselves apostles on a par with "the apostles," a few also assuming the task of perfecting Christianity, soon even becoming religious founders themselves, inventors of a new religion that will gratify the times and the world in a completely different way from Christianity's "asceticism." The age for scientific-scholarly attacks on Christianity was already over before 1848; we were already far into the age of attacks of passion, attacks by the offended. But these are not the most dangerous; the most dangerous comes when the daimonics themselves become apostles—something like thieves passing themselves off as policemen—even founders of religion, who will get a dreadful foothold in an age that is critical in such a way that from the standpoint of the eternal it is eternally true to say of it: What is needed is religiousness—that is, true religiousness; whereas from the standpoint of the daimonic, the same age says about itself: It is religiousness we need—namely daimonic religiousness.

This is my view or conception of the age, the view of an insignificant man who has something of the poet in him but otherwise is a kind of philosopher, but—yes, how often I have repeated and emphasized what is so important and crucial, my first declaration about myself—"without authority."

S. K.

—*JP* VI 6257 (*Pap.* X⁶ B 41) *n.d.*, 1849

N.B.   N.B.
N.B.

Most of my concern that the completed works might put me in a false light as an extraordinary and the like is sheer hypochondria. As far as "A Cycle of Ethical-Religious Essays"[29] is concerned, on looking through it again, I find it entirely in order. From the outset I have marked the other works: poetic attempt—without authority. In addition, "Armed Neutrality" contains this as scrupulously as possible.

The question, therefore, is on the other side: to what extent, after all, do I have the right to hold these works back?

In one sense I would prefer to be free, I would prefer to be free from sending it out into the world, just as if I suddenly had no responsibility to desist from sending it all out.—*Pap.* X^1 A 97 *n.d.*, 1849

N.B.   N.B.
N.B.

X^1
A 116
86

"A Cycle of Ethical-Religious Essays,"[30] if that which deals with Adler is omitted (and it definitely must be omitted, because to come in contact with him is completely senseless, and furthermore it perhaps is also unfair to treat a contemporary merely psychologically this way), has the defect that what as parts in a total study does not draw attention to itself (and originally this was the case) will draw far too much attention to itself now and thereby to me. Although originally an independent work, the same applies to no. 3, a more recent work.

X^1
A 116
87

But if no. 2 and no. 3[31] which are about Adler, are also to be omitted, then "A Cycle" cannot be published at all.

Besides, there should be some stress on a second edition of *Either/Or.*[32] Therefore, either—as I previously thought—a quarto with all the most recent writing or only a small fragment of it, but, please note, a proper contrast to *Either/Or*. The "Three Notes"[33] on my work as an author are as if intended for that, and this has a strong appeal to me.

If I do nothing at all directly to assure a full understanding of

my whole literary production (by publishing "The Point of View
for My Work as an Author") or do not even give an indirect
telegraphic sign (by publishing "A Cycle" etc.)—then what?
Then there will be no judgment at all on my authorship in its
totality, since no one has sufficient faith in it or time or compe-
tence to look for a comprehensive plan [*Total-Anlæg*] in the entire production. Consequently the verdict will be that I have
changed somewhat over the years.

So it will be. This distresses me. I am deeply convinced that
there is another integral coherence, that there is a comprehensiveness in the whole production (especially through the assistance of Governance), and that there certainly is something else
to be said about it than this meager comment that in a way the
author has changed.

I keep this hidden deep within, where there is also something
in contrast: the sense in which I was more guilty than other men.

These proportions strongly appeal to me. I am averse to being
regarded with any kind of sympathy or to representing myself as
the extraordinary.

This suits me completely. So the best incognito I can choose
is quite simply to take an appointment.

The enticing aspect of the total productivity (that it is esthetic—but also religious) will be very faintly intimated by the
"Three Notes." For that matter, if something is to function
enticingly, it is wrong to explain it. A fisherman would not tell
the fish about his bait, saying "This is bait." And finally, if everything else pointed to the appropriateness of communicating something about the integral comprehensiveness, I cannot
emphasize enough that Governance actually is the directing
power and that in so many ways I do not understand until afterward.

This is written on Shrove Monday. A year ago today, I decided to publish *Christian Discourses*;[34] this year I am inclined to
the very opposite.

For a moment I would like to bring a bit of mildness and
friendliness into the whole thing. This can best be achieved by a
second edition of *Either/Or* and then the "Three Notes." In fact,
it would be odd right now when I am thinking of stopping writ-

ing to commence a polemic in which I do not wish to engage by replying (a polemic that is unavoidable because of no. 1 and no. 2 in "A Cycle").

Let there be moderation on my part: if someone wants a fight, then behind this I certainly am well armed.—*JP* VI 6346 (*Pap.* X^1 A 116) February 19, 1849

N.B.   N.B.
N.B.

X^1
A 117
88

To venture looks different to me this time from the way it did before. Previously I have always been keen on publishing what I had written; now it is a matter of holding back.

X^1
A 117
89

As for "A Cycle of Ethical-Religious Essays," it dates from an earlier period. Its composition is also unusual, because it is the original larger work ["The Book on Adler"] that is chopped into pieces, and the stimulus for the whole work (Adler) is omitted, and a separate essay, No. 3,[35] added. I cannot get myself into it in such a way that I really have a desire to publish it. Moreover, it has been laid aside or put away more than once.

As far as "The Point of View" is concerned, the point there is that it was written entirely in a frame of mind in which I did not expect to live to publish it myself. It is like the confession of a dying man. It is certainly a great benefit for me to have succeeded in writing it, and if I had gone abroad last spring as first planned I very likely would never have lived to get something like that written. For that there had to be altogether different sufferings, and I had to sink into myself more deeply than ever before. In that regard the past summer has been extremely important to me. In that way it was again good that I did not travel. I have achieved a productivity that I otherwise would not have achieved. But as far as "The Point of View" is concerned, this does not mean that it must be published.

The second edition of *Either/Or* and the 3 Notes:[36] this appeals to me. It is totally in character for me to hide the best in inwardness. In the past I have endured being looked upon as a villain, although I certainly was not exactly a villain: so let me as an author also endure seeming to be an oddity, although I am not

X¹
A 117
90

exactly that. But at that time the circumstances did not torment me so much; so I was tempted to show that I was not a villain but was perhaps just the opposite. With regard to my work as an author, the circumstances have tormented me more, and moreover this is also in another sense a public relationship.

But I must remember that I now have an additional danger, one that is totally foreign to me: a little bit of security for my future. I am assuming now that the limit of risking is this: trusting in God, one ventures into the danger about which one nevertheless has the idea that one has the possibility of being able to endure it. Thus I have been and am willing (on the old conditions) to venture into battle with people, their power, their ridicule etc., because I understood myself in the possibility of being able to be victorious by God's help. But I cannot have the other danger at the same time. I am not that strong; here I consider that my venturing is for me a rash act.

My original thought has always been to break off my work as an author and then to seek a minor appointment. Even though as an author I put out money and reaped no profit, I had hoped that I nevertheless would leave it with a kind of honor. It is this, if anything, that has embittered me somewhat, that I have to leave it as one mistreated. It has pained me that my stopping as an author should be interpreted as weakness. This bitterness has possibly influenced me to want to rise a stage higher than I myself had ever imagined. True enough, one must also remember that a person receives his orders only successively and to that extent there could be some truth in the idea that I went further than I had originally thought of doing. But yet it is also a matter of being true to myself.—*Pap.* X¹ A 117 *n.d.*, 1849

N.B.　　　　　　N.B.
N.B.

My task was to pose this riddle of awakening: a balanced esthetic and religious productivity, simultaneously.

This has been done. There is a balance even in quantity. *Concluding Postscript* is the midpoint.

The "Three Notes" swing it into the purely religious.

What comes next cannot be added impatiently as a conclu-

sion. For dialectically it is precisely right that this be the end. What comes next would be the beginning of something new.
—*JP* VI 6347 (*Pap.* X¹ A 118) *n.d.*, 1849

N.B.

An understanding of the totality of my work as an author, its maieutic purpose etc., requires also an understanding of my personal existing [*Existeren*] as an author, what I *qua* author have done with my personal existing to support it, illuminate it, conceal it, give it direction, etc., something that is more complicated than and just as interesting as the whole work as an author. Ideally the whole thing goes back to "the single individual [*den Enkelte*]," who is not I in an empirical sense but is the author.

That Socrates belonged together with what he taught, that his teaching ended in him, that he himself was his teaching, in the setting of actuality was himself artistically[37] a product of that which he taught—we have learned to rattle this off by rote because we have scarcely understood it. Even the systematicians talk this way about Socrates. But nowadays everything is supposed to be objective. And if someone were to use his own person maieutically, one would think it was "*à la* Andersen."[38]

All this is part of an illumination of my position in the development. Objectivity is believed to be superior to subjectivity, but it is just the opposite. That is to say, an objectivity that is within a corresponding subjectivity is the finale. The system was an inhuman something to which no human being could correspond as author and executor.—*JP* VI 6360 (*Pap.* X¹ A 146) *n.d.*, 1849

N.B.   N.B.
N.B.

It will never do to let the second edition of *Either/Or* be published without something accompanying it. Somehow the accent must be that I have made up my mind about being a religious author.

To be sure, my seeking an ecclesiastical post also stresses this, but it can be interpreted as something that came later.

X¹
A 147
109

X¹
A 147
110

Therefore, do I have the right (partly out of concern lest I say too much about myself, partly because of a disinclination to expose myself to possible annoyances) to allow what I have written to be vague, lie in abeyance as something indefinite and thus as being much less than it is, although it no doubt will embitter various people to have to realize that there is such ingeniousness in the whole [authorship]. It is, in fact, comfortable to regard me as a kind of half-mad genius—it is a strain to have to become aware of the more extraordinary.

And all this concern about an appointment and livelihood is both melancholy and exaggerated. And a second question arises: Will I be able to endure living if I must confess to myself that I have *acted prudently* and avoided the danger that the truth could require me to confront.

Furthermore, the other books ("The Sickness unto Death," "Come Here," "Blessed Is He Who is Not Offended"[39]) are extremely valuable. In one of them in particular it was granted to me to illuminate Christianity on a scale greater than I had ever dreamed possible; crucial categories are directly disclosed there. Consequently it must be published. But if I publish nothing at present, I will again have the last card.

"The Point of View" cannot be published.

I must travel.

But the second edition of *Either/Or* is a critical point (as I did in fact regard it originally and wrote "The Point of View" to be published simultaneously with it and otherwise would scarcely have been in earnest about publishing the second edition)—it will never come again. If this opportunity is not utilized, everything I have written, viewed as a totality, will be dragged down mainly into the esthetic.—*JP* VI 6361 (*Pap.* X¹ A 147) *n.d.*, 1849

X¹
A 147
111

See 116:11–118:10:

X¹
A 152
112

[*In margin:*—**N.B.** An observation concerning two passages in note no. 2 of the Three Friendly Notes.]

X¹
A 152
113

Although "the pseudonyms expected to get only a few readers," it can still be quite all right that the esthetic productivity "was used maieutically to get hold of men." For one thing, the human crowd is inquisitive about esthetic productions; another matter is the concept of "readers" that the pseudonyms must advance. How many readers *Either/Or* has had—and yet how few readers it has truly had, or how little it has come to be "read"! —*JP* VI 6363 (*Pap.* X^1 A 152) *n.d.*, 1849

The Three Friendly Notes[40] are not to be published either. Forget them; they are still about me. For a moment I thought it was necessary, but it is not needed.—*Pap.* X^1 A 157 *n.d.*, 1849

In margin:

Witnessing is still the form of communication that strikes the truest mean between direct and indirect communication. Witnessing is direct communication, but nevertheless it does not make one's contemporaries the *authority*. While the witness's *communication* addresses itself to the contemporaries, the *witness* himself addresses God and makes him the authority.—*JP* I 670 (*Pap.* X^1 A 235) *n.d.*, 1849

N.B.

The "Three Notes" must not be published either. Nothing is to be declared directly about me; if anything is to be said, much more should be said, "The Point of View" should be published. But all such writing shall lie there finished, just as it is, until after my death.

About my personal life, and directly, nothing is to be said: (1) because after all I am essentially a poet; but there is always something enigmatical in a poet's personality and therefore he must not be presented as, and above all he must not confuse himself with, an authentically ethical character in the most rigorous sense. (2) Insofar as I am a little more than a poet, I am essentially a penitent, but I cannot speak directly of that and therefore also cannot discuss any possible extraordinariness granted me. (3) I cannot make sure for myself and for my communication that the emphasis will fall strongly enough upon God. (4) It is an inconsistency in connection with self-denial.

X^1
A 250
164

X^1
A 250
165

Therefore, to want to do it would be on my part:

(1) a piece of recklessness, wanting to speak about myself at this time, as if either I were about to die tomorrow or it had been decided that I would stop being an author, since neither is the case. (2) It would be arbitrariness and impatience (the result of my having been the one who suffered) for me to want to decide my own fate in advance or to contribute to my being forced further into the character of a martyr, even if I secretly am that but without demanding the satisfaction of being regarded as one.

It was a godsend that I did not do it, that I did not publish the "Notes" or that God did not permit it to happen. It would have disturbed my life in every way, whether I continue to be an author at present or am set to something else. Therefore I actually have to repent the time I spent bumbling around tinkering with the "Notes," one word here and a word there. I have suffered a great deal, but God is helping me also to learn something.

How much God is the one directing the whole thing I see best in the manner in which the discourses about the lily and the bird[41] came into being at the time—just what I needed! God be praised! Without being contentious with people and without talking about myself, I get much said of what has to be said, but in a moving, gentle, uplifting way.

And now to travel; I must get away from here both for a moment's recreation and for a longer period, for it is all involved with my still being essentially a poet.

If I am to make any direct communication about myself personally, I must be forced to it from the outside, although with difficulty, since my creativity is actually not my own but a higher power's.—*JP* VI 6383 (*Pap.* X[1] A 250) *n.d.*, 1849

N.B.

I have made one final attempt to say a word about myself and my whole authorship. I have written "An Appendix" that should be called "The Accounting" and should follow the "Discourses."[42] I think it is a masterpiece, but that is of no importance—it cannot be done.

The point is that I perceive with extraordinary clarity the infinitely ingenious thought present in the totality of the authorship. Humanly speaking, now would be just the right time, now when the second edition of *Either/Or* appears. It would be splendid. But there is something false in it.

For I am a genius of such a kind that I cannot just directly and personally assume the whole thing without encroaching on Governance. Every genius is preponderantly immanence and immediacy, has no "why"; but again it is my genius that lets me see clearly, afterward, the infinite "why" in the whole, but this is Governance's doing. *On the other hand, I am not a religious person of such a kind that I can directly assign everything to God.*

Therefore not a word. If anything is to be said, then just that. Or if the world wants to extort a statement and explanation from me, then this.

I suffer indescribably every time I have begun to want to publish something about myself and the authorship. My soul becomes restless, my mind is not content to be producing as it is generally; I regard every word with dreadful suffering, think of it constantly, even outside of my time for work; my praying becomes sickly and distracted, because every trifle becomes excessively important to me as soon as it gets tied in with this. As soon as I leave it alone, either produce it but with the idea of not publishing it, or produce something else, then I am calm immediately, my mind is at rest, as it is now in having written and in intending to publish the "Three Devotional Discourses."[43]

Suddenly to want to assume this enormous productivity as one thought is too much—although I see very well that it is that. Yet I do not believe that I was motivated by vanity. It is originally a religious thought—I thought I owed it to God. But this is why everything is now ready—until after my death.

I cannot assume it personally in this way. It is true, for example, that when I began as an author I was "religiously resolved," but this must be understood in another way. *Either/Or*, especially "The Seducer's Diary," was written for her sake[44] in order to clear her out of the relationship. On the whole, the very mark of my genius is that Governance broadens and radicalizes whatever concerns me personally. I remember what a pseudonymous writer said about Socrates: "His whole life was personal pre-occupation with himself, and then Governance comes and adds world-historical significance to it."[45] To take another example—I am polemical by nature, and I understood the concept of "that single individual [*hiin Enkelte*]" early. However, when I wrote it for the first time (in *Two Upbuilding Discourses*),[46] I was thinking particularly of *my* reader, for this book contained a little hint to her, and until later it was for me very true personally that I sought only one single reader. Gradually this thought was taken over. But here again Governance's part is so infinite.

The rest of the things written can very well be published. But not one word about myself.

So I must take a journey.

—*JP* VI 6388 (*Pap.* X¹ A 266) *n.d.*, 1849

A Poetical View of Myself

X¹
A 272
179

[*In margin:* Used as an "appendix" to "The Accounting."[47]]

. . . . . If, however, someone were to say to me: You who for a long time now have lived and go on living every day sur-rounded by the drivel, derision, bestiality, etc. of these thousands of people—it seems to me that there is something artificial in the silence you steadily maintain about all this, or in the tranquillity with which you speak about yourself, as if you were untouched by the wretchedness of life [*changed to*: all these matters], I would answer him like this.

X¹
A 272
180

In the first place, when I speak, there is a very exalted person listening—moreover, this is the case with every human being, but the majority do not bear it in mind—there is a very exalted person listening: God in heaven; he is in heaven and hears what every person says. I bear this in mind. No wonder then that what I say has a certain solemnity. Furthermore, I am not speak-ing with those thousands, but with the single individual before God—thus it is rather to be wondered at that what I say is not infinitely more solemn.

Second, already as a small child I was told—and as solemnly as possible—that "the crowd" spat upon Christ, who indeed was the truth. [*In margin:* that **they** spat on Christ, that **the crowd** ("those who passed by") spat on him and said: Fie on you.[48]] This I have hid deep in my heart [*penciled in margin:* even though there have been moments, yes, times, when I seemed to have forgotten it, it has always come back to me as my first thought]. In order better to conceal the fact that I hid this thought deep in my soul, I have even concealed it under the most opposite exterior, for I was afraid that I would forget it too soon, that it would be tricked out of me and be like a blank cartridge. This thought—with the aid of which I also promptly and readily understood, as the lesser difficulty, what occupied me so much in my youth: that simple wise man,[49] that martyr of *intellectuality* whom "numbers," "the crowd" persecuted and condemned to death—this thought is my life. [*In margin:* although the task so far has been intellectual but fought religiously.]

I know with the greatest possible certitude that I am on the right road from this, that the context and the marks are the drivel, derision, and bestiality of "the crowd." No wonder, then, that what I say is not without a certain solemnity and has, as I do, a tranquillity, for the road I am taking is the right one, I am on the right road, even though far behind. Assuming that those who after *voluntarily* suffering for a long time the cruelty, mistreatment, and vilification of their contemporaries (consequently after being, as it were, salted,[50] for "every sacrifice ought to be salted"), then after having been mocked, spat upon (consequently after having accepted the last ordination beforehand)—assuming that they end up being crucified or beheaded or burned or broken on the wheel—assuming, then, that in the Christian order of precedence these are in first rank, which certainly is indisputable—assuming this, I believe that without saying too much about myself I am just about lowest in the lowest rank, the eighth rank. No doubt I will rise no higher. But a teacher's comment on one of his pupils is appropriate to my life—the only thing lacking is that it was written about me—"He is going backward, yet not without great diligence." Certainly this was not felicitously expressed by the teacher. Only in a very special situation such as my own can such a judgment be said to be felicitously expressed. Yet "not without great diligence" is perhaps

X'
A 272
181

saying too little, for I am applying myself very diligently, am extremely busy and hardworking, and I am going backward for sure, and it is also certain that the more diligent I am, the more I go backward—thus I am in truth going backward with great diligence.

In this way I hope to enter into eternity, and from a philosophical point of view how would it be possible to enter into eternity except by going backward; from an essentially Christian point of view, how would it be possible to enter into eternity except by having things go backward for one more and more? After all, Christ, who was the truth, was spat upon—and if I forgot everything, I will never forget, just as up to now I have not forgotten for a moment, what was said to me as a child and the impression it made on the child. It sometimes happens that a child while still in the cradle is pledged [*forloves*] to the one who someday will be his wife or her husband—religiously understood, I was pre-pledged [*for-lovet*] early in childhood. Ah, I have paid dearly for misinterpreting my life at one time and forgetting—that I was pledged. On the other hand, I once experienced in my life the most beautiful, blessed, and to me indescribably fulfilling satisfaction because in the step I took at that time, in the danger I voluntarily exposed myself to at that time, I completely understood myself and realized that I was pre-pledged. Pledged, pledged to the love that, despite all my errors and sins, has surrounded me from the beginning and until this moment, surrounded me, of whom it can be said with complete truth that he sinned much, but of whom it perhaps may not be completely false to say: he loved much[51]—surrounded by a love that infinitely exceeds my understanding, by a fatherly love "compared with which the most loving father is but a stepfather."[52]

Just one thing more, something upon which I, if possible, with a dying man's last will, put the strongest emphasis of earnestness. I no doubt have a grave and sad advantage (when I consider myself in relation to those glorious ones, to whom I stand in only the most distant possible relation, down below as the very lowest in the lowest rank, in eighth rank), yet in one sense an advantage over them with regard to having to endure. For it seems to me

X¹
A 272
182

that if one is oneself pure, perfect, and holy, the opposition of the world to the truth would make a person so sad that he quickly would die of sadness. But I am not a saintly person; I am a penitent, for whom it can be indescribably suitable to suffer something and for whom personally, precisely as a penitent, there is a satisfaction in suffering. Yes, if I were a contemporary of a more pure person, I would be happy to turn all the scorn and mistreatment of *the crowd* from him to myself. I look upon it as an advantage that I, who have the honor of serving the truth by personally being a penitent (for what I may have done wrong earlier and for what offense I personally have committed) in this way (but only in this way), find mistreatment by people to be in the right place when it is turned against me. [*In margin:* for whom the deception has certainly been extraordinarily successful, the deception that to a certain degree was possibly the invention of depression, the deception of being regarded as the most light-minded of all.]

X¹
A 272
183

—*JP* VI 6389 (*Pap.* X¹ A 272) *n.d.*, 1849

The Total Production with the Addition of the
Two Essays by H. H.[53]

X¹
A 351
228

The authorship conceived as a whole (as found in "A Note Concerning My Work as an Author,"[54] "Three Notes Concerning My Work as an Author," and "The Point of View for My Work as an Author") points definitively to "Discourses at the Communion on Fridays."[55]

X¹
A 351
229

The same applies to the whole structure. "Three Devotional Discourses"[56] comes later and is supposed to accompany the second edition of *Either/Or* and mark the distinction between what is offered with the left hand and what is offered with the right.

"Two Ethical-Religious Essays" does not belong to the authorship in the same way; it is not an element in it but a point of view. If there is to be a halt, it will be like a point one projects in advance in order to have a stopping place. It also contains an apparent and an actual eminence: a martyr, yes, an apostle—and a genius. If any information about me is to be sought in the essays, then it is this: that I am a genius—not an apostle, not a martyr. The apparent eminence is included in order to determine all the more accurately the actual one. For most people the category "genius" is so indiscriminate that it can mean anything; for that very reason it was important to define this concept, as the two essays do by means of defining that which is infinitely qualitatively higher.

Thus the two essays appropriately have the character of a signal. But it is dialectical. It could signify: here is the stopping place; and then could signify: here is the beginning—but always in such a way that above all I take precautions not to occasion any conceptual confusion but remain true to myself in being no more or no less than a genius, or in being a poet and thinker with a quantitative "more" not customary in a poet and thinker with regard to being what one writes and thinks about. A quantitative "more," not a qualitative "more," for the qualitative "more" is: the truth-witness, the martyr—which I am not. And even qualitatively higher is the apostle, which I have not fancied myself to be any more than that I am a bird. I shall guard myself against blasphemy and against profanely confusing the religious sphere, which I devoutly am doing my utmost to uphold and secure against prostitution by confused and presumptuous thinking.—*JP* VI 6407 (*Pap.* X¹ A 351) *n.d.*, 1849

X¹
A 351
230

X¹
A 422
268

Just as the Guadalquibir [*sic*] River at some place plunges underground and then comes out again, so I must now plunge into pseudonymity, but I also understand now how I will emerge again under my own name. The important thing left is to do something about seeking an appointment and then to travel.

(1) The three ethical-religious essays[57] will be anonymous; this was the earlier stipulation. (2) "The Sickness unto Death" will be pseudonymous and is to be gone through so that my name and the like are not in it. (3) The three works, "Come Here, All You," "Blessed Is He Who Is Not Offended," and "From on High He Will Draw All to Himself" will be pseudonymous. Either all three in one volume under the common title, "Practice in Christianity, Attempt by ————," or each one separately. They are to be checked so that my name and anything about me

etc. are excluded, which is the case with number three. (4) Everything under the titles "The Point of View for My Work as an Author," "A Note," "Three Notes," and "Armed Neutrality"* cannot conceivably be published.

These writings properly remain pseudonymous. Here there is the dialectical tension and tightening with respect to the doctrine of sin and redemption, and then I begin with my own name in a simple upbuilding discourse. But it is one thing for a work of such a dialectical nature to appear pseudonymously and something quite different if it appears over my name, in character, as the finale of the whole effort.

After all, there is no hurry about publishing. But if it is to be in character and as a finale, it must be done as soon as possible, something that has pained me frightfully and that has now become almost an impossibility, because today, June 4, I spoke with Reitzel,[58] who said he dared not take on anything new for publication. On the whole the man has plagued me unbearably with his miseries, which perhaps are exaggerated anyway.

A battle of ideas has taken place here. In actuality the whole matter of publishing with or without my name perhaps would be a bagatelle. But to me in my ideality it is a very taxing problem, that above all I do not falsely hold myself back or falsely go too far but truly understand myself and continue to be myself.

I have struggled and suffered fearfully. Yet one who fights for the "You shall" as I do must also suffer at this point. But yet at times I probably have not been far from pressing this "You shall" in an almost melancholy-frantic way. But now I understand myself. You shall—this is eternally true—but it is not less true and it is also a "You shall" that with God you shall understand your limits and beyond them you shall not go or you shall abandon such desires.

But, gracious God, how I have suffered and how I have struggled. Yet it is my consolation that the God of love will let this be to my good, and in a certain sense it consoles me that I have endured this suffering, because in this very suffering I have become convinced of the way I am to turn.

X¹
A 422
269

X¹
A 422
270

---

*See this journal, p. 157 [*Pap.* X¹ A 450, p. 278 (p. 301)].

My misfortune always has been that it is so difficult for me to take an appointment. My depression, which is almost a quiet derangement, has been a hindrance to me all along, my consciousness of sin, too. This has aided me continually in venturing, for it has assured me that I was at least not being guided by vanity and the like. But now in God's name I must turn in this direction.

Strangely enough, incidentally, I have written so much in journal NB[10] [*Pap.* X[1] A 82–294] and in this journal [NB[11], *Pap.* X[1] A 295–541], but there is on a loose sheet [*Pap.* X[1] A 424 (pp. 196–97)] something I have not wished to enter in the journal and that I still really regard as the most decisive and also one of the earliest—I now end with precisely this.—*JP* VI 6416 (*Pap.* X[1] A 422) June 4, 1849

X[1]
A 424
271

This is the loose sheet mentioned on page 129 of this journal [*Pap.* X[1] A 422 (p. 196)]. To be written transversely in the journal.

If I had the means, I would venture further out—of course, not with the intention of being put to death (for that, after all, is sinful), but nevertheless, with that possibility in mind, believing that eventually my life might take a still higher turn.

Now I cannot, and I cannot defend venturing in the way that would give my life such a turn that I really would not recognize myself, whereas I fully recognize myself in the kind of persecution, if it may be called that, which I have suffered. Yes, from earliest childhood I have had the presentiment in my soul that things would turn out this way for me, that in a certain sense I would be regarded even with a certain solemnity as somewhat extraordinary and yet be laughed at and regarded as a bit mad.

Now I cannot. Now all my original plans go against me: to be a writer for only a few years and then to seek an appointment, to practice the art of being able to stop—all the more so since it was my intention, never as definite as last year when I sold the house and made a little on it, to stop in earnest (I did not even rent rooms; this I did only much later) and to travel; and the Friday discourses[59] have always seemed to me to be a suitable terminating point. Perhaps I should have done that. I suffered much in

1848, but I also learned much and in that case I would scarcely have learned to know myself in this way.

Now I cannot. Suddenly to be forced to sustain a very perceptible financial loss,[60] perhaps at a time when I am about to take the most decisive step—and then perhaps not be put to death anyway and thus to have bungled the whole and myself—no, that I cannot do. To my mind it would be tempting God if I, spoiled by having had financial means, were now, with this new danger, to venture to a degree previously untried.

In addition, I now have a misgiving about myself that I would not have if I had financial means: is there possibly a connection between this almost martyr-impatience of mine and another kind of impatience, that I rather shrink from the humiliating task of actively seeking an appointment and from the humiliation implicit in all such things and in the whole mode of life? Moreover, I do have perhaps a trace of life-weariness.[61] Perhaps it is also an exaggeration in the direction of expressing that I have suffered injustice and therefore could wish that they would put me to death.

Finally, there is a big question whether I, with my differential mental capacities,[62] am not intended to live, because the more there is of scientific scholarly nature and the like, the less pertinence there is to work in that way.

Finally, it is part of being human not to become the very highest that one has envisioned—patience and humility in this respect. But one will be wounded by this highest, and that I have been, through having been so close to it in thought.

Consequently I do not take the least little step in that direction.—*JP* VI 6418 (*Pap.* X¹ A 424) *n.d.*, 1849

In God's name, then! What worries me most is "The Point of View for My Work as an Author." It can still easily be kept back; indeed, it will be a good while until I arrive at printing it; but at that time I will no doubt find the strength to let it be included.

This time I am learning what it means that I would pray that I might be spared making this step—ah, and this is why I for a period hoped that death would release me. And I am learning what it is to sigh: Would that this fire be kindled.[63]

X¹
A 424
272

However, no reflections! Now they will only exhaust and confuse me. As taciturnly as possible I will cling to this: In God's name.—*Pap.* X^1 A 501 *n.d.*, 1849

No, it cannot be done!

I cannot do it, it is too high for me! "The Point of View" cannot be published—and therefore when the other discourses already finished are published is unimportant or less important.

There is really something that continually troubles me—that there is something untrue about hurling myself into such decisions at the same time as I have an entirely different concern.

—*Pap.* X^1 A 508 *n.d.*, 1849

X^1
A 510
327

The other alternative[64] is perhaps more rash, perhaps bolder, perhaps a more daring venture, but this does not make it more true for me—and to be true is of first importance.

X^1
A 510
328

If I consider my own personal life, am I then a Christian or is my personal life purely a poet-existence, even with an addition of something demonic. In that case the idea would be to take such an enormous risk that I thereby make myself so unhappy that I would get into the situation for really becoming a Christian. But does this give me the right to do it dramatically so that the Christendom of a whole country gets involved. Is there not something desperate in the whole thing, something like the treachery of starting a fire in order to throw oneself into the arms of God—perhaps, for perhaps it would nevertheless turn out that I would not become a Christian.

All this about my person as author cannot be used at all, for it is clear that it only will involve me more in the interesting instead of getting me out of it, and this is also the effect it will have on my contemporaries. The simple transition is very simple: to be silent and then to see about getting an appointment.

There is no question but that I will stop being an author now, but I would still like to dispense with the interesting: put down the period myself and officially in character. The simple way to do it is to cross over to the new in complete silence; this solemn determination to put down a period is an extremely dangerous thing; the elemental point is that there in fact comes to be a period.

I regret—and I blame myself for it—that in several previous entries in this journal there are attempts to overstrain myself, for which God will forgive me.

Until now I have been a poet, absolutely nothing else, and it is a desperate struggle to will to go out beyond my limits.

The work "Practice in Christianity" has great personal signifi- x^1 cance for me—does it follow that I should publish it right away? A 510 329 Perhaps I am one of the few who need such strong remedies— and I, I should then, instead of benefiting from it and myself beginning in real earnestness to become a Christian, I should first publish it. Fantasy!

The work and other works are ready;[65] perhaps the time may come when it is suitable and I have the strength to do it and when it is truth in me.

In many ways it is true that the entire authorship is my up-bringing—well, does that mean that instead of being in earnest about becoming a true Christian I am to become a phenomenon in the world?

Consequently *The Sickness unto Death* appears at this time, but pseudonymously and with me as editor. It is said to be "for upbuilding." This is more than my category, the poet-category: upbuilding.[66]

Just as the Guadalquibir [*sic*] River (this occurred to me earlier and is somewhere in the journal [*Pap.* X^1 A 422 (p. 194)]) at some place plunges underground, so is there also a stretch, the upbuilding, that carries my name. There is something (the es-thetic) that is lower and is pseudonymous, and something that is higher and is also pseudonymous, because as a person I do not correspond to it.

The pseudonym is Johannes Anticlimacus [*sic*] in contrast to Climacus, who said he was not a Christian. Anticlimacus is the opposite extreme: a Christian on an extraordinary level—if only I myself manage to be just a simple Christian.

"Practice in Christianity" can be published in the same way, but there is no hurry.

But nothing about my personality as a writer; it is false to want to anticipate during one's lifetime—this merely converts a person into the interesting.

X¹
A 510
330

On the whole, I must now venture in quite different directions. I must dare to believe that through Christ I can be saved from the power of depression in which I have lived; and I must dare to try to be more economical.—*JP* VI 6431 (*Pap.* X¹ A 510) *n.d.*, 1849

X¹
A 541
344

De se ipso [About oneself]

Actually, something else will happen than what I originally had in mind.

When I began as the author of *Either/Or*, I no doubt had a far more profound impression of the *terror* of Christianity than any clergyman in the country. I had a fear and trembling such as perhaps no one else had. Not that I therefore wanted to relinquish Christianity. No, I had another interpretation of it. For one thing I had in fact learned very early that there are men who seem to be selected for suffering, and, for another thing, I was conscious of having sinned much and therefore supposed that Christianity had to appear to me in the form of this terror. But how cruel and false of you, I thought, if you use it to terrify others,

X¹
A 541
345

perhaps upset ever so many happy, loving lives that may very well be truly Christian. It was as alien as it could possibly be to my nature to want to terrify others, and therefore I both sadly and perhaps also a bit proudly found my joy in comforting others and in being gentleness itself to them—hiding the terror in my own interior being.

So my idea was to give my contemporaries (whether or not they themselves would want to understand) a hint in humorous form (in order to achieve a lighter tone) that a much greater .pressure was needed—but then no more; I aimed to keep my heavy burden to myself, as my cross. I have often taken exception to anyone who was a sinner in the strictest sense and then promptly got busy terrifying others. Here is where *Concluding Postscript* comes in.

Then I was horrified to see what was understood by a Christian state (this I saw especially in 1848); I saw how the ones who were supposed to rule, both in Church and state, hid themselves like cowards while barbarism boldly and brazenly raged; and I experienced how a truly unselfish and God-fearing endeavor (and my endeavor as an author was that) is rewarded in the Christian state.

     That seals my fate. Now it is up to my contemporaries how they will list the cost of being a Christian, how terrifying they will make it. I surely will be given the strength for it—I almost said "unfortunately." I really do not say this in pride. I both have been and am willing to pray to God to exempt me from this terrible business; furthermore, I am human myself and love, humanly speaking, to live happily here on earth. But if what one sees all over Europe is Christendom, a Christian state, then I propose to start here in Denmark to list the price for being Christian in such a way that the whole concept—state church, official appointments, livelihood—bursts open.

     I dare not do otherwise, for I am a penitent from whom God can demand everything. I also write under a pseudonym because I am a penitent. Nevertheless, I will be persecuted, but I am secure against any honor and esteem that from another side could fall to me.

     For some years now I have been so inured to bearing the treachery and ingratitude of a little country, the envy of the elite and the insults of the rabble that I perhaps—for want of anything better—am qualified to proclaim Christianity. Bishop Mynster can keep his velvet robe and Grand Cross.—*JP* VI 6444 (*Pap.* X[1] A 541) *n.d.*, 1849

X[1]
A 541
346

     Thank God I did not publish the book about my work as an author or in any way try to push myself to be more than I am.

X[1]
A 546
348

     The Sickness unto Death is now printed,[67] and pseudonymously, by Anti-Climacus.

     "Practice in Christianity" will also be pseudonymous. I now understand myself completely.

     The point in the whole thing is this: there is a zenith of Christianity in ethical rigorousness and this must at least be heard. But no more. It must be left to everyone's conscience to decide whether he is capable of building the tower so high.

But it must be heard. But the trouble is simply that practically all Christendom and all the clergy, too, live not only in secular prudence at best but also in such a way that they brazenly boast about it and as a consequence must interpret the life of Christ to be fanaticism.

This is why the other must be heard, heard if possible as a voice in the clouds, heard as the flight of wild birds over the heads of the tame ones.

But no more. That is why it must be pseudonymous and I merely the editor.

Ah, but what I suffered before arriving at this, something that was essentially clear to me earlier but I had to understand for the second time.

God will certainly look after the rest for me.

If I now continue to be an author, the subject must be "sin" and "reconciliation" in such a way that in upbuilding discourse I would now make use of the fact that the pseudonym has appropriately jacked up the price.

For this, pseudonyms will be used continually. I entertained this idea once before, particularly regarding that to which Anti-Climacus is assigned, and it is somewhere in the journals, no doubt in NB¹⁰ [*Pap.* X¹ A 422 (pp. 194–96)].

The fearful stress and strain I have experienced lately are due to my wanting to overexert myself and wanting too much, and then I myself perceived that it was too much, and therefore I did not carry it out, but then again I was unable to let the possibility go and to my own torment held myself on the spearhead of possibility—something, incidentally, that without any merit on my part has been an extremely beneficial exercise for me.

Now there has been action, and now I can breathe.

It was a sound idea: to stop my productivity by once again using a pseudonym. Like the river Guadalquibir [*sic*]—this simile appeals to me very much.

So not a word about myself with regard to the total authorship; such a word will change everything and misrepresent me.—*JP* VI 6445 (*Pap.* X¹ A 546) *n.d.*, 1849

In margin:

It is absolutely right—a pseudonym had to be used.

When the demands of ideality are to be presented at their maximum, then one must take extreme care not to be confused with them himself, as if he himself were the ideal.

Protestations could be used to avoid this. But the only sure way is this redoubling.

The difference from the earlier pseudonyms is simply but essentially this, that I do not retract the whole thing humorously but identify myself as one who is striving.—*JP* VI 6446 (*Pap.* X^1 A 548) *n.d.*, 1849

So I turned off the tap; that means the pseudonym Anti-Climacus, a halt.

An awakening[68] is the final goal, but that is too high for me personally—I am too much of a poet.—*JP* VI 6450 (*Pap.* X^1 A 557) *n.d.*, 1849

In margin:

Now *The Sickness unto Death* is published and pseudonymously.[69] So an end has been put to the confounded torment of undertaking too great a task: wishing to publish everything at one time, including what I wrote about the authorship, and, so to speak, taking the desperate step of setting fire to established Christendom.

Now the question of when the three other books[70] come out is of less importance (and the one about my authorship will not appear at all), because now there is no question of the force of one single blow.

Now I will rest and be more calm.

—*JP* VI 6451 (*Pap.* X^1 A 567) *n.d.*, 1849

If it could be done and if I had not virtually ceased being an author, it would give me much joy to dedicate one of my books to the memory of Councilor Olsen.[71] In fact, for that purpose the book "From on High He Will Draw All to Himself" could pro-̇ vide the opportunity.—*JP* VI 6455 (*Pap.* X^1 A 571) *n.d.*, 1849

What an accomplishment the *Concluding Postscript* is; there is more than enough for three professors. But of course the author was a someone who did not have a career position and did not seem to want to have one; there was nothing worthy of becoming a paragraph in the system—well, then, it is nothing at all.

The book came out in Denmark. It was not mentioned anywhere at all. Perhaps fifty copies were sold; thus the publishing costs for me, including the proofreader's fee (one hundred rix-dollars), came to about four or five hundred rix-dollars, plus my time and work. And in the meantime, I was caricatured by a scandal sheet that in the same little country had three thousand subscribers, and another paper (also with wide circulation, *Flyveposten*) continued the discussion about my trousers.[72]—*JP* VI 6458 (*Pap.* X^1 A 584) *n.d.*, 1849

The two works by Anti-Climacus[73] ("Practice in Christianity") can be published immediately.

With this the writing stops; essentially it has already stopped (that which is wholly mine) with "The Friday Discourses."[74] The pseudonymous writer[75] at the end is a higher level, which I can only suggest. The second-round pseudonymity is precisely the expression for the halt. *Qua* author I am like the river Guadalquibir [*sic*], which at some place plunges underground; there is a stretch that is mine: the upbuilding;[76] behind and ahead lie the lower and the higher pseudonymities: the upbuilding is mine, not the esthetic, nor that for upbuilding,[77] and even less that for awakening.[78]—*JP* VI 6461 (*Pap.* X^1 A 593) *n.d.*, 1849

"Practice in Christianity" will be the last to be published. There I shall end for now.

Consequently the year 1848 will be included, since the things by Anti-Climacus[79] are all from 1848. The remainder is from 1849. According to decision, writing concerning the authorship will be shelved.

If "Practice in Christianity" is published, what has been intimated many places elsewhere will be carried out—namely, to set
forth the possibility of offense. This is also related essentially to
my task, which is continually to jack up the price[80] by bringing
a dialectic to bear. But for this reason, too, a pseudonym had to
be used. That which represents the dialectical element has always
been by a pseudonym. To want to make it my own would be
both untrue and an all too frightful and violent means of awakening.—*JP* VI 6464 (*Pap.* X^1 A 615) *n.d.*, 1849

My Writings Considered as a "Corrective" to the Established Order

The designation "corrective" is a category of reflection just as:
here/there, right/left.

The person who is to provide the "corrective" must study the
weak sides of the established order scrupulously and pene-
tratingly and then one-sidedly present the opposite—with expert
one-sidedness. Precisely in this consists the corrective, and in
this also the resignation in the one who is going to do it. In a
certain sense the corrective is expended on the established order.

If this is done properly, then a presumably sharp head can
come along and object that "the corrective" is one-sided and get
the public to believe there is something in it. Ye gods! Nothing
is easier for the one providing the corrective than to add the
other side; but then it ceases to be precisely the corrective and
itself becomes an established order.

Therefore an objection of this nature comes from a person
utterly lacking the resignation required to provide "the corrective" and without even the patience to comprehend this.—*JP* VI
6467 (*Pap.* X^1 A 640) *n.d.*, 1849

As soon as the category "the single individual" goes out,
Christianity is abolished. Then the individual will relate himself
to God through the human race, through an abstraction, through
a third party—and then Christianity is *eo ipso* abolished. If this
happens, then the God-man is a phantom instead of an actual
prototype.

Alas, when I look at my own life! How rare the man who is so

X^1
A 646
401

endowed for the life of the spirit and above all so rigorously schooled with the help of spiritual suffering—in the eyes of all my contemporaries I am fighting almost like a Don Quixote—it never occurs to them that it is Christianity; indeed, they are convinced of just the opposite.

Christendom as it is now makes Christ into a complete phantom as far as existence is concerned—although they do profess that Christ was a particular human being. They have no courage to believe existentially in the ideal.

Yes, it is true, the human race has grown away from Christianity! Alas, yes, in quite the same sense as a person grows away from ideals. For the young person the ideal is the ideal, but he relates himself to it with pathos. For the older person, who has grown away from the ideal, the ideal has become something quixotic and visionary, something that does not belong in the world of actuality.

In the hour of my death I shall repeat again and again, if possible, what every word in my writings testifies to: Never, never, with a single word have I given occasion for the mistaken notion that I personally mistook myself for the ideal—but I have been convinced that my striving has served to illuminate what Christianity is.

The understanding, reflection, has taken the ideal away from people, from Christendom, and has made it into something quixotic and visionary—consequently, being a Christian must be set a whole reflection further back, being a Christian now comes to mean loving to be a Christian, striving to be one: so enormous has the ideal now become.

In reference to this, see the essay, "Armed Neutrality," where I have paralleled this with the transition from being called σοφοί [wise men] to being called φιλόσοφοι [lovers of wisdom].[81]

—*JP* II 1781 (*Pap.* X¹ A 646) *n.d.*, 1849

In margin:

"Practice in Christianity" certainly should be pseudonymous.[82] It is the dialectical element and would be much too strong if I brought it out personally.

So "The Sickness unto Death," "Practice in Christianity," "The Point of View for My Work as an Author," and "Three Notes" belong to the year 1848.

To 1849 "From on High He Will Draw All to Himself,"[83] "Armed Neutrality," and other small things, including the one about Phister.[84]

Even if I wanted to publish "From on High" under my name, it is nevertheless definite that the conception of my writings finally gathers itself together in the "Discourses at the Communion on Fridays,"[85] since "The Point of View," after all, is from 1848.

> N.B. And in order that "From on High," which is somewhat polemical, not be the last work, some additional discourses for the Communion on Fridays could be written, a second series of them. One, and as good as two, are already finished, and some suggestions for a few more are in one of the new folders bookbinder Møller[86] has made.

—*JP* VI 6487 (*Pap.* X¹ A 678) *n.d.*, 1849

On the Year 1848

X²
A 66
51

In one sense 1848 has raised me to another level. In another sense it has shattered me, that is, it has shattered me religiously, or to say it in my own language: God has run me ragged. He has let me take on a task that even trusting in him I cannot raise to its highest form; I must take it in a lower form. For this reason the matter actually has contributed inversely to my religious or further religious development. In one sense I want so much to venture; my imagination beckons and goads me, but I will simply have to agree to venture in a lower form. Without a doubt it is the most perfect and the truest thing I have written;[87] but it must not be interpreted as if I am supposed to be the one who almost censoriously bursts in upon everybody else—no, I must first be brought up myself by the same thing; there perhaps is no one who is permitted to humble himself as deeply under it as I do before I am permitted to publish it. I, the author, who myself am nothing (the highest) must not be permitted to publish it under my own name,[88] because the work is itself a judgment. In one way or another I first must have arranged myself in life and have admitted that I am weak like everyone else—then I can publish it. But that which tempts my imagination is to get permission to do it before I, humanly speaking, can pay the price. Quite true, the blow would then be all the more powerful, but I would also gain a false high position. It is poetry—and therefore my life, to my humiliation, must demonstrably express the opposite, the inferior. Or perhaps I should even be an ascetic who can live on water and bread. —And yet this mortification I would willingly submit to, if only I will be able to undertake an appointment. In a still deeper sense this is my difficulty. And there may be still greater humiliation here before it becomes possible, if it becomes possible.

Economic concerns came suddenly and all too close. I cannot bear two such disparate burdens, the hostility of the world and concern for the future, at the same time. My idea when I rented the apartment on Tornebuskegaden was to live there a half year, quietly reflecting on my life, and then seek an appointment.

Then suddenly everything was thrown into confusion. In a matter of months I was in the situation where tomorrow, perhaps, I would not own a thing but be literally in financial straits. It was a severe drain on me. My spirit reacted all the more strongly. I wrote more than ever, but more than ever like a dying man. Without question, in the context of Christian truth it certainly is the highest that has been granted to me. But in another sense it is too high for me to appropriate it right off in life and to walk in character.

This is the deeper significance of the new pseudonym, which is higher than I am myself.

Oh, I know I have not spared myself; even to the point of overstrain I have wanted to force myself to venture something rash, but I cannot do it, I cannot justify it.

This is how Governance continually keeps his hand on me— and governs. I had never considered getting a new pseudonym. And yet the new pseudonym—but note well that it is higher than my personal existence—precisely that is the truth of my nature,

X^2
A 66
52

X^2
A 66
53

it is the expression for the limits of my nature. Otherwise I would finally become veritably more than human.—*JP* VI 6501 (*Pap.* X² A 66) *n.d.,* 1849

The Basic Error

in Christendom is actually that people have wanted to make all religious education Christian with the aid of the ridiculous presupposition that all people are Christians because they are baptized as children.

Just as Christianity historically entered the world after having a whole prehistoric religious development in the background, so a person, if one is going to have a decisive impression of Christianity, must first of all go through a whole religious school. Christianity is truly too spiritual for a person to begin with it right off. What discipline is presupposed in order to understand in such a way that it is truth in oneself: that sin is the only tragedy, and that Christ is a Savior only in relation to that.

In Christendom it would be most proper to build a number of chapels for the teaching of Jewish piety without ever naming the name of Christ; for many this in itself would be considerable.

This is my unswerving position: the little bit of piety in Christendom is Jewish piety (a clinging to this life, a hope and faith that God will bless them in this life, etc., so the evidence that a person is God's friend is that things go well with him in this world), and yet they always put Christ's name to this.—*JP* IV 4456 (*Pap.* X² A 80) *n.d.,* 1849

About the Completed Unpublished Writings[89] and Myself X²
A 89
69

The difficulty in publishing anything about the authorship is and remains that, without my knowing it or knowing it positively, I really have been used, and now for the first time I understand and comprehend the whole—but then I cannot, after all, say: *I.* At most I can say (that is, given my scrupulous demand for the truth): This is how I now understand the writings of the past.* The flaw, again, is that if I do not do it myself, there is no one who can present it, because no one knows it the way I do. No one can explain the structure of the whole as I can.

But this is my limitation—I am a pseudonym. Fervently, incitingly, I present the ideal, and when the listener or reader is moved to tears, then I still have one job left: to say, "I am not that, my life is not like that."[90]

Quite true: I think the effect would be stronger if at this moment one person stepped forward and spoke in his own name and gesticulated with his life: but perhaps Governance does not think this way—I must in truth learn that there is something higher that I perhaps am able to think but do not dare to venture.

"From on High He Will Draw All to Himself"[91] must be done pseudonymously.

X^2
A 89
70

*Note. The truest statement, however, is that there is an "also," because I have understood a part from the beginning and always understood in advance before I did it.—*JP* VI 6505 (*Pap.* X^2 A 89) *n.d.*, 1849

On "That Single Individual," My Work as an Author, My Existing

The movement the entire authorship describes is: **from** the public **to** the single individual. It appears for the first time in the preface to *Two Upbuilding Discourses*—and the second time, or raised to the second power, at the most crucial moment, in the dedication to *Upbuilding Discourses in Various Spirits*. (Concerning this, see the little article, which is finished and ready, "The Accounting," to be found with "On My Work as an Author.")

As an esthetic author I went out of my way, as it were, to catch hold of the public—and my personal existing, including living on the streets and byways, expresses the same thing—this describes the movement: *from* the public *to* the single individual, and it ends quite consistently with my living, myself the single individual, in rural solitude in a country parish.

Well, enough of that. Even if I were not compelled for external reasons to do it, it would still be the most appropriate thing to do. Oh, but Governance always helps me—this I continually see—by looking back.—*Pap.* X^2 A 96 *n.d.*, 1849

With Regard to the Idea of My Life as an Author

X^2
A 98
73

This was also my idea, all in the course of time. The truth must never become an object of pity; serve it as long as you can, to the best of your ability with unconditioned recklessness; squander everything in its service—and then you can quit. Indeed, a person accomplishes much more, if so it be, by serving the truth with genuine recklessness for just one year than by botching it up and compromising it with: "out of concern for myself and the truth"—and putting a whole life into this mixture. No, it must be clear where I am serving the truth and where I am serving myself.

Of course, I have nothing against a person's working for a living and the like—I aim to do it myself, and I by no means pass myself off as pure spirit—but it must be clear that it is not in order to serve the truth. The truth does not stand in need at all of my becoming a man of distinction and the like; it is totally indifferent to whether I live on dry bread—thus it cannot be for the sake of truth. That it should be, as the saying goes, "in order to be more effective by virtue of my office and position," well, that makes a mockery of Christ and all truth-witnesses, who alone have shown how to be most effective for the truth. If despite this I still want the high office—well, then one admission, it is for my own sake.—*Pap.* X^2 A 98 *n.d.*, 1849

X^2
A 98
74

Concerning the Writings on
My Work as an Author

X^2
A 104
79

They contain something that makes their publication dubious. Yet it is a view, a later view; I cannot say that I thought of it that way before. There is a poetic aspect to it. I have also put myself into carrying through my work as an author. It is certainly true that I repeat and emphasize this again and again in the books, but I still continually fear that by publishing them I may infringe upon God, whereas at times it really seems to me that I would infringe upon God by not publishing them.

Basically it is like this. My nature has been the possibility of being a writer. It is Governance who always has arranged the situations for me in such a way that they seemed to press the writing out of me, and yet almost all my situations are such that I, freely acting, brought myself into them. But the point is that I was a long way from understanding their implications until I perceived them later.

It is true that I have been willing to venture, to make a sacrifice, to expose myself to dangers; it is true that the thought of my personal guilt and the hope of possibly doing something good in return have been with me—but I must also confess that my whole life has been an indescribable joy or satisfaction, which is also why in praying to God I always thank him for the indescribable good he has done to me, far more than I had expected.

Fundamentally, to be an author has been my only possibility. The thought of becoming a rural pastor has always been in my mind, but the trouble is that in one sense, in an unhappy sense, I am not a human being and therefore find it very difficult to take on something like that. But even if I could have done it, I still would not have been able to do it at first, since my need to write was too great and writing satisfied me too much.

That is why I am refraining from publishing these writings; it is preferable to say too little about myself by being silent than by speaking to say too much. But it is certain and true that: I did not become an author in order to be a success in the world—oh, I hated myself when I began writing *Either/Or,* I can say that I wished that everybody would rise up against me. But I have so much knowledge of the religious that I cannot straightforwardly call this pure religiousness—it was a kind of intoxicated religiousness.—*Pap.* X^2 A 104 *n.d.,* 1849

[margin: X^2 A 104 80]

About Myself as Author

[margin: X^2 A 106 81]

Once again I have reached the point where I was last summer,[92] the most intensive, the richest time I have experienced, where I understood myself to be what I must call a poet of the religious, not however that my personal life should express the opposite—no, I strive continually, but that I am a "poet" expresses that I do not confuse myself with the ideality.

[margin: X^2 A 106 82]

My task was to cast Christianity into reflection, not poetically to idealize (for the essentially Christian, after all, is itself the ideal) but with poetic fervor to present the total ideality at its most ideal—always ending with: I am not that, but I strive. If the latter does not prove correct and is not true about me, then everything is cast in intellectual form and falls short.

Given the momentum of my writing a year ago I also managed to comprehend the total authorship and myself. I realized that I was a poetic reflector of Christianity with the capacity to set forth the Christian qualifications in all their ideality; I understood how in wonderful ways I had been led to this early in my life. I understood, God be praised, what I understand so unaltered that I can never thank God sufficiently for the good he has done for me, indescribably much more than I had expected. All this I understood, and the total structure of the authorship, and I put it all down in the book on my work as an author.

Then for a time I misunderstood myself, although not for long. I wanted to publish this book. The understanding of my life as an author and of myself was, if I may say so, a gift of Governance to me, which should also be a supporting point of view in going ahead in becoming more truly a Christian—and the misunderstanding was that I wanted to publish it, forgetting that this would be an overstepping of my limits. If I state that I am this poetic reflector and striver, then I am making myself out to be more than I say I am: in one way or another I myself come to be the ideal and claim to be that. The whole thing would then be in the realm of the interesting, and my contemporaries would then be made accomplices in my intrigue—but I have no right at all to call it that, since it is also my own development.

X^2
A 106
83

In the most curious ways I have been prevented from publishing. And now the turn has been made, the new pseudonym[93] established. I deserve no credit whatever, because once again it seems that a Governance has helped me do the right thing.

Many times I was all set to publish the writings about myself, but—no. I was able to write them with the same calmness I customarily have in my work, but the minute I took them out with the thought of publishing them, I felt an uneasiness, a tension that I had never sensed before.

That was my boundary. To publish them would have produced a great confusion. Despite all the disclaimers in the writings, it would not have been possible to prevent my being regarded as an extraordinary Christian, instead of being only a genius; eventually I perhaps would have made the error of regarding myself as an extraordinary Christian. The truth of the matter, however, which I have learned precisely with the help of the writing, is that I am far, far from being an extraordinary Christian, that there is still an element of the poetic in me that from a Christian point of view is a minus. Publishing them would have been a bewildering poet-confusion. In one sense the understanding I arrived at elevated me to a perception of what extraordinary endowments had been granted to me, and how an infinitely loving Governance had been leading me from the very beginning, but the same understanding humbled me in another way by giving me to understand how far I still was from being a Christian in a stricter sense. But this very understanding was gained through the suffering of wanting to publish but not being able to do it. If I had not been prevented, if I had been permitted to storm ahead with the publishing, a confused darkness undoubtedly would have entered my soul.

If things were to take such a turn that the age would demand an explanation from me, I certainly could give it, but not until I had first asked permission to speak quite unguardedly. It is a different matter if I, so requested, explain what in this case is implicit in the matter itself, how I now understand myself, rather than what would still have become the end of it despite all my objections: to press on with my own life development transformed into my purpose.—*JP* VI 6511 (*Pap.* X² A 106) *n.d.*, 1849

X²
A 106
84

X²
A 124
94

Lines about Myself

If someone were to say that I as a religious author am very severe with my contemporaries, I would (yet without altogether admitting it to be so) answer: But why are you so severe with me? Consider my life as an author, my diligence, my exertions—and then the judgment is supposed to be that I am a kind of eccentric, an exaggerator—while those who carry on the most contemptible literary trade live in abundance and have power, while everyone with a finite goal is rewarded with this and in addition is regarded as earnest.

Is this not being severe with me? Well, my life is in rapport with ideas, and I personally feel myself to be religiously committed. Halfheartedness and blather I cannot endure; my life is either/or everywhere. If I am supposed to be an ornament for my country, well, then express it. But if everything against me is supposed to be permitted, well, then I also must express that I live in my native country as a piece of folly—and I must have the idea with me; I cannot do without the essentially Christian: ergo, I must raise the price of being a Christian.[94] If wantonness and rudeness and envy are permitted to treat a literary endeavor, respectable in every regard, the way I have been treated, well, then people will have to put up with my suspicions about the right such a country has to call itself totally Christian, will have to put up with my jacking up what it is to be Christian.

I may very well suffer for it, but I will not relinquish the idea. If the pressure on me is increased, well, then I will suffer more, but I cannot relinquish the idea, and so the counter pressure that I provide will be even stronger. I find no pleasure in this situation, but with regard to the idea I cannot do otherwise, and I feel myself to be religiously committed.

Or has it become a crime for me to be an author? To take just one example. Three years ago, *Concluding Postscript* was published. It is the capstone to an earlier splendid literary endeavor; it is itself the fruit of one or one-and-a-half years of diligence, and diligence that I call diligence; it cost me between five and six hundred rix-dollars to publish. Sixty copies of the book were sold. It was not mentioned in one single place. On the other hand, to the delight of the rabble, I was caricatured and insulted in the *Corsair,* in *Kjøbenhavnsposten,* P. L. Møller poured insults on it and me; in *Flyve-Posten,* in order to incite the rabble's ridicule, they wrote about my trousers, that they had now become too long.[95]

And then they want to complain that I am too severe—but the severity that is shown to me, no mention must be made of that.

—*Pap.* X² A 124 *n.d.,* 1849

X²
A 124
95

On My Authorship

The heterogeneity must definitely be maintained, that here is an author, that objectively it is not a cause but that it is a cause for which an individual has stood alone, suffered, etc. But just as it has not been understood why *Concluding Postscript* has a comic design—and just as the matter is thought to be improved by taking particular theses and translating them into the didactic—so it will probably end with treating me, unto new confusion, as a cause and translating everything into the objective, making it into something new, that here is a new doctrine, rather than that the new is that here is personality. . . .—*Pap.* X² A 130 *n.d.*, 1849

X²
A 147
110

The Turn in the Authorship, How the New Pseudonym (Anti-Climacus) Was Introduced

My intention was to publish all the completed manuscripts in one volume,[96] all under my name—and then to make a clean break.

This was a drastic idea, but I suffered indescribably in persistently wanting to cling to it; I penciled notes here and there (especially in the books about the authorship), and at the same time I continually overtaxed myself on the whole project, especially on the added point that I should existentially alter my course and yet in a way conceal that there was something false about my stepping forth in character on such a scale—by withdrawing entirely.

X²
A 147
111

Finally it became clear to me that I definitely had to consider my future and that it was beyond my ability to manage both at once—to arrange such a production of writing and also to have financial difficulties. So I decided to lay aside the entire production that lay finished and ready until a more propitious time— and then not to write anymore and to make a move with regard to appointment.

Then the idea came to me again that it might be unjustifiable for me to let these writings just lie there, and I also became somewhat impatient when I thought of how difficult it is for me to become an officeholder, even if willing to do everything, and so I make futile visits to both Madvig and Mynster.[97] Then I tackled the matter again—sent the first part of the manuscript to the printer under my name, so it would now be possible to arrange the whole project. My idea was to let actuality put the pressure on me and to get a close perspective of the matter, and I committed myself to God, that he would help me.

Meanwhile Councilor Olsen[98] died, and this raised a host of difficulties—I realized also that it was rash and excessive to instigate a *coup* of that nature—with the result that *The Sickness unto Death* was made pseudonymous.

This led me to understand myself and my limitations; I gained an ingeniousness with respect to the structure of the authorship, which again is not my original idea; I realized that it was practically desperation on my part to want to venture that far out toward being a kind of apostle, and in so curious a manner that I simultaneously would break off and with the same step possibly wipe out my future.

If this had not happened, if I had let all that I had written lie there, I no doubt would have come back every week to the thought of carrying out that reckless idea, and I probably would have unhinged myself, for it still would not have been carried out.

Now the writing has begun to move, the pseudonym is established, I can breathe again and am released from the ghost of tension.—*JP* VI 6517 (*Pap.* X^2 A 147) *n.d.*, 1849

X^2
A 147
112

On My Authorship as a Totality

In a certain sense there is a problem of choice for my contemporaries: They must choose either to make the esthetic the total idea and interpret everything in that way or choose the religious. Precisely in this there is some awakening.—*JP* VI 6520 (*Pap.* X^2 A 150) *n.d.*, 1849

A New View of the Relation Pastor—Poet in the Sphere of Religion

X^2
A 157
121

Christianity has of course known very well what it wanted. It wants to be proclaimed by *witnesses*—that is, by persons who proclaim the teaching and also existentially express it.

The modern notion of a pastor as it is now is a complete misunderstanding. Since pastors also presumably should express the essentially Christian, they have quite rightly discovered how to relax the requirement, abolish the ideal.

What is to be done now? Yes, now we must prepare for another tactical advance.

First a detachment of poets; almost sinking under the demands of the ideal, with the glow of a certain unhappy love they set forth the ideal. Present-day pastors may now take second rank.

These religious poets must have the particular ability to do the kind of writing that helps people out into the current.

When this has happened, when a generation has grown up that from childhood on has received the pathos-filled impression of an existential expression of the ideal, the monastery and genuine witnesses of the truth will both come again.

This is how far behind the cause of Christianity is in our time.

The first and foremost task is to create pathos, with the superiority of intelligence, imagination, penetration, and wit to guarantee pathos for the existential, which "the understanding" has reduced to the ludicrous.

Here is my task. A young person, an utterly simple person can be used for the highest level of the existential—for that the ethical alone is the sole requirement. But when "the understanding" and the power of the understanding have triumphed in the world and made the genuinely existential almost ludicrous, then neither a young person nor a simple person is able to cut through at once. Then there must first be a maieutic, an old person in a certain sense, eminently possessing all the gifts of mind and spirit—and these he applies to create pathos for the pathos-filled life.

Any young girl can truly fall in love. But imagine an age that has sunk to such depths of commonsensicality that all the brilliant minds etc. applied their talents to making love ludicrous—then no young girl is able to cut through at once. There must only be an older person who can crush this commonsensicality and create pathos—and then, hail to thee, O youth, whoever you are— then there is a place for youth's in a sense far inferior powers. And yet in one sense the relation is such, as it always is in the pseu-

X²
A 157
122

donymous works, that the young person stands higher than the older one.[99]

Alas, my own life demonstrates this. Only now do I see where the turn must be made—now after almost overstraining myself for seven years, now when I must begin to carry a new kind of burden, concern for making ends meet. Oh, why was there no older person who related to me as I do to the youth.

Yet in a certain degree I myself still belong to the old, but I guarantee pathos.

Mynster's[100] error was not the sagacity etc. he has used. No, the error was that, beguiled by the workings of his sagacity in the world of temporality, beguiled by his power and influence, he actually let the ideal vanish. Were there in Mynster's preaching but one thing—a constant and deep sorrow over not having been spiritual enough himself to become a martyr, I would have approved of him; I would then have said of him what I say of myself: He did not become a martyr, but he is able to bring forth martyrs.

No one can take what has not been given to him—and neither can I. I also am marked by having been born in Christendom, spoiled in my upbringing, etc. If I had not been brought up in Christianity, if I had stood outside Christianity, it might perhaps have the power to swing me a stage higher, if, note well, Christianity itself were represented as in its earliest times, when there was pathos in abundance.

But no one can take what has not been given to him.

How true it is to me now that all my recent productivity has actually been my personal upbringing, my humiliation. Youthfully I have dared—then it was granted to me to set forth the requirement of ideality in an eminent sense—and quite rightly I am the one who feels humbled under it and learns in a still deeper sense to resort to grace. Moreover, this which I now again have experienced even more personally has already been called to mind in the works themselves, for Anti-Climacus says in the moral to "Come Here, All You Who Labor and Are Burdened":[101] The prototype must be presented so ideally that you are humbled by it and learn to flee to the prototype, but in an entirely different sense—namely, as to the merciful one.

X^2
A 157
123

But all must relate themselves to the ideal; and no matter how far below and how far away I am, there must still be in my glance and in my sighing a direction that indicates that I also am related to the ideal—only in that way am I one who strives.

And then, as Anti-Climacus says: then no overrash impetuosity.

Yet how different to begin as a youth can begin, and then in the best years of his life still to have belonged to the old.

One thing, however, remains—we are still all saved by grace.
—*JP* VI 6521 (*Pap.* X² A 157) *n.d.,* 1849

The Position of Christianity at the Present Moment

... What Christianity needs for certain is traitors. Christendom has insidiously betrayed Christianity by wanting not to be truly Christian but to have the appearance of being so. Now traitors are needed.

But this concept, traitors, is dialectical. The devil also, so to speak, has his traitors, his spies, who do not attack Christianity but attack the Christians—with the express purpose of getting more and more to fall away. God, too, has his traitors: God-fearing traitors, who in unconditional obedience to him simply and sincerely present Christianity in order that for once people may get to know what Christianity is. I am sure that established Christendom regards them as traitors, since Christendom has taken illegal possession of Christianity by a colossal forgery.

Strangely enough, I always understand best afterwards. Dialectically Johannes Climacus[102] is in fact so radical a defense of Christianity that to many it may seem like an attack. This book makes one feel that it is Christendom that has betrayed Christianity.

This book has an extraordinary future.

And I, the author, am in a way held up to ridicule as always. I manage to do things the entire significance of which I do not understand until later. This I have seen again and again. For that very reason I cannot become serious in the trivial sense in which serious people are serious, for I realize that I am nothing. There is an infinite power that, as it were, helps me; when I turn to it, I pray—this certainly is earnestness; but when I turn to myself, I almost have to laugh at the thought that I, a wretched nobody etc., seem to be so important. I cannot quite make myself intelligible to others, for whatever I write they promptly categorize as pertaining to me. In my own consciousness, where I understand the way things really hang together, at every alternate moment jest can scarcely be avoided. But it is a pious jest, for precisely in smiling at myself in my nothingness there is again an expression of devotion. To use a metaphor and example, it is as if a little miss were loved by someone whom she feels to be very superior to her intellectually. In the ordinary sense of the word this relationship does not become serious. The like-for-like that provides finite security and earnestness is lacking. She cannot help smiling at herself when she thinks of being loved by—him, and yet she feels blissful during every moment of his visit. Nor does she dare tell herself "in earnest": He loves me, for she will say: My relationship to him is actually nothing; he would do no wrong whatsoever in leaving me this moment, for there is no relationship between us, but the relationship is blissful as long as it lasts.

But my relationship has the peculiar quality of being reflective, so that I do not see it until later—see, there I have been helped again. I take my pen, commend myself to God, work hard, etc., in short, do the best I can with the meager human means. The pen moves briskly across the paper. I feel that what I am writing is all my own. And then, long afterwards, I profoundly understand what I wrote and see that I received help.

It is easy to see that dialectically Johannes Climacus's defense of Christianity is as radical as it can be, for dialectically the defense and the attack are within a single hair of being one.

"Johannes Climacus" was actually a contemplative piece, for when I wrote it I was contemplating the possibility of not letting myself be taken over by Christianity, even if it was my most honest intention to devote my whole life and daily diligence to the cause of Christianity, to do everything, to do nothing else but to expound and interpret it, even though I were to become like, be like the legendary Wandering Jew—myself not a Christian in the final and most decisive sense of the word and yet leading others to Christianity.—*JP* VI 6523 (*Pap.* X^2 A 163) *n.d.,* 1849

X^2
A 163
131

A line by Thomas à Kempis that perhaps could be used as a motto sometime. He says of Paul: Therefore he turned everything over to God, who knows all, and defended himself solely by means of patience and humility . . . . . He did defend himself now and then so that the weak would not be offended by his silence.

Book III, chapter 36, para. 2, or in my little edition, p. 131.[103]

—*JP* VI 6524 (*Pap.* X^2 A 167) *n.d.*, 1849

X^2
A 171
136

If the writings on my work as an author are published by a pseudonymous author, it could be done this way.

see p. 41 [*Pap.* X^2 A 192 (p. 229)].

Magister Kierkegaard's Work as an Author
Viewed by the Author
A Poetical Attempt by A-O

Preface

Just as in a mathematical equation one factor is given and a second is to be found, so also with this poetical venture. *The given* is: (1) all the writings on my work as an author, which I have scrutinized very carefully; (2) Magister K.'s personal existing, which has been the focus of my attention for some time and which I daresay I know as fully as is possible for any third person. *What is to be found* is: an author-personality, an indwelling unity corresponding to the given work as an author.

X^2
A 171
137

I realize that work as an author such as the one given, which in all respects points to personality, requires for definitive completion that the author himself be brought in at the end. It seems to me, however, that dialectically it is really impossible for Magister K. himself to do it, since by doing it himself he dialectically breaks the dialectical structure of the entire work as an author.

Thus I now risk making this poetical venture. The author himself speaks formally in the first person, but remember that this author is not Mag. K. but my poetical creation.

I certainly do ask Herr Magister's pardon for venturing right under his nose, so to speak, poetically to construe him, or to poetize him. But nothing more than to make this apology to him. In other respects I have poetically emancipated myself from him completely. Yes, even if he were to pronounce my interpretation factually incorrect in some details, it does not follow that it is poetically untrue. The conclusion could indeed also be turned around: ergo, Magister K. has not corresponded to or realized what would be right poetically.

A-O

This transformation or poetical communication is categorically entirely right and corresponds to everything that I have understood at the time and that is found written down most likely in journal NB[11] or NB[12] [*Pap.* X^1 A 295–541; X^1 A 542–682 and X^2 A 1–68]: (1) that I am essentially a poet; (2) that my authorship has been my own upbringing; (3) that I am sheer reflection, therefore always facing backward; (4) that I am a penitent, and inasmuch as I am unable to speak altogether uninhibitedly about that I cannot speak about its correlative either, the inwardness of the God-relationship; (5) that I have reached my boundary, that the turning under the new pseudonym (Anti-Climacus) and now the new pseudonym—I am amazed at the ingenuity of this, although it is not my doing—is dialectically the completely consequent expression that I have reached my boundary, that I have been granted the indescribably good fortune of fully understanding my boundary, of taking my boundary into consideration. Oh, how can I ever thank Governance sufficiently!

X^2
A 171
138

Ordinarily poetizing is done in such a way that something more is deceptively ascribed [*tillyve*]; here the poetizing is done in such a way that something is deceptively taken away [*bortlyve*]—so that the whole thing is in fact actual.

But I am no apostle or anything like that. And if I use direct communication here, it is of no use with all the restrictions etc.

No, but here again an amazing consistency—God knows it is not my invention; I had scarcely dreamed of it from the very beginning—again the inversion, which all my life is: to poetize here means falsely to take away a something more; by being poetized, it becomes one key lower than the actuality.

This is how pressure is to be applied to my contemporaries. It becomes a purely spiritual pressure.

For me there remains the simple thing to do: quite simply to accept an official appointment, and now I have the doctrine of sin and grace.

If anyone asks me directly about my work as an author, I must say: I cannot speak of it directly, since the difficulty is that it is my own upbringing and that I myself am nevertheless the author.

X^2 A 171 139 In this way I will step forth very simply as the simple one. But I will not take this step with the momentum of the whole authorship, whereby the whole thing would remain within the realm of the interesting. The authorship is separated from me by the chasmic abyss of indirect communication—it is not my own; it belongs to one higher.

Moreover, there is a fearful border skirmish involved here. It was a poet-existence* that by a hairsbreadth escaped making a wrong turn into actuality. But just to think of the dialectical difficulties of this collision—to me it seems that one could become an old man merely by contemplating that a head has been able to endure all this.—*Pap.* X^2 A 171 *n.d.*, 1849

Marginal addition to Pap. X^2 A 171:

**Note*. Mainly with regard to my having had independent means and consequently not having been tried in that kind of actuality, together with having lived prodigally, which yet in turn is related to my productivity and its poetical impetus; there certainly has been meaning and thought in this prodigality, but mostly poetical.—*Pap.* X^2 A 172 *n.d.*, 1849

X^2 A 174 139

The Significance of the Whole Authorship

is its *calling attention* to the essentially Christian.

Attention is not to be called to me, and yet it is to existence as
X^2 A 174 140 a person that attention is to be called, or to the significance of existence as a person as crucial for the essentially Christian. Therefore, my existence as a person is also utilized, but always in

order to point beyond me at the decisive moment: I am not that.[104]

To call attention this way is to place the essentially Christian in the relationship of possibility for people, to show them how far we all are from being Christians.—*JP* VI 6525 (*Pap.* X² A 174) *n.d.*, 1849

The New Pseudonym Anti-Climacus

X²
A 177
141

Since all the writing under the title "Practice in Christianity" was poetic,[105] it was understood from the very first that I had to take great pains not to become confused with an analogy to an apostle. Generally my hypochondria has also had a part in all the later works, for even though things undeniably have become more clear, they were not understood this way from the beginning.

When the book "Come Here, All You Who Labor etc." was written, "A Poetic Attempt—Without Authority—For Inward Deepening in Christianity" was placed on the title page at the outset. And then came my name. And the same with the others.

But as time went on it became clear to me (in this connection see journal NB¹¹ or NB¹² [*Pap.* X¹ A 295–541; X¹ A 542–682 and X² A 1–68], but more particularly NB¹¹) that if possible there must be an even stronger declaration that it was poetic—and that it was best to have a new pseudonym. This became clear to me. Meanwhile I wanted to wait and see, during which time I suffered very much, constantly undertaking too much with the whole writing project and tormented by the fixed and desperate idea of publishing it all in one single swoop and then leaping aside and vanishing, something I basically understood could not be done but which nevertheless captivated my imagination so that I really did not want to give up the possibility, although it became more and more clear that if I were to get room to move, it would have to be split up.

Finally, I decided to lay the whole project aside and seek an appointment; and when that had been done, I would publish gradually, in small lots, what was completed.

I then went to Madvig and Mynster[106] and met neither of them, and since in another way I was strongly influenced in the opposite direction, I took it to be a hint from Governance that I was about to make a mistake, that I simply should venture everything. Now came the reaction. I wrote to the printer and engaged typesetters and said that they "should speed ahead." I get word from the printer[107] that all is clear and could they have the manuscript. At the very same time I learn that Councilor Olsen[108] has died. That affected me strongly; if I had known about it before I wrote to the printer, it would have prompted a postponement. But now, after so frequently being on the verge of it, fearfully overtaxed as I was, I was afraid I would be incapacitated if I backed out after taking this step.

X² A 177 142

I was under great strain and slept badly, and, strangely enough, a phrase came to my mind, as if I myself wanted to hurl myself into disaster.

In the morning I pondered the matter again. It seemed to me that I had to act. Then I decided to submit the whole matter to God: to send the first manuscript ("The Sickness unto Death") to the printer without saying anything about what else there was to be printed. My intention was to allow actuality to test me; it was possible that the sum total could be printed, and it was possible that there could be a turning aside.

Under that tension I began to see that it should be published under a pseudonym, something I understood earlier but postponed doing because it could be done at any time.

In the middle of the typesetting there was trouble with Reitzel, which made me extremely impatient. Once again I had the thought of withdrawing the whole manuscript, laying it aside, and waiting once again to see if I should have everything published at the same time, and without the pseudonymity, since the pseudonymity was not established as yet, inasmuch as the title page was not printed, because, contrary to my practice, I had originally ordered it to be printed last. I went to the printer. It was too late. The composition was as good as finished.

So the pseudonym was established. That is how one is helped and helps oneself when it is so difficult to act.—*JP* VI 6526 (*Pap.* X² A 177) *n.d.*, 1849

The New Pseudonym (Anti-Climacus)

X²
A 184
145

The fact that there is a pseudonym is the *qualitative* expression that it is a poet-communication, that it is not I who speaks but another, that it is addressed to me just as much as to others; it is as if a spirit speaks, while I get the inconvenience of being the editor. What he has to say is something we human beings prefer to have cast into oblivion. But it must be heard nevertheless. Not that everyone should do it, nor that eternal happiness depends upon my doing it—oh, no. I realize, after all, that my life does not express it either, but I humble myself under it; I regard this as an indulgence, and my life has unrest.

X²
A 184
146

With respect to ethical-religious communication (that is, along the lines of depicting the requirement of ideality—which is different from grace and what is involved in it, different in that rigorousness creates a tension to the point that one feels the need of grace, without, however, being permitted to take it in vain), I am not permitted to communicate more than what I, the speaker, am, that is, in my own factual first person, no more than what my life existentially but fairly well conforms to. If I place the requirement higher, I must express that this presentation is a poetic one. It is altogether appropriate for me to present it, since it may influence another to strive more, and I myself must define myself as one who is striving in relation to it, thereby distinguishing myself from the typical poet, to whom it never occurs to strive personally in relation to the ideality he presents.

Incidentally, what is so terrible here is that the requirements of ideality are presented by people who never give the remotest thought to whether their lives express it or that their lives do not express it at all. That I have been aware here is indicated by my calling this a poetic communication—even though I am striving.

That the communication is poetic may be expressed **either** by the speaker's saying in his own person: This is poetic communication, that is, *what I am saying is not poetic,* because what I am saying is the very truth, but *the fact that I am saying it* constitutes the poetic aspect, **or** *qua* author he can do it with the help of pseudonyms, as I have done now for the first time[109] in order to make matters clear.

But the difference between such a speaker-author—and a typical poet—is that the speaker and author himself defines himself as striving in relation to what is being communicated.

X²
A 184
147
And this whole distinction pertaining to poet-communication is related again to Christianity's basic category, that Christianity is an existence-communication [*Existents-Meddelelse*] and not doctrine, as Christianity has unchristianly and meaninglessly been made to be, so that the question in relation to a doctrine is simply: Is my interpretation of the doctrine true, the true interpretation, or not, like, for example, an interpretation of Plato's philosophy. No, the question is: Does or does not my personal life express what is communicated? As long as my life expresses what is communicated, I am a teacher; when this is not the case, I am obliged to add: What I say is certainly true, but *my* saying it is the poetic aspect; consequently it is a poet-communication, which, however, is meaningful both for keeping me awake and keeping me striving, and, if possible, for encouraging others.

In book No. 1 ("Come Here, All You Who Labor and Are Burdened") the *qualitative* rigorousness is the in one sense Christianly untrue thesis (because it is almost solely metaphysical)— that Christ came to the world because he was the absolute, not out of human compassion or for any other reason, a thesis to which corresponds the absolute "You shall." At the same time, however, on the other side it holds true Christianly that Christ came to the world out of love **in order** to save the world. The fact that he had to break up the world, as it were, the fact that, humanly speaking, enormous, humanly speaking, suffering came from accepting him, certainly is due to his being the absolute, but joy over the fact that he came **in order** to save must completely surmount all this suffering. These two theses (he came because he was the absolute, and he came out of love **in order** to save the world) make the difference between Christianity's being proclaimed in *law* or in *grace*.

In book No. 2 ("Blessed Is He Who Is Not Offended") the *qualitative* rigorousness is the *necessity* with which offense is joined together with all that is essentially Christian.

In book No. 3 ("From on High He Will Draw All to Himself") the *qualitative* rigorousness is the *necessity* with which abasement is added to being Christian, that unconditionally every true Christian is abased in this world.—*JP* VI 6528 (*Pap.* X² A 184) *n.d.*, 1849

[*In margin:* See p. 10 (*Pap.* X² A 171)]

> *Pseudonymous Publication of the Writings on My Work as an Author*

But it is not necessary to publish them pseudonymously; it is not even right to do so, inasmuch as the matter does not become sufficiently simple.

The category: that I myself am the one who has been brought up, that it all is my own upbringing, is decisive enough.

The first idea to publish all the books (including those which have become pseudonymous) in my name and in one volume[110] along with the writings about my work as an author was still vague and unclear (as it was impatient), because the writings about my work as an author go only to the Friday discourses in *Christian Discourses*, and therefore no impression is conveyed of all the new production contained in the same volume.

No, the new pseudonym, *Anti-Climacus*—which in the dialectical sphere contains a new dialectical contribution that must be completed by an upbuilding discourse on "grace"—provides "the stopping place." And *within* the stopping place, then, comes the communication about my work as an author.—*JP* VI 6530 (*Pap.* X² A 192) *n.d.*, 1849

Ordinarily the religious ought to be kept just as lenient as rigorous. God wants to be the ruler, but in the form of grace, concession, etc.; he wants to attend to a person as carefully and as solicitously as possible. To suffer is to be as a joy, a matter of honor; one comes to God and asks permission—and God says: Yes, indeed, my little friend. But of course it does not follow from this that one may not suffer. On the contrary, in the profoundest sense one may suffer indescribably, also have one's thorn in the flesh, but despite this, assuming that this suffering cannot be taken away, one can find joy in getting permission to be active in this way, to live for an idea.

It is different with *the apostle*: he is constrained.

Moreover, I again understand here why it is so important that I hold myself back and do all I can to prevent being confused with something *à la* an apostle: precisely because I am able to provide a point from which the qualifications of an apostle may in some measure be scrutinized. But what disarray if I myself were to cause the confusion.

It is not at all surprising, also to me, that Socrates has made such a deep impression upon me.

It may be said that there is something Socratic in me.

Indirect communication was my native element. By means of the very things I experienced, what I went through, and thought through last summer with respect to direct communication, I have set aside a direct communication (the one on my work as an author, with the category: it is all my upbringing) and have also acquired a deeper understanding of indirect communication, the new pseudonymity.

There is something inexplicably felicitous in the antithesis: Climacus—Anti-Climacus; I recognize so much of myself and my nature in it that if someone else had invented it I would believe that he had secretly observed my inner being. —The merit is not mine, since I did not originally think of it.—*JP* VI 6532 (*Pap.* X² A 195) *n.d.,* 1849

X²
A 195
154

To me it was also remarkable that Councilor Olsen's death[111] coincided with my intention to make a turn away from the authorship and to appear in the character of a religious author from the very beginning (see a slip[112] in journal NB[13] [*Pap.* X² A 69–163]). And when I appear in the character of the whole authorship as religious, a dedication would essentially relate to *her.*[113]
                                   —*JP* VI 6543 (*Pap.* X² A 215) *n.d.,* 1849

The words of John the Baptizer, "I am a voice,"[114] could be applied to my work as an author. To prevent any mistaken identity, that I myself would be taken for the extraordinary, I always withdraw myself, and the voice, that is, what I say, remains. But I always withdraw myself only in such a way that I do own up to striving. Thus I am like a voice, but I always have one more auditor than speakers generally have: myself.—*JP* VI 6561 (*Pap.* X² A 281) *n.d.*, 1849

Concerning the publication of a couple of writings about myself.

X²
A 378
270

I had again taken out the matter I had considered: The Accounting, the Three Notes, and the first part of The Point of View. I modified a couple of particular points.

Meanwhile all my old doubts rose up again, essentially centering in this: it is inconsistent and impatient to bring myself in during my lifetime, and especially right now when I wish to stop, and then thereby rather to risk getting new momentum even though by an earlier editing from a time in 1849 I had done everything to introduce the two determinants: that the whole work as an author is for myself my own upbringing and that it is intended to make aware.—*Pap.* X² A 378 *n.d.*, 1850

X²
A 378
271

From draft of On My Work; *see 12:1–30:*

For

X⁵
B 211
393

"The Accounting"

Postscript

[*Deleted:* Dear Reader! I have wished to say and have thought I ought to say this, and precisely at this time, prompted chiefly by the fact that the first has come again, the second edition of *Either/Or*, which previously I had not wanted to have published (*same as 12:3–5).*]

X⁵
B 211
394

[*Essentially the same as Pap.* X⁵ B 168, *pp. 290–94*]

March 1849

X⁵
B 211
397

Note. But this I know, that both originally and continually without change it has been my thought to be an author for not many years and then to take a position as a country pastor.

—*Pap.* X⁵ B 211 March 1849

Deleted addition to Pap. X⁵ B 211:

N.B. Perhaps a passage is still to be added with a dash before the date; it is in fair copy in the little packet with loose pages for "The Accounting."—*Pap.* X⁵ B 212 *n.d.*, 1849

From draft of "The Accounting" *in* On My Work as an Author:

X⁵
B 217
404

Yet I owe it to the truth to admit that in the beginning it was by no means my thought to become a religious author in the sense I have become that; on the contrary, it was truly my intention in the beginning to become a rural pastor the moment I laid down my pen. I profoundly understood that I belonged to the religious, that it was a deception on my part, albeit a pious deception, to pass myself off as an esthetic author, and I sought an energetic expression for my belonging in the strictest sense to the religious and thought to find this in leaping away from being an esthetic author—and at once becoming a rural pastor. My first thought was to stop with *Either/Or*—and then at once a rural pastor. It did not happen; but since it did not happen, there was promptly a religious signaling (*Two Upbuilding Discourses*). Then

X⁵
B 217
405

for a time my thought was to break off with *Concluding Postscript*—and then rural pastor. That did not happen, but then, too, the authorship became decidedly religious. Now these seven years have passed. It is again, unchanged, my thought to become a rural pastor, but a point has also been reached from which I can survey the totality of the authorship. . . . My thought was to deceive by becoming an esthetic author and then promptly to become a rural pastor, accentuating the religious doubly strongly by the contrast. Something else happened: the religious found its expression in my becoming a religious author, but consequently a religious author who began with an esthetic productivity as a deception. The point was that the religious found its expression unconditionally at the same time the esthetic deception was initiated—otherwise there would have been a show of justification in saying that originally I was not conscious that the esthetic productivity was a deception and that the explanation would be that in the beginning I wanted to be an esthetic author and then later changed. But the presence of the religious at exactly the same time found its expression not as I had thought by my becoming a rural pastor but by the publication of *Two Upbuilding Discourses.*[115]—*Pap.* X⁵ B 217 *n.d.*, 1849

X⁵
B 217
406

From draft of On My Work:

[*Deleted:* This is approximately the same postscript as originally
   N.B. written for the "Three Notes" and thus cannot be used
      both places.]

Postscript.

Dear Reader. I have wished to say and have thought I ought
   to say this, and precisely at this time. This is scarcely the
   place [*same as 12:3–12:6*] the many books.
Yet in one sense [*essentially the same as Pap.* X⁵ B 168, *291:23–
294:29*].

March 1849
—*Pap.* X⁵ B 222 March 1849

On folder for mss. of Point of View *and* On My Work *as
An Author:*

On My Work as an Author

X⁵
B 141
343

Contents

1. The Point of View for My Work as an Author.
2. 3 Notes on ———
3. (1 Note) ——— The Accounting
4. an Appendix to (this one Note) The Accounting
5. The Whole in One Word.
6. a few slips of paper with regard to the publishing
   of all the manuscripts at one time in one volume.

Which must in no way be published now.

NB

X⁵
B 141
344

The common main title will be:
On My Work as an Author
written in 1848 (or the fruit of 1848)

The contents will be
the 5 numbers

1. The Point of View   2. 3 Notes   3. The Accounting
4. Appendix   5. The Whole in One Word.

Epigraph: If for the lily, when the time has come when it is to
blossom, it really seems as unfortunate as possible, the obedient
lily simply understands only one thing: that it is now the moment. See 3 Devotional Discourses[116] by S. K.—*Pap.* X^5 B 141
n.d., 1849

From draft of The Collected Works of Completion:

X^5 B 143 344	The (Collected) Works of Completion.[117] The fruit of the year 1848. [*Deleted:* or the end.]

Vol. I   "The Sickness unto Death."

X^5 **Vol. II**   [*In margin:* and here as appendix:
B 143
345   Armed Neutrality]
Practice in Christianity
An Attempt
Part One
    Come Here, All You.
Part Two
    Blessed Is He Who Is Not Offended.
Part Three
    From on High He Will Draw All to Himself.

Vol. III

On My Work as an Author.

No. 1. *The Point of View.* N.B. perhaps not yet.
But the first part could possibly be used, yet
so that it would not then remain no. 1, but
the three Notes and the one Note would
precede.

No. 2. *3 Notes.*

No. 3. *1 Note.* but best to leave out note p. 9. [*Pap.* X^5
B 145]; the postscript, however, could possi-
bly be used.

No. 4. *The Whole in One Word*[118]
—*Pap.* X⁵ B 143 *n.d.*, 1849

From draft of "The Collected Works of Completion":

To come at the very end, with a title page of its own, after "One Note":

X⁵
B 144
345

The Whole in One Word

What I have written is, from first to last, a religious, a Christian religious development, or a development to religiousness, Christian religiousness.

Just as in one sense what I have written could be attributed to me as my design, in another sense it is my own development and upbringing. If the matter is posed to me as a dilemma, that I must say either that the whole is my design or the whole is Governance's, then I unconditionally say the latter.

In relation to my contemporaries, I, the author, do not call myself a teacher, an educator, but a learner; I myself am the one who is being brought up.

X⁵
B 144
346

No one, unconditionally not a single contemporary, has been attacked by me with regard to whether it is indeed true that he is a Christian or not. This has happened not because I disapprove of such attacks but because they lie outside my rights, I who— existentially—have essentially been a poet* and, as I have said from the very beginning: have been without authority.

As for the established order, with regard to change in externals, I have had nothing, unconditionally nothing, to propose, not one single word, unconditionally not one single word to say but have observed the silence of one who is dead. All that I have said, the many works, are a modest contribution to renewal in the religiousness that is: the inwardness in the single individual.

In margin: *(although just this is my difference from "the poet"—that I have been aware of the dubiousness of that kind of existing.)

—*Pap.* X⁵ B 144 *n.d.*, 1849

For

Vol. III,[119] at the outset on a sheet by itself, a *note*.

Note. It is observed here at the outset that all that follows about my authorship is something later, a little by little subsequently acquired understanding or an additional understanding and interpretation. I dare not say that I had from the beginning such an overview of the whole authorship, which, even though it is my production, is also my religious upbringing and development. Neither would I dare to want, by crossing my boundary, to falsify my nature, which essentially is reflection and therefore never proclaims, prophesies, but essentially understands itself first in what has gone before, in what has been carried out.—*Pap.* X^5 B 145 *n.d.*, 1849

What is presented here is all done in the names of the pseudonymous authors; yet it must be remembered that I, the author, now understand it far better than when I did it—it is also my own development.—*Pap.* X^5 B 146 *n.d.*, 1849

See 1–3:

X^5
B 147
347

See journal NB[14] p. 10 and p. 41 [*Pap.* X^2 A 171, 192 (pp. 222–24, 229)]

If the writings on my work as an author are published [*deleted: during my lifetime, it could be done in this way*] by a pseudonym, it could be done in this way.

Mag. Kierkegaard's Work as an Author

Viewed by the Author

A Poetical Attempt

by

A-O

Preface

Just as [*essentially the same as Pap.* X^2 *A 171 (pp. 222:16–223:25)*] Governance sufficiently!

See p. 41 in the same journal [*Pap.* X^2 A 192 (p. 229)]
[*The same as Pap.* X^2 A 192, 229]

X^5
B 147
348

—*Pap.* X^5 B 147 *n.d.*, 1849

On folder for ms. of Point of View:

The Point of View for My
Work as an Author

X^5
B 154
355

Fair copy

N.B. All tenses, provided they are not that (which is the case in only a single passage at the beginning and at the very end), must be made into the past or present tense, not one single future.

See Journal NB^9 p. 115 [*Pap.* X^1 A 56] and others.

N.B.   [*Deleted:* Pp. 24–50 removed, which are, together with what is to be published, "The Accounting" and "Three Notes."]

written after the middle of the year 1848; the several small changes* (which are found by comparing this with the draft**), occasioned by thinking more carefully about publishing, are from Feb. 1849.

X^5
B 154
356

*which, however, are of no importance.
**which lies in my desk.

—*Pap.* X^5 B 154 *n.d.*, 1849

On folder for ms. of Point of View:

What was not [*deleted:* used] to be used from
     "*The Point of View for My Work as an Author*"
     if it had been published in the spring of '49.

1. The whole section about my *vita ante acta* [earlier life]
2. The conclusion of the epilogue.
3. A conclusion after "Supplements," which does not exist even in rough draft.

—*Pap.* X^5 B 155 *n.d.*, 1849

For *"The Point of View"*

See to it that all the tenses become past. For example, immediately in the introduction: "but make me weary of defending the truth *no one can do*" to be changed to "no one *has been able to do*," because I—not *am* myself but *was* myself a penitent.[120]—*Pap.* X⁵ B 156 *n.d.*, 1849

If *The Point of View for My Work as an Author* is to be published now, the whole preface or introduction goes out, together with the words on the title page "Report to History."
          But perhaps the words "Report to History"
                  could remain.
                 —*Pap.* X⁵ B 157 *n.d.*, 1849

The part of "The Point of View" I once considered publishing with "The Accounting" and "Three Notes" was:

the [*deleted:* first section] first chapter* of Part Two of a book "The Point of View for My Work as an Author." 1848.
    from p. 24—to near the end of p. 51 [*SV* XIII 521–43]
        [*Deleted:* *Yet in such a way that the last passage, which begins with "And what does all this mean etc.,"[121] is not used.]
                1848.
Why the authorship begins with
the esthetic works, or what this authorship,
understood as a whole, means.
              —*Pap.* X⁵ B 158 *n.d.*, 1849

On folder for mss. of Point of View *and* On My Work:

        "The Accounting" and "Three Notes"
        also the final version of "The Accounting"

"Three Notes" could *perhaps* be changed quite simply to theses; thus there would not be a word about myself, but merely: theses about "the crowd" and "the single individual." Most of the passages are already revised as theses; so only the passages that treat of me need to be deleted.—*Pap.* X⁵ B 159 *n.d.*, 1849

Pages from "The Accounting" and "Three Notes" or loose slips with regard to publication that were removed.

Also the draft of a few additions to "The Accounting" and the draft and fair copy of one that has not yet been used, together with a preface to "Three Notes."—*Pap.* X⁵ B 160 *n.d.*, 1849

x⁵
B 160
357

x⁵
B 160
358

Information about where the drafts of particular small pieces or particular inserted passages are to be found—*Pap.* X⁵ B 161 *n.d.*, 1849

Addition to Pap. X⁵ B 161:

Dec. 2, '49

1. The draft of the Appendix to "The Accounting" is in one of the journals from last year or the year before, older than NB¹³. (It is NB¹⁰, pp. 236 ff. [*Pap.* X¹ A 272 (pp. 190–93)] under the heading: Poetical about myself, a somewhat longer passage.

2. The draft of the conclusion of the piece "About the Relation of My Authorship to That Single Individual" is in one of the older journals [*Pap.* VIII¹ A 482 (pp. 154–56)] from last year or the year before.

3. The draft of several small passages in "Three Notes" is in the Bible case that is in the desk.

4. The drafts of other small things are either in this Bible case or in the red box that is in the desk.

5. The draft of the dedication to that single individual (belonging to *Upbuilding Discourses in Various Spirits* and used for the first note of "Three Notes" is in the journal [*Pap.* VII¹ A 176 (pp. 151–53)] from that period.

In margin: The draft of some other minor things is perhaps in the packet that lies in the mahogany box, on which packet is written: Loose papers from 1848 that were in the Bible case that is still in the desk.—*Pap.* X⁵ B 162 December 2, 1849

Addition to Pap. X⁵ B 161:

> **N.B.** What was in the Bible case Dec. 2, 1849, is now in an
> envelope labeled: What was in the Bible case; the en-
> velope lies in the second of the three large drawers in
> the desk.
>
> —*Pap.* X⁵ B 163 *n.d.*, 1849

On folder for mss. of Point of View, Supplement, "The Single
Individual," two "Notes":

> [*Deleted:* 3 notes]
> 2 notes

The preface mentioned on the title page of the Two Notes is in
a separate little packet labeled "Loose pages for the Accounting
and Three Notes," which packet in turn is in the larger packet
labeled "On My Work as an Author," which is in this (mahogany) box

[*Deleted:* The third Note [*Pap.* IX B 63:14] is used as the preface
to the Friday Discourses;[122] hence the title becomes: Two Notes.

The two pages lying here and numbered 15–18[123] are the postscript to "The Accounting."]—*Pap.* X⁵ B 164 *n.d.*, 1849

> "Three Notes on My Work as an Author"
> Draft
> The third Note is used as the preface to
> Friday Discourses.[124]
> —*Pap.* X⁵ B 165 *n.d.*, 1849–50

For
The Three Notes

If "The Point of View" is to be published and also these 3
Notes, some of the later additions should of course be taken out
since everything is said in "The Point of View."

> Of course, the postscript to Note 3
> or to the whole little book should be removed,
> so that it ends right after Note 3.
>   —*Pap.* X⁵ B 169 *n.d.*, 1849

From draft of Point of View:

> For 3 Notes.   **N.B.**

the addition (pp. 1–5) [*Pap.* IX B 63:13 (pp. 280–83)] to
p. 298 [*Pap.* IX B 63:6] can be omitted if they are published now.
                    —*Pap.* X⁵ B 178 *n.d.*, 1849

From draft of Point of View:

If "Three Notes" and "The Accounting" are to be published
together, in the third Note delete the sentence:

> giving thanks for whatever favor and good will
> have been shown me, willingly forgetting what-
> ever of the opposite has been my lot.
>   —*Pap.* X⁵ B 183 *n.d.*, 1849

From draft of "The Accounting":

N.B. If "The Accounting" should accompany the three Friday discourses (The High Priest etc.)[125] or be published separately, the printing should be: (1) the part that should be printed
in columns should have its own special type; (2) "The Accounting" itself should be printed like the three discourses; (3) the
Notes in the smallest possible brevier; (4) the "Postscript" with a
slightly larger brevier.—*Pap.* X⁵ B 227 *n.d.*, 1849–50

Note. Recently a new pseudonym appeared: Anti-Climacus.
But this implies precisely a halt; this is how one goes about dialectically effecting a halt: one points to something higher that
examines a person critically and forces him back within his
boundaries.

October 1849

The note that accompanies the final draft in the mahogany
box reads something like this.

—*JP* VI 6518 (*Pap.* X⁵ B 206) October 1849

The Sagacious and Sensible—
the Good and True

Take a certain fraction of the good or of the true—this is the
sagacious and sensible way to be a success in the world. Take the
good or true whole, and the exact opposite occurs and you run
completely counter to the world.

I have an example of that.

I have considered inserting "her"[126] [*in margin:* see enclo-
sure[127]] in an enigmatic dedication to the writings about my
work as an author. It cannot be done now, for other reasons,
since no matter how enigmatic it is, it nevertheless will be easily
understood, and therefore I not only have no guarantee at all
that it will be respected, but there is the strongest probability that
a newspaper will pick it up and mention her name, and then
everything is stirred up and I perhaps would have done incalculable harm. But I would like very much to do it, because I
would also like to have it all in order, if possible, before my
death.

Yet there is another matter I want to explain now. Assuming
that I did do it, what then? Well, it would not have been sagacious and sensible. Why? Because it aims too high. The story is
now forgotten; I was a scoundrel, but now that is forgotten
and everything is all right again in that respect; it should not be
stirred up now. Yes, but I was not an utter scoundrel; the whole
affair has a far deeper meaning. It would be futile, that is precisely
the trouble, and that is also what would make such a step unwise.
That is, it would aim so high that it would seem to be an attempt
to rip people out of their cozy routines for a moment by being
able to explain everything and having explained everything; then
they would be annoyed, and thus one would run counter to
them.—*JP* VI 6583 (*Pap.* X² A 427) *n.d.*, 1850

Concerning the Publishing of "The Accounting" and the
"Three Notes" at This Time

"The Accounting" perhaps can be published and in its latest version.

As for "Three Notes," I have come back to the original understanding: since I cannot present myself in my misery, no attempt should be made to present myself in my possible extraordinariness; for me personally both factors are accurate correlatives; if the one is taken away, the other becomes false. "Three Notes" therefore can either be left lying, or the important thought-categories in them can be used simply as theses without mentioning me in a single word: the thesis "the crowd" is untruth and the thesis about "the single individual."

In its present version, "The Accounting" has essentially nothing about me; if any objection is to be raised to it, it must, if anything, be that I am made too insignificant. But after all my significance cannot be truly represented without counterbalancing it with my being a penitent, and I cannot as long as I live go that far in presenting my personality, not even out of respect for "her,"[128] who suddenly would be hurled into the reinterpretation of the past, which perhaps would thoroughly disturb her.—
Pap. X^2 A 450 *n.d.*, 1850

About Myself

X^2
A 586
417

When I think back on it now, it is wonderful to think of that stroke of a pen with which I hurled myself against rabble-barbarism!

And this was my mood when I took that step. I thought of stopping writing with *Concluding Postscript*, and to that end the manuscript in its entirety was delivered to Luno. Grateful, unspeakably grateful for what had been granted to me, I decided— on the occasion of that article in *Gæa*[129]—to take a magnanimous step for "the others." I was the only one who had the qualifications to do it emphatically, the qualifications along these lines: (1) Goldschmidt had immortalized me[130] and saw in me an object of admiration, (2) I am a witty author, (3) I have not sided with the elite or with any party at all, (4) I have a personal virtuosity for associating with everybody, (5) a shining reputation that literally did not have one single speck of criticism or the like, (6) I altruistically used my own money to be an author, (7) I was unmarried, independent, etc.

So, religiously motivated, I did it. And look, this step was determinative for my continuing to write! And what significance it has had, how I have learned to know myself, learned to know "the world," and learned to understand Christianity—yes, a whole side of Christianity, and a crucial side, which very likely would not have occurred to me at all otherwise, and except for that the situation for coming into the proper relation to Christianity myself perhaps would not have been my fortune, either.

But what a range: an established consummate reputation as an author, and then suddenly almost beginning all over again!—*JP* VI 6594 (*Pap.* X² A 586) *n.d.*, 1850

The Misunderstanding of My Position as an Author

My contemporaries have only worldly categories; thus they expected and expect either that I would escape my mistreatment[131] by taking a journey, for example, or that I will defend myself.

I am, however, engrossed with the religious prototypes, whose identifying mark is suffering. I do not know if it is permissible for me to make my situation easier, since it is clear that the more I suffer the more deeply I will wound my contemporaries and the influence of my life will become all the greater.

This is how I myself (by not doing the expected) cooperate to make the situation more difficult.

But they do not really know me.—*Pap.* X² A 621 *n.d.*, 1850

My Concern with Regard to the Publication
of the Writings That Are Finished[132]

Although I realize that with almost exaggerated care I have made a movement in the direction of inwardness and never in

X²
A 586
418

X²
A 621
445

X²
A 621
446

the direction of a pietistic or ascetic awakening that wants to realize it externally, I nevertheless continually fear that communication of this sort somehow obligates me promptly to express it existentially, which is beyond my capability, nor is that what I mean, which is that it be used to intensify the need for grace; but, even if I were more spiritual than I am, I have an indescribable anxiety about venturing so far out or so high up.

But as long as I am leading the life I now lead, it easily could be misinterpreted, as if I thought I already realize such a thing.

That is why I have thought that first of all I ought to assure myself of a pastoral appointment or something like that, to show that I do not make myself out to be better than others.

But that again has its own special difficulties, and that is why the time has passed and I have suffered exceedingly.—*JP* VI 6646 (*Pap.* X³ A 190) *n.d.*, 1850

Intensification in Being a Christian

What is called humanity today is not purely and simply humanity but a diffused form of the essentially Christian.

Originally the procedure was this: with "the universally human consciousness" as the point of departure, to accept the essentially Christian. Now the procedure is this: from a point of origin that already is a diffused form of the essentially Christian—to become a Christian.

Ergo, to become a Christian is intensified.

Here, as I have developed in "Armed Neutrality,"[133] it is apparent that the procedure turns out to be one of instituting reflection on a full level deeper and more inward, something like the change from σοφοί [wise men] to φιλόσοφοι [lovers of wisdom], simply because the task has become enormously greater.
—*JP* VI 6649 (*Pap.* X³ A 204) *n.d.*, 1850

Wilhelm Lund[134]

The similarity between his life and mine occurred to me today. Just as he lives over there in Brazil, lost to the world, absorbed in excavating antediluvian fossils, so I live as if outside the world, absorbed in excavating Christian concepts—alas, and yet I am living in Christendom, where Christianity flourishes, stands in luxuriant growth with 1,000 clergymen, and where we all are Christians.—*JP* VI 6652 (*Pap.* X³ A 239) *n.d.*, 1850

Mynster[135]—Luther

Somewhere in his sermons Luther declares that three things belong to a Christian life: (1) faith, (2) works of love, (3) persecution for this faith and for these works of love.[136]

Take Mynster now. He has reduced faith oriented toward tension and inwardness. He has set legality in the place of works of love. And persecution he has completely abolished.—*JP* VI 6653 (*Pap.* X³ A 249) *n.d.*, 1850

Regarding a statement in the postscript to "Concluding Postscript" *with respect to publishing the books about my work as an author*

The statement is: "Thus in the pseudonymous books there is not a single word by me. I have no opinion about them except as a third party, no knowledge of their meaning except as a reader, not the remotest private relation to them, since it is impossible to have that to a doubly reflected communication. A single word by me personally in my own name would be an arrogating self-forgetfulness that, regarded dialectically, would be guilty of essentially having annihilated the pseudonymous authors by this one word."[137]

Now it could be said that in "The Accounting,"[138] for example, there is indeed direct discussion of the pseudonymous authors, pointing out the principal idea that runs through the whole.

With regard to that, it must be observed *both* that what I wrote then can be altogether true and that what I wrote later just as true, simply because at that time I was not as advanced in my development, still had not come to an understanding of the definitive idea for all my writing, still did not even dare to declare definitely whether or not it would possibly end with my finding something that would push me back from Christianity, although I still continued with religious enthusiasm and to the best of my ability to work out the task of presenting what Christianity is. *And* it may also be noted that I do not discuss the pseudonyms directly in the books about my authorship or identify with them but merely show their significance as maieutic method. Finally, I must add: This is how I understand the totality *now*, by no means did I have this overview of the whole from the beginning, no more than I dare to say that I immediately perceived that the τέλος of the pseudonyms was maieutic, since this, too, was like a phase of poetic emptying in my own life-development.—*JP* VI 6654 (*Pap.* X³ A 258) *n.d.*, 1850

When I had published *Concluding Postscript*, I intended to withdraw and devote myself more to my own relationship to Christianity.

X¹
A 318
231

But in the meantime external situations involved my public life in such a way that I existentially discovered the Christian collisions.

X¹
A 318
232

This is an essential element in my own upbringing.—*JP* VI 6660 (*Pap.* X³ A 318) *n.d.*, 1850

Jottings

This year, August 9 (the date of Father's death[139]) happened to fall on a Friday. I went to Communion that day.

And, strangely enough, the sermon in Luther[140] I read according to plan that day was on the verse "All good and perfect gifts etc." from the Epistle of James.[141]

The day I sent the manuscript[142] to the printer, the Luther sermon[143] I read according to plan was on Paul's verse on the tribulations of the day etc.[144]

This strikes me as very curious; I myself am also oddly moved, since I do not remember beforehand which sermon is to be read according to the schedule.

September 8 (which I really call my engagement day[145]) is on a Sunday this year, and the Gospel is: No one can serve two masters.[146]—*JP* VI 6666 (*Pap.* X³ A 391) *n.d.*, 1850

The Judgment of My Contemporaries
upon Me

Now there will again be an uproar claiming that I proclaim only the law, urge imitation too strongly, and the like (although in the preface to the new book, *Practice in Christianity*, I presented grace). And they will say: We cannot stop with this; we must go further—to grace, where there is peace and rest.

You babble nonsense. For the average person, Christianity has shriveled to sheer meaninglessness, a burlesque edition of the doctrine of grace, that if one is a Christian one lets things go their way and counts on God's grace.

But because everything that is essentially Christian has shriveled to meaninglessness this way, they are unable to recognize it again when pathos-filled aspects are delineated. They have the whole thing in an infinitely empty, abstract summary—and thus think they have gone further than the successive unfolding of the pathos-filled aspects.

Nothing can be taken in vain as easily as grace; as soon as imitation is completely omitted, grace is taken in vain. But that is the kind of preaching people like.—*JP* II 1878 (*Pap.* X³ A 411) *n.d.*, 1850

X³
A 413
284   *Indirect Communication*

It is not true that direct communication is superior to indirect communication. No, no. But the fact is that no human being has
X³
A 413
285   ever been born who could use the indirect method even fairly well, to say nothing of using it all his life. We human beings need each other, and in that there is already a directness.

Only the God-man is in every respect pure indirect communication from first to last. He did not need people, but they infinitely needed him; he loves people, but according to his conception of what love is; therefore he does not change in the slightest toward their conception, does not speak directly in such a way that he also surrenders the possibility of offense—which his existence [*Existents*] in the guise of servant is.

When a person uses the indirect method, there is in one way

or another something daimonic—but not necessarily in the bad sense—about it, as, for example, with Socrates.

Direct communication indeed makes life far easier. On the other hand, the use of direct communication may be humiliating for a person who has used indirect communication perhaps self-ishly (therefore daimonically in a bad sense).

I have frequently felt the need to use direct communication (although it must be remembered, of course, that even when I did use it, it was far from being carried through completely and indeed it was only for a short time), but it seemed to me as if I wanted to be lenient with myself, as if I could achieve more by holding out. Whether there is pride here as well, God knows best—before God I would dare neither to affirm nor to deny this, for who knows himself well enough for this?

When I look back on my life, I must say that it seems to me not impossible that something higher hid behind me. It was not impossible. I do not say more. What have I done, then? I have said: For the present I use no means that would disturb this possibility, for example, by *premature* direct communication. The situation is like that of a fisherman when he sees the float move—maybe it means a bite, maybe it is due to the motion of the water. But the fisherman says: I will not pull up the line; if I do, I indicate that I have surrendered this possibility; perhaps it will happen again and prove to be a bite.

For me indirect communication has been instinctive within me, because in being an author I no doubt have also developed myself, and consequently the whole movement is backward, which is why from the very first I could not state my plan directly, although I certainly was aware that a lot was fermenting within me. Furthermore, consideration for "her"[147] required me to be careful. I could well have said right away: I am a religious author. But how could I risk that after having made the pretense that I was a scoundrel in order if possible to help her? Actually it was she—that is, my relationship to her—who taught me the indirect method. She could be helped only by an untruth about me; otherwise I believe she would have lost her mind. That the collision was a religious one would have completely deranged her, and therefore I have had to be so infinitely careful. And not

X¹
A 413
286

until I had her engaged again and married did I regard myself as somewhat free in this regard.

Thus, through something purely personal, I have been assisted to something on a far greater scale, something I have gradually come to understand more and more deeply.—*JP* II 1959 (*Pap.* X³ A 413) *n.d.*, 1850

The Established Church—My Position

From the highest Christian point of view, there is no established Church, only a Church militant.

This is the first point.

The second, then, is that factually there is such a one. We must in no way want to overthrow it, no, but above it the higher ideality must hover as a possibility of awakening—in the strictest sense there actually is no established Church.

This has now taken place through me, with the aid of a pseudonym, in order that it all might be a purely spiritual movement. There is not a shred of a proposal pertaining to the external.

And while the pseudonym lifts his hand for this big blow, I stand in between parrying; the whole thing recoils on me for being such a poor Christian, I who still remain in the established Church. In this way the whole thing is a spiritual movement.

O my God, I am almost tempted to admire myself for what I am managing to do—but, God be praised, you help me to trace everything back to you in adoration, I who never can thank you sufficiently for the good that has been done for me, far more than I ever expected, could have expected, dared to expect.—*JP* VI 6671 (*Pap.* X³ A 415) *n.d.*, 1850

The eighth of September![148] The Gospel: No man can serve two masters (my favorite Gospel)![149] My favorite hymn:[150] "Commit Thy Ways Confiding," which Kofoed-Hansen[151] selected today!

How festive, and how relevant to me, occupied as I have been these days with publishing "On My Work as an Author"[152] and the dedication[153] in it.—*JP* VI 6673 (*Pap.* X³ A 422) *n.d.*, 1850

The Publication of the Book:
"On My Work as an Author"

"On My Work as an Author" still must be kept back. I feel that it would come disturbingly close to "Practice in Christianity,"[154] so that they would mutually diminish each other, even if in another sense I feel it could be more impressive.

But the main point is that the spirit has not moved me to a firm and fixed conviction that now is the time, something I did feel about the timing of the publication of "Practice in Christianity."

The difference between being moved by the spirit or not, between being completely at one with myself or not, I know at once, because in the latter case I cannot stop thinking about details, changing something, this detail or that. In the other case this never occurs to me, because the whole attention of my mind is solely and unanimously concentrated on the fact that the whole matter has now been commended into God's hand, I have relinquished it.

God knows that I would in one sense gladly publish "On My Work as an Author" now, and then be completely free, but since I cannot find the unqualified sanction within me, I dare not do it. It may be a mistake on my part not to find this sanction; perhaps without quite detecting it I am seeking to spare myself. Or precisely this is the right thing, and I do right in not giving in to an impatience that in another sense nags me to publish it now. This I do not know, but I commend myself to God; surely he will see to it that when the time has come I will find in myself complete unanimity about publishing it.—*JP* VI 6674 (*Pap.* X^3 A 423) *n.d.*, 1850

[*In margin:* Anti-Climacus.]
Concerning the Impression Anti-Climacus's Latest Book
(Practice in Christianity) *Will Make*

Today I talked with Tryde.[155] He told me that it was too strong to say that Christianity had been abolished through "observation."[156] He himself had stressed the subjective, and that was true also of all the more competent preachers.

O my God, how I have had to put up with this, that I was purely subjective, not objective, etc.—and now the same people claim that they also emphasize the subjective.

Moreover, the point is that in defining the concept "preaching," the sermon, one never gets further than a speech, talking about something; consequently one does not pay attention to existence at all. An officeholder—shackled in seventeen ways to finitude and objectivity—achieves nothing, no matter how subjective he makes his talk. A nobody who preaches *gratis* on the street—even if he makes observations that are ever so objective—remains a subjective and vivifying person; and one who is ever so subjective but is trapped by his position and the like in all possible secular considerations, his preaching remains essentially nothing but observation, for it is easy to see that he has made it impossible for himself to actualize even moderately that which he preaches about.

But I have to say one thing about Tryde, something splendid about him: that he said, that he did not deny, that he had been predisposed to be objective.—*JP* VI 6687 (*Pap.* X³ A 530) *n.d.,* 1850

[*In margin: Johannes Climacus—Anti-Climacus*]
Johannes Climacus—Anti-Climacus

Just as Johannes Climacus dialectically formulated the issue so sharply that no one could directly see whether it was an attack on Christianity or a defense, but it depended on the state of the reader and what he got out of the book, so also Anti-Climacus has carried the issue to such an extreme that no one can see directly whether it is primarily radical or primarily conservative, whether it is an attack on the established order or in fact a defense.—*JP* VI 6690 (*Pap.* X³ A 555) *n.d.,* 1850

X³
A 586
384

Regarding Practice in Christianity *and Its Relation to an Established Order*

It is altogether conservative, wants only or is able only to preserve the established order.

X³
A 586
385

But the point is that its author is not an appointed official or a person who as a matter of course attaches himself to the established order so as to make a professional career.

My whole view, which I have always avowed, is that the evil is not the government but the crowd; therefore the true extraordinaries would have to aim against the crowd in favor of the government.

But on the other hand an extraordinary is something else and different from an appointed official. Thus he first of all has to take his position by means of a dialectical crossing so that he does not conceal the irregularities of the established order—and then he finds out whether the established order perhaps wants to reject him and if possible identify him with a movement in the sense of opinion.

In former days the extraordinaries aimed against the government and sought support from the people. This is no longer the case. The new way will be for the extraordinary to take the opposite position but not allow the confusion such as when an appointed official identifies serving the established order with getting ahead etc.

The question is whether an established order is true enough to recognize such an extraordinary.

For the person concerned, operating in this manner is extremely taxing, sheer fear and trembling. It is especially so for me—I who have so much of the poet in me and therefore am not an extraordinary in the strictest sense, something I have always emphasized, but yet I am so kindred to it and so full of presentiment about it that I can at least make aware.—*Pap.* X^3 A 586 *n.d.*, 1850

Faith

It is clear that in my writings I have supplied a more radical characterization of the concept faith than there has been up until this time.—*JP* VI 6698 (*Pap.* X^3 A 591) *n.d.*, 1850

The Christian Emphasis

Christianly the emphasis does not fall so much upon to what extent or how far a person succeeds in meeting or fulfilling the requirement, if he actually is striving, as upon his getting an impression of the requirement in all its infinitude so that he rightly learns to be humbled and to rely upon grace.

To scale down the requirement in order to be able to fulfill it better (as if this were earnestness, that now it can all the more easily *appear* that one is earnest about wanting to fulfill the requirement)—to this Christianity in its deepest essence is opposed.

No, infinite humiliation and grace, and then a striving born of gratitude—this is Christianity.—*JP* I 993 (*Pap.* X³ A 734) *n.d.*, 1851

From draft of On My Work; *see 1–3:*

"The Accounting."
   Will have the main title: On My Work as an Author,
                     and then on the next page
                        The Accounting
   On the overleaf of the first title page the epigraph is to be placed:
                  Wer etc. [*same as p. 2*]
                        —*Pap.* X⁵ B 259 *n.d.*, 1849–50

From draft of On My Work; *see 1:*

X⁵
B 207
388

                  On My Work as an Author
                           By
                     S. Kierkegaard
            Format as in *Philosophical Fragments*, but
            smaller type and set more closely;
            525 copies; 30 copies on vellum.
            Copenhagen, 1850.

   To the typesetter: To be printed in columns.

Perhaps someone is amazed when he has read these books, but no one more than I when I turn around now (after having been an author for approximately seven years and just as if in one breath) and look at what has been accomplished and with almost a shiver of amazement see that the whole thing is actually only one thought, something I quite clearly understand now, although in the beginning I had not expected to go on being an author for so many years, nor did I have such a grand objective. Philosophically, this is a movement of reflection that is described backward and is first understood when it is accomplished. Religiously, this indicates to me personally in what an infinite debt of gratitude I am to Governance, who like a father has benevolently held his hand over me and supported me in so many ways. This also signifies to me personally my own development and upbringing, for however true it is that when I began I had basically understood that I essentially belonged to the religious, in various ways this relationship still needed development and upbringing, which I need now also.

Since, however, the *interpretation* of my work as an author that I shall communicate here is not something pasted on but is simply a demonstration and explanation of what has actually been done, and since from the beginning I have understood some of this in advance and gradually more and more of the whole, I have structured the production as if the whole from the beginning was a conscious thought. In one sense I am indeed myself the author who has done everything that has been done; humanly speaking, in a human judgment I must call the authorship predominantly my own production, even though helped and supported in numerous ways by a higher being; divinely understood, before God I call it my own development and upbringing, but not in the sense as if I were now complete or completely finished with regard to needing upbringing and development.

But lest I in any way—alas, ungratefully—cheat Governance, as it were, of the least little thing or falsely attribute anything to myself, I let what is set forth here come first. This is truly more important to me than the whole authorship, and it is closer to my heart to express this as honestly and as strongly as possible, something for which I can never give thanks sufficiently and something that I, when at some time I have forgotten the entire authorship, will eternally and unalterably recollect: how infinitely more Governance has done for me than I ever had expected, could have expected, or dared to have expected. This feeling is indescribably blessed; at times it has overwhelmed me in such a way that it has taught me to understand to some degree the

X⁵
B 207
389

words of the apostle: "Depart from me, for I am a sinful man"[157]—that is, this very immensity makes me feel all the more deeply my own unworthiness.

Upbringing in Christianity is what is needed everywhere. In this regard I believe that my work as an author has importance. In no way do I, the author, call myself *the teacher;* I myself am the one who is being brought up. *Authority* I have never used; on the contrary, from the very first moment (the preface to *Two Upbuilding Discourses* [1843]) I have stereotypically repeated, pointed out "that I am without authority." *To make aware* with respect to the religious, more specifically the Christian, is actually the category for my authorship; the three rubrics above are also categorically appropriate to this category.—*Pap.* X⁵ B 207 *n.d.*, 1850

From draft of On My Work; *see 3:*

> For
>   "The Accounting."
>   The dedication[158] will read
>   To One Unnamed[159]
>   whose name will one day be named
>   is dedicated
>   etc.
>   Then the line "and will—*be named*" goes out.
>   —*Pap.* X⁵ B 261 *n.d.*, 1849–50

From draft of On My Work; *see 3:*

X⁵
B 262
429

For "The Accounting"
Other versions of the dedication,
but which could not be used.

1

A dedication for which I here merely reserve the place until the moment comes when it can be filled in with a name that will inseparably follow my authorship as long as it is remembered, be it for a long time or short.

    or only: until the moment comes when it
    can be filled in with a name.

2

X⁵
B 262
430

    Dedicated to an unnamed person[160]
    whose name as yet must be withheld
    but which history eventually will name,
    and, be it a long time or short,
    just as long as mine.

etc.

3

A Dedication*

Note. By reason of circumstances this inscription cannot as
    yet be filled in with a name, but nevertheless it must
    already now have its place.

4

One unnamed
    whose name will one day be named,
        and will—*be named*

—*Pap.* X⁵ B 262 *n.d.*, 1849–50

From draft of On My Work; *see 3:*

    The Dedication to Regine Schlegel,[161]
if there can be such a thing during my *lifetime*, could very well be
used in the front of a small collection of Friday discourses but
properly belongs to the writings on my work as an author. Inasmuch as I appear so decisively in the character of the religious,
which I have wanted from the very beginning, at this moment
she is the only important one, since my relationship to her is a
God-relationship.

    The dedication could read:
        To R. S.—with this little book is dedicated an au-
    thorship, which to some extent belongs to her,
    by one who belongs to her completely.

Or with a collection of Friday discourses:
To R. S. is dedicated this little book.
—*JP* VI 6675 (*Pap.* X⁵ B 263) *n.d.*, 1849–50

From draft of On My Work; *see 3:*

To a contemporary,[162]
whose name must still be concealed,
but history will name
—be it for a short time or long—
as long as it names mine,
                    is dedicated
                              with this little book
                              the whole authorship, as it
                              was from the beginning.
          —*JP* VI 6676 (*Pap.* X⁵ B 264) *n.d.*, 1849–50

From draft of On My Work; *see 5:3; 290–94:*

For "The Accounting"

In the "Postscript" where there is mention of my personal life,
omit:
                    its errors—and later: its repentance and regret

And at the very beginning where it reads
                    The Accounting
          Copenhagen, March   S. Kierkegaard
omit my name.
                              —*Pap.* X⁵ B 252 *n.d.*, 1849–50

From draft of On My Work; *see 5:1 9:7:*

X⁵
B 191
375

                    Appendix
          The Accounting

Copenhagen, the fifth of May [*changed to:* April, *changed to:*
March] 1849

                                        S. Kierkegaard

When a country [*essentially the same as 5:4–27*].

When I, religiously resolved, began as an author, it was my thought not to be that for many years, but in the few years devoted to it to be that with my life and soul, night and day, "willing only one thing,"[163] and in relation to this one thing rejecting and renouncing all else. What determined me in this resolve is the following. In my view, to be an author was and is to be regarded as a kind of uncommon existence; therefore it was in character to keep as free as possible from any more commonplace determination of finitude. It ought to be, I thought, the flower of a person's life. —I have now been an author for seven years, the seven years that also are ordinarily regarded as the richest: from age 28 to 35. This is one side; on the other side, it was my wish from the beginning eventually to step into the modest position of a rural pastor[164]—something I have also still considered as my life's finite destination.

These two thoughts are the law for the speed with which I have worked as an author. Regarded as a totality, the whole authorship could be said to be predicated upon the second of these two thoughts, as if the authorship and my personality had some finite relation to each other, rather than that my finite personality is infinitely indifferent to the authorship. . . .

X^5
B 191
376

When I began writing *Either/Or*, I was just as profoundly moved by the religious as I am now at the end, except that the work has been for me a second upbringing, and I have become more mature. . . .

Consequently, the task of the entire authorship was: to arrive at the simple, to become simple, simplification. In this regard it would then be a consistency in my personal life if I, the author, [*deleted:* now] became a rural pastor.

X^5
B 191
377

I do not, however, mean to say by what is stated here that I intend today or tomorrow to seek to become a rural pastor or that it is decided. Prompted by the second edition of *Either/ Or*,[165] which until now I have not allowed to be published, and also feeling obligated, I have only wanted to give the reader, "that single individual whom I with joy and gratitude call my reader,"[166] this view of the thought of my work as an author. I have hereby actually not said a word about what will happen, about the future. I have only said hereby and say hereby that this has been my thought.—*Pap.* X⁵ B 191 *n.d.*, 1849

X⁵
B 191
378

From draft of On My Work; *see 5:27:*

X⁵
B 228
412

For

"The Accounting"

To the first passage in what is in columns could perhaps be added the following, which then is also to be added to the earlier writing, a fair copy now reduced to a draft.

From childhood rigorously brought up in Christianity, by filial piety indissolubly bound to it, deeply inward a sufferer, in possession of unusual gifts, financially independent so that I could serve an idea, easily convinced by my first look at the world that what is being proclaimed in the world under the name of Christianity actually is not Christianity or in any case seems to be meaninglessly unrecognizable by the illusion—I understood it as my task to work in pious devotion every day of my life with all my soul and all my power to get Christianity presented. With regard to what pertains to me personally, there was something—in me or in Christianity for me—especially at the beginning, something, a difficulty, that pained me, under which I suffered, something that would hold me back from completely devoting myself to Christianity; but even if I were to become seventy years old and this difficulty continued unaltered, I would still understand this unalterably and unconditionally unalterably to be my life task to which I was committed; I dared to believe that I, humanly speaking, could do a good deed by presenting Christianity, partly because I was unusually well informed about what Christianity is, and partly because I had a more than ordinary gift to be able to present it, and finally because I saw so clearly that I had the

X⁵
B 228
413

solution to the customary doubts about Christianity. Moreover, understood in this way (bearing in mind that something and that difficulty for me personally), I call my work as an author my upbringing and development.—*Pap.* X⁵ B 228 *n.d.*, 1849–50

From draft of On My Work; *see 5:29:*

. . . The whole authorship, regarded in its entirety, is planned with this wish in mind [to become a rural pastor]. The movement it describes is: from "the poet," from the esthetic—from the philosopher, from the speculative—to the intimation of the most inward interpretation of the essentially Christian; **from** the **pseudonymous** *Either/Or,* which was immediately accompanied by *Two Upbuilding Discourses* with *my name* as author, **through** *Concluding Postscript* with my name as editor, **to** *Discourses at the Communion on Fridays*[167] [*here a double dagger in red crayon, in margin a double dagger and:* see the attached], the latest work I have written, and "of which two have been delivered in Frue Church." . . .

In a sense the whole authorship can be considered, if I may speak this way, as my program for becoming a rural pastor. If this should seem strange to anyone, this would not be due to the matter itself. Christianly, it is entirely in order. The movement is the right one. Not until now have I reached the higher level, because Christianly it is a matter of *arriving at* the simple, to become more and more simple. . . .—*Pap.* X⁵ B 201 *n.d.*, 1849

X⁵
B 201
382

X⁵
B 201
383

From draft of On My Work; *see 6:34–35:*

Authority is appropriate to the "ordained" pastor, and to the preaching of sin and grace in the decisive sense. But from the very beginning (preface to *Two Upbuilding Discourses* [1843]) I have stereotypically repeated that I was without authority and even at the end, in the preface to the discourses at Communion,[168] pointed out that these were not sermons, because I have not yet decisively advanced the doctrine of sin and grace in the strictest sense and as the decisive element.—*Pap.* X⁵ B 204 *n.d.*, 1849

X⁵
B 204
385

X⁵
B 204
386

From draft of On My Work; *see 6:41:*

For p. 9 in a "Note" on
my authorship.

X⁵
B 249
421

    Note.

Lest I, by continually speaking about my authorship only in this moderate, subdued tone and never in any other way, lest I

X⁵
B 249
422

thereby become guilty of what surely in God's eyes is just as culpable as presumptuousness—a false and unseemly modesty—then in faithfulness to the truth the other side of the matter must also be touched upon. When at some time this authorship takes its place in history, it will then be said there. This authorship contains the movement of a turning point, and its author has experienced the turning point's conflict between the two moments. When the author began, what the age had gone astray and bogged down in was "the interesting." Religiously the task was to move from the interesting and to arrive at the simple. To that end the author must be eminently in possession of the interesting. That he was indeed; unconditionally no Danish author can claim the predicate "the interesting" as he can; as an esthetic author he is entitled to it as a distinctive feature, while other authors are in the same way entitled to other predicates. What "the moment" wanted was the interesting; what the author was capable of was the interesting—thus he would have had it in his power to become the hero and the idol of "the moment." If "the moment" had become preponderant for him, if he had forgotten the "next thing" (to come to the simple), if he had wanted to adulterate his task within "the moment"—then he would have become the idol of "the moment." If not—then, then he would have to become a martyr of "the moment," because "the moment," which wanted the interesting, was too decisively aware of him, who could be the very one whom the moment craved, to let him go without further ado. Faithful to his task, he became a martyr of the moment—the best or rather the only proof that can be adduced that he, eternally understood, was victorious. And his martyrdom, which he himself freely determined and chose, categorically corresponded exactly to the conflict between the two categories, the interesting—the simple; corresponded exactly to the conflict of the turning point that he experienced: the conflict between the interesting and the simple.

Yet the author cannot inwardly have any merit. He has by no means been entirely free: from the beginning he has had a thorn in the flesh*—the only feature of an apostle[169] he has had—it has taught him obedience; and in an anguished consciousness** of his own personal guilt he has had a constraint that could even further constrain him in absolute obedience.

$\quad$*—this is historical—

$\quad$**—this is historical—

$\qquad\qquad\qquad\qquad\qquad$—*Pap.* X^5 B 249 *n.d.*, 1849–50

Deleted from final copy of On My Work; *see 9:19–24:*

Note. And since the public, to take an example, that was jabbed was a public corresponding to the press of literary contemptibility, the tone became what it became. And since the speaker was a pseudonym, his words, accordingly also the poetical replies, became esthetic, in his character of an imaginatively constructing humorist. . . .—*Pap.* X^5 B 289:11 *n.d.*, 1850–51

From draft of On My Work; *see 10:15:*

In "The Accounting," regardless of which version is used, to be added to the passage that the movement is from the public to the single individual

$\quad$a note.

Note. This again (just like the circumstance of a religious author's *beginning* with esthetic production) is the dialectical movement, or it is dialectical: in *working* also to *work against* oneself, which is the reduplication and the heterogeneity of all true godly effort to worldly effort. To strive or to work directly is to work or strive directly in the immediate context of an actual situation; the dialectical is the *reverse*: in working also to work against oneself, a redoubling that is* like the pressure on the plow that determines the depth of the furrow, while the direct striving is** a

X^5
B 249
423

smoothing over that is both more speedily taken care of and is far, far more gratefully received—that is, it is worldliness, homogeneity.

 *"Earnestness,"
 **Superficiality, . . .

—Pap. X⁵ B 234 n.d., 1849–50

Deleted from margin of final copy of On My Work; *see 10:16:*

†*Note.* And especially in our time this had to be and must be ethically and existentially emphasized as decisively as possible, especially in our time, metaphysically or ethically dissipated, whose specific evil and particular demoralization are precisely to want to do away with the foundation of all morality, upbuilding, and religiousness—*the single individual*—and substitute the race, one or another abstraction, fantastical social categories, etc., something the world revolution in 1848[170] has made even clearer and more obvious. Thus it is already fairly easy to see that *the single individual* is the point of view of the future pointing toward rescue, just as *the single individual* is also the passage through which "Christendom" must go—this enormous illusion, turning all the Christian concepts upside down, which, if it is to be thoroughly revised and raised up, must pose the task: to introduce Christianity into Christendom.—*Pap.* X⁵ B 289:13 *n.d.*, 1850–51

From draft of On My Work; *see 10:21:*

> To be *added* in "The Accounting" (if it is to be published now and separately) at the end of what it says in the *text* about the single individual, but not a new ending.

— —this about the *single individual.* Yes, it was this about the single individual, which in the past was considered a foolish exaggeration by systematicians, politicians, journalists, by the public, by every Tom, Dick, and Harry, by which I had even made myself a laughingstock—until the year 1848[171] showed that it was the truth; truly, a poor solitary thinker cannot possibly ask for greater support from existence. Neither can an author, who in the year 1846 takes it upon himself to portray the future, and in the same way as I did it in *A Literary Review*,[172] cannot possibly ask for more than 1848. Finally, for the sake of recollection, if a thinker can be engaged in concentrating and having concentrated all his intellectual activity in one single thought—this has been granted to me. My whole intellectual activity as an author has been concentrated on this one thought, *the single individual*, the category that eventually will become the point of view of the future, the category whose meaning (political, ethical, religious) the future will more and more make manifest.—*Pap.* X^5 B 247 *n.d.*, 1849–50

From draft of On My Work; *see 10:37–40:*

. . . *Note.* And insofar as there is the *congregation* in the religious sense, this is a concept that lies on the other side of *the single individual; the single individual* must with ethical decisiveness have gone in between as the middle term in order to make sure that *the congregation* is not taken in vain as synonymous with "the public," "the crowd," etc., although we still must remember what is well-known, that it is not the single individual's relationship to the congregation that determines his relationship to God, but it is his relationship to God that determines his relationship to the congregation. Then finally (in order to include this) there is the supreme relationship, in which *the single individual* is absolutely higher than *the congregation*, the single individual κατ' ἐξοχήν [in the eminent sense], the God-man; in the Old Testament, the judge; in the New Testament, the apostle, even if these god-fearingly admit that they have their divine authority in order to serve *the congregation*. But *religiously* (in contrast to "the public," "the crowd," etc., which *politically* can have validity), there is only the single individual. And Christianly-religiously, is anything but "the crowd," "the public," etc. (which had, have, and can have validity in paganism and worldliness), because the *possibility of offense*, which Christianly is the *middle term* in relation to

X^5
B 208
392

becoming a Christian, first unconditionally makes human beings *the single individual* qualitatively, whereby this concept *the Christian congregation* is safeguarded as something qualitatively different from "the public," "the crowd," etc., whereas of course unconditionally every human being can be the single individual.

I do not, however, mean to say by what is stated here that I intend today or tomorrow to seek to become a rural pastor or that it is decided. I have only wanted—also thinking myself *obligated* to it—to give the reader [*deleted:* , that single individual,] this view of the thought behind my work as an author. I have hereby actually not said a word about the future, about what is going to happen; I have only said hereby and say hereby that this has been my thought.—*Pap.* X⁵ B 208 March 1849

In margin of Pap. X⁵ B 208:

Note. I did not at the beginning think of expressing the contrast (between my beginning as an esthetic author although I belonged essentially to the religious) by becoming a religious author, which did happen, or for so long a time or on so great a scale, but rather by becoming a rural pastor immediately after being an esthetic author, by becoming as far as possible a rural pastor the moment I laid down my pen as an esthetic author, thereby expressing that I was conscious that my having been an esthetic author was a deception, but a pious deception.—*Pap.* X⁵ B 209 March 1849

See 12:21:

For

the passage in

"The Accounting," **without authority** to make aware etc., could perhaps be added at the end:

and I regard myself rather as a *reader* of the books, not as the *author*.

—*Pap.* X⁵ B 258 *n.d.,* 1849–50

Deleted from final copy of On My Work; *see 12:30:*

No, in that regard I certainly have very much left, although I *perhaps* am now finished as author.—*Pap.* X⁵ B 289:21 *n.d.*, 1850–51

From draft of On My Work; *see 13:1:*

To "On My Work as an Author"
could be added

Two Appendices. (This is a separate page)
To be used here the two essays: My Position as a Religious Author in "Christendom" and My Strategy and On Herr Professor Nielsen's Relation to My Work as an Author.[173]
                                    —*Pap.* X⁵ B 271 *n.d.*, 1850

From draft of On My Work; *see 15:1–2:*

My Position as a Religious Author in "Christendom" and My Strategy.
                                    Draft.
November 1850.
                                    —*Pap.* X⁵ B 272 *n.d.*, 1850

From draft of On My Work; *see 13:1; 15:1–2:*

Appendix
[*Deleted:* by
The Editor]

My Position as a Religious Author in "Christendom" and My Strategy . . .
                                    —*Pap.* X⁵ B 273 November 1850

Deleted from final copy of On My Work; *see 15:1–2:*

My Position as a Religious Author in "Christendom" and My Strategy

An appendix to "Practice in Christianity" by the editor.
[*Deleted:* Draft and] final copy
November 1850
—*Pap.* X⁵ B 290 November 1850

Deleted from final draft of On My Work; *see 16:37:*

But I accuse no one, judge no one, no more than I establish parties or the like. I want only that the requirements of infinity be heard, *regarding everything as if spoken to me,* and otherwise leaving entirely up to each one what use he wants to make of these presentations (among which the most recent ones by Anti-Climacus[174] have in one place used a poetical presentation that ventures to say everything and a dialectical presentation that shies away from no consequences, in order, if possible, to disturb the illusions), otherwise leaving it entirely up to each one what use he wants to make of these presentations—but not in one case, if anyone should want to use them for judging others, that they are not true Christians etc., rather than for judging oneself, because in that case I intend, if the opportunity is given, to take the part of those attacked, and if I am prevented, if this does not happen, then this is nevertheless what I would do.

> *Deleted:* Editor [*changed from:* S. Kierkegaard]
> —*Pap.* X⁵ B 291:17 *n.d.,* 1850–51

Deleted from first page proofs of On My Work; *see 18:19:*

I, a poor private person, have, strangely enough, more or less undertaken the very tasks that actually are up to government and public officials to undertake—*Pap.* X⁵ B 293:19 *n.d.,* 1851

Deleted from final draft of On My Work; *see 19:9:*

What it means to govern, to rule, to be a teacher in obedience to God, in fear and trembling before the responsibility of eternity, is more or less forgotten, and instead governing is done more or less in the fear of people and with secular sagacity. If it is once again to amount to anything, the best thing to do is make an admission. "An admission," do I hear someone say, "then even more admissions must be made to the opposition, governing must be cut down even more." No, no, the admission will be made with regard to God and Christianity, that we have inadmissibly scaled down. It is more or less forgotten that all governing, especially in the ecclesiastical sphere, is from God, that to govern is to be obedient to God, and not a matter of summarily identifying with being a public official, and perhaps as such immediately tyrannizing if one sees one's chance, or, if the wind turns, haggling and bargaining and pretending to be sagacious—this is more or less forgotten, and therefore we more and more miss out on what is still the greatest blessing for us human beings: a God-fearing government that by fearing God is sufficiently strong and powerful not to fear people. [*In margin:* because to have its strength essentially in secular sagacity is simply and essentially to lack strength.]—*Pap.* X^5 B 291:41 *n.d.,* 1850–51

Deleted from final draft of On My Work; *see 19:1:*

    . . . . . —so let it be forgotten, forgotten, forgotten—as if it had been rendered totally unusable—the art of governing (which in every case is still unconditionally preferable to the art of governing by means of balloting and tossing a coin), the art of governing whose strength was secular sagacity, which, of course, in a deeper sense was exactly its lack of strength, the art of governing that in its craving for power at times pettily tormented people and in its fear of people at times pettily bargained with them.
              —*Pap.* X^5 B 291:44 *n.d.,* 1850–51

X^5
B 291:44
448
X^5
B 291:44
449

From final draft of On My Work; *see 19:14:*

[*Deleted:* no, insofar as the single individual needs it, it is only necessary that a change in his inner being take place]—but perhaps an internal transformation in the direction of becoming steadfast by fearing God. [*Deleted:* Then the forward step will be made, and there will be (*bestaa*) an established order (*bestaaende*) whose maxim will be: to govern is to obey God; and this maxim will denote that it lies on the other side of the year 1848. The mistake from above was simply that governing in the high sense was not being done; the fault from below was to want to do away with all government.] Certainly the mistake from above was that on the whole the strength throughout the government from top to bottom was essentially secular sagacity, which essentially is precisely the lack of strength. The fault from below was to want to do away with all government. The punishment, since the mode of the sin is always the mode of the punishment, the punishment is: that which comes to be most bitterly missed is precisely—government. [*Deleted:* What most of us all surely needed to learn by its absence was: how necessary it is for us human beings that there be government; and what the government surely had to learn was what it actually means to govern, that it is, in the fear of God, the responsibility to be strong and powerful enough not to fear people and "number," that it is in self-denial not to love governing but to love *the neighbor*, the true humanity and the true human equality.]—*Pap.* X⁵ B 291:47 *n.d.*, 1850–51

Deleted from draft of On My Work; *see* 20:25:

. . . , to speak Lutheranly, despite Satan, the public, and the newspapers, . . .

—*Pap.* X⁵ B 287 *n.d.*, 1850

From draft of On My Work; *see* 20:26:

If

"My Position as a Religious Author in Christendom and My Strategy"

is published separately, the following *conclusion* could perhaps be added

———

Since I have noticed, not without pain nor without indignation, all too frequently how a "gracious address to the reading public" is at times used by *Stüverfängere* [catchpennies], at times by partisans, at times by bootlickers and slaves of the people, in short, in various ways but in the service of shabby interests; since

I on the whole believe that a communication like this in these times can easily be misunderstood, exactly as dedications in former times to kings and royal personages—I have never made use of anything like this but have always addressed myself to "the single individual."

People have used this against me, interpreted it as pride, arrogance, and *pro virili* [with all their might] have tried to cast odium upon me. No doubt there is a misunderstanding here; what I am convinced of, indeed know, what the more honest, soberminded, and insightful have understood and, exactly the reverse, have given me credit for, is that I have been too proud to want to be confused with *Stüverfängere* etc.—something, incidentally, that not only I but everyone should be and ought to be—whereas both my life and my writings certainly bear the unmistakable mark of altruistic kindness and affection for, if possible, every single human being, which is why I also as a religious author have always addressed myself to "the single individual," religiously understood of course, consequently understood in such a way that everyone, unconditionally everyone, and everyone unconditionally can be that.—*Pap.* X^5 B 288 *n.d.*, 1850

From final copy of Point of View; *see 95:13–97:32:*

Conclusion

IX
·B 57
347

[*In margin:* **N.B.**

It would perhaps be better to use this in the introduction itself at the end, in which case the first two endings[175] drop out.]

The present work is an *interpretation* of something past, something traversed, something *historical.* Thus in a way it itself belongs to the past; therefore various things have to be said that I should prefer not to have said but that *historically* must not and cannot be forgotten or suppressed.

This is now completed; the historical truth gets its due by way of a *direct* communication, but—and this of course does not be-

IX
B 57
348

long to the past—for this very reason my whole relationship as an author is altered. The accounting has been made; on the other hand, with the direct communication contained in this work, I have abandoned the character of polemical subtlety—it would be a contradiction to want to be subtle and direct at the same time.

Consequently, in order to call the introduction to mind at the conclusion, to speak as definitely, as directly, as openly, as reconcilingly, as amicably as possible. Now, since I religiously regard it as my duty to speak, with God's help I shall speak in this spirit, honestly and also to the best of my ability. My heart expands—not as if it had ever been constricted in my breast, but the intensity that has been in my life and that I believed would be my death, has gotten a breathing spell, the dialectical bond has been broken, I dare to speak directly.

I ask everyone who has the cause of Christianity at heart (and I pray to God that the time might come when this would be the case with everyone) to give earnest attention to my whole endeavor as an author. I am convinced that there is present on my side a combination of conditions that are rarely found joined, conditions for elucidating and presenting Christianity exactly in the way now made necessary at this moment. I say this without any vain joy. After all, from the very first I have been and still am sacrificed for the cause I serve. Yet this does not trouble me if only the cause—and this occupies me indescribably [*changed from:* infinitely]—may serve to God's honor. Yet also in this regard everything is present. My weakness, spineless fellow that I am; my feebleness and powerlessness, dying man that I am; my errors and sins, penitent that I am—yes, even if I were ungrateful and enough of a scoundrel to want to take the honor for the whole thing, it would be impossible. On the other hand, God be praised, it is impossible for anyone who with any reflection at all attends to my work as an author not to have to become aware of God and to be somewhat constrained, if he does not do it with joy, to give God the honor—God be praised! What do I care about the world's honor and glory, and what do I care about its ridicule and scorn, indeed, what do I care about myself if only God may be honored. Give me the whole world—and I will instantly give it back again if God will allow me to do the least thing to his honor.

"You are raving." Oh, no, I certainly am not raving. Or is it then raving to add: If anyone can show that at this moment there is living in our country one other man, an author, who has as many qualifications for throwing light upon the cause of Christianity as I have, then I will at once subordinate all my work under him.—*Pap.* IX B 57 *n.d.*, 1848

From final copy of "Three Notes Concerning My Work as an Author"; *see 101:1–5:*

> Three [*deleted:* Friendly] "Notes" Concerning
> My Work as an Author.
> [*Deleted:* To the single individual.]
> By
> S. Kierkegaard.
> —*Pap.* IX B 58 *n.d.*, 1848

Addition to Pap. IX B 58:

To the typesetter

The *title page* is to be set as written. A blank page is to be placed *between each number.* [*Deleted:* The *preface* is to be set in the smallest possible brevier.] Each number should begin approximately in the middle of the page, not at the top. The *footnotes* are to be set in the smallest possible brevier.—*Pap.* IX B 59 *n.d.*, 1848

Addition to Pap. IX B 58:

30 copies on thin vellum.

> —*Pap.* IX B 60 *n.d.*, 1848

Deleted addition to Pap. IX B 58:

A smaller format, for example, like *Philosophical Fragments* but in smaller type.

> —*Pap.* IX B 61 *n.d.*, 1848

Addition to Pap. IX B 58:

N.B. A preface to this is in the little pack of loose sheets for "The Accounting" and "Three Notes."—*Pap.* IX B 62 *n.d.*, 1848

Deleted from final draft of "Three Notes"; *see 101:1–5:*

Three "Notes" Concerning
My Work as an Author

Supplement

by
S. Kierkegaard.

—*Pap.* IX B 63:1 *n.d.*, 1848

Deleted from final draft of "Three Notes"; *see 101:1–5:*

To the typesetter
The book is to be set in larger print, with a blank page between each number.—*Pap.* IX B 63:2 *n.d.*, 1848

From final draft of "Three Notes"; *see 101:5:*

Contents
No. 1. For the Dedication to "That Single Individual."
No. 2. A Word about the Relation of My Work as an Author to "That Single Individual."
No. 3. Preface to "Friday Discourses."[176]

—*Pap.* IX B 63:3 *n.d.*, 1848

From draft of Point of View; *see 101:1–5:*

Note no. 3 has been used;[177] so it will be only
"Two Notes"
Perhaps the title of the book could be:
"The Single Individual."
Two Notes Concerning My Work as an Author.

—*Pap.* X⁵ B 187 *n.d.*, 1851

From draft of Point of View; *see 100:*

> For
>
> Three Notes.
>
> If it is found used here as an epigraph:
>> *Wer glaubet, der ist gross und reich*[178]
>> etc.
>
> it should be deleted here, since it will be used in "The Accounting."[179]
>
> —*Pap.* X⁵ B 170 *n.d.*, 1849

Deleted from final draft of "Three Notes"; *see 111:33:*

> . . . I for my part, with regard to every single human being who lives in this country with me, unconditionally every single human being, if I could manage to do so, was [*changed from:* am] willing in God's name to humble myself, both orally and in writing, as deeply before him as possible and like a suppliant plead that he think about his relationship to God. To honor every single human being is to fear God, whereas on the other hand every assemblage consciously or unconsciously has a propensity to want to make itself God for the individual, so that one should fear it more than God. Therefore if it were an assemblage of ten thousand with a claim to be the authority with regard to *the truth*, and if it were a public of hundreds of thousands with a claim to be the authority with regard to *the truth*—I would pray [*changed from:* pray] to God (and if I prayed rightly, he would do it) to give me, the weakest of all, the vigor to express [*deleted:* all my disgust] that "the crowd" as an authority is untruth. . . .—*Pap.* IX B 63:4 *n.d.*, 1848

IX
B 63:4
355

IX
B 63:4
356

From draft of "Three Notes"; *See 113:1:*

> A Word on the Relation of My Work as an Author
>> To That Single Individual
>>> used for Note no. 2 in Three Notes.
>>> The conclusion of the piece[180] is no doubt also found in one of the journals

[see Supplement, pp. 154–56 (*Pap.* VIII¹ A 482); *Pap.* VIII² B 195] from '47, or one earlier, because it is not later.

—*Pap.* VIII² B 190 *n.d.*, 1848

From draft of Point of View; *see 115:4–29:*

This is how it is used. The subject of the single individual appears in every book by the pseudonymous writers, but the price put upon being a single individual, a single individual in the eminent sense, rises. The subject of the single individual appears in every one of my upbuilding books, but there the single individual is what every human being is. This is precisely the dialectic of "the single individual" [*changed from:* the particular]. The single individual can mean the most unique of all, and it can mean everyone. Now if one desires to stimulate attention, one will use this category in rapid succession but always in a double-stroke. The pride in the one thought incites a few, the humility in the other thought repels others, but the confusion in this doubleness provokes attention, and yet this is the idea of "the single individual." The pride in the one thought eggs on a few who in that sense of the word could very well desire to be the single individual of the pseudonyms. But then they are repelled in turn by the thought of "the single individual" in the sense of the upbuilding.*

In margin: *That is, the point of departure of the pseudonymous writers is continually in the differences—the point of departure in the upbuilding discourses is in the universally human.

—*Pap.* VIII² B 192 *n.d.*, 1847–48

From draft of "Three Notes"; *see 119:26–120:10:*

IX
B 64
377

[*Essentially the same as 119:15–25*]: that it **was an age of disintegration**. That it was an age of disintegration, an esthetic, enervating disintegration, and therefore, before there could be any question even of merely introducing the religious, the ethically strengthening Either/Or had to precede. That it was an age of disintegration, that "the system" itself (according to which this author pushes forward in historical sequence), like overripe fruit, was a sign of downfall and did not, as the systematicians self-complacently interpreted it, signify that completion was now attained. That it was an age of disintegration and therefore not, as the politicians thought, that "government" was the evil,* which would have been a curious self-contradiction for the viewpoint "the single individual," but that the crowd, the public, was the evil, which coincides with the viewpoint, the single individual. That it was an age of disintegration, that it was not nationalities that should be advanced but Christianity, and a Christianity relating to the single individual, that no particular class could be the stake but "the crowd," and that the task was to make it into individuals. That it was an age of disintegration, a critical time, that history was about to make a turn, that it was a matter of having heard right, of being in propitious rapport with the age and the turn that should be made—that it was the ethical that should be advanced, but above all that the ethical should not again be systematically muddled up or conglomerated with the old order, consequently that it was not simply a question of teaching the ethical objectively but of accentuating the ethical, of ethically putting into action the qualitative force of the ethical, "the single individual," and of supporting it fairly well by personal existing (again in qualitative contrast to system, didacticizing instruction, and everything related to them), yet consistently to continue for the time being to hide in the careful incognito of a *flâneur* [idler]. This puts the writings over into another sphere, since "that single individual" will become a historical point of view.

This is why I do not call myself a *truth-witness*. By such a term I do not actually understand everyone who says something true. Thank you, no; then we would have truth-witnesses enough. No, in a truth-witness the personal existing must be seen in relation to what was said. The word "witness" refers to the personal life—a consideration that, it is entirely right to say, the systematizing and the didacticizing and the characterlessness of the age

IX
B 64
378

---

*Note. And now in '48 this certainly is well understood.

have abolished completely. My life has indeed accurately expressed the ethical, what was ethically accentuated: to be the single individual; I have associated with countless people, but I have always stood alone, unconditionally alone. For the sake of this, my category, I have also ventured in various ways, made more than one sacrifice, exposed myself to one and another danger—and, note well, to precisely the kind of danger that categorically corresponds to *the single individual*—exposed myself to the "crowd," "the public," to blather and laughter. But even if there was no other hindrance, I have had independent means. That alone is enough; therefore I do not call myself a truth-witness; this is a preferential position that places me down in a lower class. But in addition I have also had too much imagination and much too much of a poet to dare to be called a truth-witness in the strict sense. I have been far from having an overview of everything from the beginning but have been aided both by a fortunate immediacy and by Governance, which on more than one point have helped me immediately to apprehend correctly. Thus the writings have also been my own development, and I have successively become aware of having apprehended correctly. I have had too much to do with the ethical to be a poet, but I am too much of a poet to be a truth-witness; I am a *confinium* [border territory] in between. I am, to allude to the highest, neither the one awaited nor the forerunner of the one awaited, but a prescient figure who with categorical exactitude has been related to the future of history, to the turn that should be made and that will become the future of history. It will go with me as with all such figures—the very thing for which my contemporaries rejected me and were angry with me, precisely that, literally the same, will become my eulogy in the future: he is eccentric, refractory, and proud; he will not reduce the price, will not yield. —This was the charge, and the eulogy will read literally the same: he would not scale down, he would not yield. Consistency of character always affronts the egotism of contemporaries, who, opposing such a person, do not think of becoming informed about him but only want to have power over him. The future, which is interested only in the idea and not in the personal, will find no affront in the fact that there lived a thinker who was consistent;

IX
B 64
379

on the contrary, the future will regard this as magnificent, although, of course, in its own capacity of the contemporary public it will behave like every contemporary public.—*Pap.* IX B 64 *n.d.*, 1848

Addition to Pap. IX B 64:

That it is an age of disintegration—a dizziness occasioned by and in a mounting fever fomented by continually wanting, with finite sagacity and operating with the numerical, to aid the moment by means of the momentary, and with the impatience of the moment to demand to see the result in that very moment—a condition that only leads, if possible, to making it dreadfully manifest that what is needed is the very opposite: the eternal and the single individual.—*Pap.* IX B 65 *n.d.*, 1848

From draft of "Three Notes"; *see 119:26:*

In Three Notes
Note no. 2, the passage: That it was an age of disintegration; an esthetic disintegration[181]—the following lines are to be deleted and the passage will read:
> an esthetic disintegration, that before the decisively religious is introduced a beginning must be made *maieutically* with esthetic works, yet ethically oriented: Either/ Or.
> —*Pap.* X⁵ B 173 *n.d.*, 1849

Sharpened
A Double-Edged Weapon

In times of tranquillity, the category "the single individual" is the category of awakening; when everything is tranquillity, security, and indolence—and the ideal has vanished—then the single individual is the awakening. In times of commotion, when everything is tottering, the single individual is the category of composure. The person who knows how to use this category will appear quite different in times of tranquillity than in times of commotion, and yet he will be using the same weapon. The difference is the same as that between using a sharp and pointed instrument to wound and using it to clean out a wound. But never will this category, "the single individual," rightly applied, cause damage to the established order. Used in a time of tranquillity, its purpose will be to awaken inwardness to heightened life in the established order without changing anything in externals. In times of commotion, its purpose will be to support the established order more directly by leading the single individual to be indifferent to external change and thus to support the established order. Earthly reward, power, honor, and the like can never be involved in the proper application, because what is rewarded in the world is, of course, only changes and working for changes in externals—inwardness does not interest the world.—*JP* II 2014 (*Pap.* IX B 66) *n.d.*, 1848

Deleted from draft of "Three Notes"; *see 123:7:*

. . . *Note.* The most zealous defenders of Christianity betray it, of course without noticing it themselves, perhaps do more harm to it than all the attackers, because these defenders have missed the point, are not dialectically attentive, do not see that the only thing that is needed (neither a new religion nor the abolition of Christianity) is simply and solely what I would call a new theological science of arms . . .—*Pap.* VIII^2 B 195 *n.d.*, 1847–48

From draft of "Three Notes"; *see 124:9:*

IX
B 63:13
372

[*In margin:* for p. 298 (*Pap.* IX B 63:6 *end*).]

Only *the martyr*, this *martyr of the future* (*the missionary*), who uses the category *the single individual* educationally, will by all means have within himself what is appropriate to the age ("the age of reflection")—a superior reflection and, in addition to the faith and the courage to risk, will need the work or the preliminary work of infinite reflection in *becoming* or in order to *become* a martyr. [*Deleted:* In this he will be different from any previous martyr (of immediacy), who required only the faith and courage to risk his life.] Differing from all previous martyrs, the martyr of the future will possess a superior reflection as a servant to determine freely (of course unconditionally obedient to God, yet freely) what kind of mistreatment and persecution he will suffer, whether he will fall or not, and if he will fall, the place where he will fall, so that he succeeds, dialectically, in falling at the right place so that his death wounds the survivors in the right spot. It will not be "the others," as it was previously, who assault the martyr, who only has to suffer—no, *the martyr* will be the self-determiner of the suffering. Just as in a parade the provost marshal gives the orders and marches with his staff at the head of the procession, just as the forestry expert goes ahead when trees are to be cut and points: "Cut there, and there, so and so much"—so this martyr of the future will himself be the one who goes ahead of his persecutors and—knowing the specific sickness of the particular age, knowing how it is to be healed, together with the kind of suffering to which he will have to expose himself—arranges everything himself with the cunning of a superior reflection. He will be just like that hero who himself gave the firing orders [*deleted:* to the soldiers] at his own execution. Actually, the persecutors only obey his orders, but the real truth of the matter is hidden from their eyes. Sick as they are, they do what they do according to their sickness. —Whole volumes could be written about this alone.

IX
B 63:13
373

The first form of rulers in the world was *the tyrants*; the last will be *the martyrs*. In the development of the world this is the movement [*deleted:* from worldliness to religiosity] [*in margin:* toward a growing worldliness, since worldliness is greatest, must have achieved a frightful upper hand, when only the martyrs are able to be rulers. When one person is the tyrant, the mass is not completely secularized, but when "the mass" wants to be the tyrant, then worldliness is completely universal, and then only the martyr can be the ruler]. No doubt there is an infinite difference between a tyrant and a martyr; yet they have one thing in common: the power to constrain. The tyrant, with a craving for power, constrains by force; the martyr, personally unconditionally obedient to God, constrains by his own sufferings. Then the tyrant dies, and his rule is over; the martyr dies, and his rule begins. The tyrant was the egotistic individual who inhumanly ruled over the masses, made the others into a mass and ruled over the mass. The martyr is the suffering single individual who in his love of mankind educates others in Christianity, converting the mass into single individuals—and there is joy in heaven for every single individual he thus rescues from [*deleted:* what even the apostle calls the "animal-category"]: the mass. —Whole volumes could be written about this alone, even by me, a kind of poet and philosopher, to say nothing of the one who is coming, the philosopher-poet or the poet-philosopher, who, in addition, will have seen close at hand the object of my presentiments at a distance, will have seen accomplished what I only dimly imagine will be carried out sometime in a distant future.

There are *really* only two sides to choose between—Either/ Or. Well, of course, there are many parties in the busyness of the world [*in margin:* —but it is not really, it is only *figuratively* that there is any question of "choosing" here, since what is chosen makes no difference and is equally wrong]. [*Deleted:* In the busyness of the world there are many parties; there are the liberals and the conservatives etc.—and all the strangest combinations, such as the rational liberals and rational conservatives. Once there were four parties in England, a large country; this was supposedly also the case in smaller Odense. But] In the profoundest sense there really are only two parties to choose between—and here lies the category "the single individual": *either* in obedience to God, fearing and loving him, to take the side of God against men so that one loves men in God—*or* to take the side of men against God, so that by distortion one humanizes God and does not "sense what is God's and what is man's" (Matthew 16:23). There is a struggle going on between man and God, a struggle unto life and death—was not the God-man put to death! —About these things alone: about what constitutes earnestness and about "the single individual," about what constitutes the daimonic, whether the daimonic is the evil or the good, about silence as a factor contributing to evil and silence as a factor contributing to good, about "deceiving into the truth," about indirect communication, to what extent this is treason against what it is to be human, an impertinence toward God, about what one learns concerning the daimonic by considering the God-man—about these things

IX
B 63:13
374

alone whole volumes could be written, even by me, a kind of philosopher, to say nothing of him who is coming, "the philosopher" who will have seen "the missionary to Christendom" and at first hand will know about all this of which I have only gradually learned to understand at least a little.—*JP* III 2649 (*Pap.* IX B 63:13) *n.d.*, 1848

From final draft of For Self-Examination:

Preface.[182]

X⁶
B 4:3
14

My dear reader, read aloud if possible. If you do so, allow me to thank you for it; if you not only do it yourself, if you influence others to do it, allow me to thank each one of them, and you again and again!

August [*changed from:* June] 1851
[*Deleted: Preface.*

What I have understood as the task of the authorship has been done.

It is one idea, this continuity from *Either/Or* to Anti-Climacus, the idea of religiousness in reflection.

X⁶
B 4:3
15

The task has occupied me totally, for it has occupied me religiously; I have understood the completion of this authorship as my duty, as a responsibility resting upon me. Whether anyone has wanted to buy or to read has concerned me very little.

At times I have considered laying down my pen and, if anything should be done, to use my voice.

Meanwhile, I came by way of further reflection to the realization that it perhaps is more appropriate for me to make at least an attempt once again to use my pen but in a different way, as I would use my voice, consequently in direct address to my contemporaries, winning people, if possible.

The first condition for winning people is that the communication reaches them. Therefore I must naturally want this little book to come to the knowledge of as many as possible.

If anyone out of interest for the cause—I repeat, out of interest for the cause—wants to work for its dissemination, this is fine with me. It would be still better if he would contribute to its well-comprehended dissemination.*

A request, an urgent request to the reader: I beg you to read aloud, if possible; I will thank everyone who does so; and I will thank again and again everyone who in addition to doing it himself influences others to do it.

Just one thing more. *I hardly need say that by wanting to win people it is not my intention to form a party, to create secular, sensate togetherness; no, my wish is only to win people, if possible all people (each individual), for Christianity.]

June 1851 S. K.

—*JP* VI 6770 (*Pap.* X⁶ B 4:3)

See 12:26–30:

X⁴
A 85
52

For "The Accounting." Something, however, that is not to be included.

[*Deleted:* Concerning Myself.]

Inasmuch as before God I regard my entire work as an author as my own upbringing or education, I could say: But I have remained silent so long lest, in relation to what I understand before God to be my own education, by speaking prematurely I become guilty of talking out of school. This could then be added to the passage in the final draft of "The Accounting": Before God I call this my upbringing or education etc.[183]

I would have liked very much to use this very expression; lyrically, it would have gratified me to use this expression. But there is something else that holds me back. As is frequently the case, the most humble expression seen from another angle is the very one that is apt to say too much, and so it is here. Precisely this humble expression would accentuate the fact that it is my upbringing, almost in the sense of my being an authority. It is simpler as it stands in "The Accounting," with the addition that I need further upbringing, and the tone is such that it can be said of every human being.—*JP* VI 6737 (*Pap.* X⁴ A 85) *n.d.*, 1851

X⁴
A 85
53

X⁴
A 351
203

About Myself

Now they are printed.[184] Oh, I feel inexplicably, unspeakably happy and calm and confident and overwhelmed.

X⁴
A 351
204

Infinite Love! I have suffered much during the past days, very much, but then it comes again. Once again an understanding of my task is clear to me but with greater vividness, and even though I have blundered seventeen times—nevertheless an infinite love in its grace has made it all completely right.

Infinite Love! It is blessed to give thanks, but a person perhaps never feels his wretchedness and sin more than when he is overwhelmed in this way, just as Peter said: Depart from me, for I am a sinful man[185]—on the very occasion of the great catch of fish.—*JP* VI 6772 (*Pap.* X^4 A 351) *n.d.*, 1851

Conversation with Mynster[186]

X^4
A 373
220

August 9, 1851

As I entered I said, "Welcome home from your visitation; I dare say Your Reverence has already visited me as well through the two little books[187] I sent you." He had read only the one (and, to be honest, for a moment I thought how strange if it had been the two discourses), but no, sure enough, he had read the book on my work as an author. "Yes, it is a clue to the whole," he said, "but spun later, but, after all, you do not say more than that yourself." I answered that the point to bear in mind was this, to have been so devoted, over many years and in much writing, to one thing, that my pen had not made one single deviation. To which he said he thought the little review of *Two Ages*[188] was an exception. I did not say any more to this, for it is in fact discussed in the little book about my work as an author, but I did make the remark that this review is essentially part of the whole authorship and that I attributed it to another because there were certain things I wanted to have said and at the time felt unable to say them as well myself. —I got the impression from Mynster that basically he was impressed by the little book and therefore he was not saying much.

X^4
A 373
221

We went on talking. He was in agreement with me, and what I said about the government[189] was fully his opinion. We spoke a little about that. I said it was not so pleasant to have to say such things and therefore no one was willing to do it, but they had to be said, and so I had done it.

He was pleased and gratified and agreed with me.

Then I told him that I really was happy to talk with him today because today was the anniversary of my father's death[190] and I wanted everything to be as it should be on this day.

Then a few words were dropped about the pastoral seminary,[191] but he avoided the subject and thought it was best for me to begin at once to establish a pastoral seminary myself.

The conversation was very friendly and not without emotion. Then I once again said a word disapproving of what he said about Goldschmidt[192] in his latest book,[193] something I felt I had to say, especially when I expressed such high regard for him.

Then we parted with his customary "Good-bye, my dear friend."—*JP* VI 6777 (*Pap.* X ^{4} A 373) August 9, 1851

X⁴
A 383
230

"On My Work as an Author"
The Significance of This Little Book

The state of "Christendom" is as follows: the point of view of Christianity and of what Christianity is has been completely shifted, has been cast in terms of the objective, the scholarly, and differences such as genius and talent have been made crucial.

This little book reverses the whole thing. It says (precisely because this enormous productivity preceded it): Forget genius, talent, scholarship, and all that—Christianity is the existential, a character-task. And now it is turned that way.

For that reason this little book is not a literary work, a new literary work, but an act, and therefore it was important that it be as short as possible, that it not mark a new productivity that people could then discuss. This little book is μετάβασις εἰς ἄλλο γένος [a shifting from one genus to another] and makes clear the extent to which it was already present in my total work as an author.

Even if I had fathomed or surveyed in advance my total work as an author down to the smallest detail, what I say in this book about my authorship never could have been said at the beginning, because it would have shifted the point of view, and the interest of the reading world would have shifted to curiosity as to whether I actually took the direction and fulfilled what I predicted.

No, it has to come at the conclusion, in order with one single stroke to do what the sailor calls tacking, the turn.

The little book is not a literary work but an act. It is an intensive act that will not readily be understood, no more than the action I took in the past against *The Corsair.*[194] It may even be found that I have made too little of myself, I who could preen myself on being a genius, a man of talent—and instead I say it is "my own personal development and upbringing." But precisely this is the turn in the direction of Christianity and in the direction of "personality."

Consequently, here is a single individual who relates to Christianity and not in such a way that he is now going to proceed to be a genius and a man of talent and to achieve something—no, just the reverse.

Here the listed price of Christianity is so low, so lenient, that it is terrible—but nevertheless it is an authentic relationship to Christianity; here there is no trick, no illusion. The Mynsterian approach[195] is *in toto* illusion and, from a Christian point of view, is tenable only by means of what I propose: admissions. I resort to grace; it is not Christianity in the more rigorous sense—something Mynster is silent about and wants to have suppressed. In my approach, however, Christianity truly is turned as the unconditional, and the whole viewpoint is utterly different: that we come to admit that in the most rigorous sense we are not Christians. In short, the cast of the whole thing is as different as possible from the official delineation, and yet it is even milder. But what is there is truth; it is not appearance and illusion.

Without this little book the whole authorship would be changed into a new doctrine.—*JP* VI 6780 (*Pap.* X^4 A 383) *n.d.*, 1851

X^4
A 383
231

4651.

X^4
A 408
248

In *Flyve-Posten*[196] for September 16 or 17, someone using 4651 as his signature—no doubt to be striking—took it upon himself to orient (it is usually the passion of the disoriented whereby they are identified) my readers or even to warn them against being confused by my little book *On My Work as an Author.* The only thing I find meriting attention, and especially as the orientating factor, is the signature: 4651. It is striking, persuasive, and overpowering. If the dreadful thing happens (and how easy!) that

X^4
A 408
249

someone now comes along who signs himself 789,691, I will be shattered.—*JP* VI 6785 (*Pap.* X⁴ A 408) *n.d.*, 1851

From unpublished reply to [Ludvig Jacob Mendel Gude,]
Om Magister Kierkegaards Forfattervirksomhed. Iagttagelser
af en Landsbypræst *(Copenhagen: 1851):*

X⁶
B 145
202
. . . As is well-known, my authorship has two parts: one pseudonymous and the other signed. The pseudonymous writers are poetized personalities, poetically maintained so that everything they say is in character with their poetized individualities; sometimes I have carefully explained in a signed preface my own interpretation of what the pseudonym said. Anyone with just a fragment of common sense will perceive that it would be ludicrously confusing to attribute to me everything the poetized personalities say. Nevertheless, to be on the safe side, I have expressly urged once and for all that anyone who wants to quote something from the pseudonyms will not attribute the quotation to me (see my postscript to *Concluding Postscript*[197]). It is easy to see that anyone wanting to have a literary lark merely needs to take some quotations higgledy-piggledy from "The Seducer," then from Johannes Climacus, then from me, etc., print them together as if they were all my words, show how they contradict each other, and create a very chaotic impression, as if the author

X⁶
B 145
203
were a kind of lunatic. Hurrah! That can be done. In my opinion anyone who exploits the poetic in me by quoting the writings in a confusing way is more or less either a charlatan or a literary toper.

The little book *On My Work as an Author* declares: "It must end with direct communication,"[198] that is, I began with pseudonymous writers representing the indirect communication I have not used over my signature. And somewhat earlier (in my preface to *Practice in Christianity*, whose author, the last pseudonymous writer, Anti-Climacus, again discourses on indirect communication) there is the statement: I understand the whole (whole book) as addressed to me so that I may learn to resort to *grace.*[199] Consequently, it ends with direct communication. . . .

—*JP* VI 6786 (*Pap.* X⁶ B 145) *n.d.*, 1851

Unrecognizability———Recognizability

Particularly toward the end of *A Literary Review* I said that none of the "unrecognizable ones" dares at any price to communicate directly or to become recognized[200]—and yet in *On My Work as an Author* I made myself responsible for the esthetic foreground of my authorship and said: "The whole thing is my own upbringing."[201] How is this to be understood?

In this way: assume that the illusion "Christendom" is truth, that it must be left standing: then unrecognizability is the maximum. If, however, the illusion must go, then it gets down to this: you actually are not Christians—then there must be recognizability. And here I have suggested the lowest: that it is I who am being brought up in Christianity.

If the illusion "Christendom" is truth, if the preaching prevalent in Christendom is as it should be, then we are all Christians and we can only speak of becoming more inward: then the maieutic and unrecognizability are the maximum.

But suppose now (something I was not aware of at first) that the preaching prevalent in Christendom leaves out something essential to the proclamation of Christianity—"imitation, dying away to the world, being born again, etc."—then we in Christendom are not Christians, and here the emphasis must be on recognizability. As stated, my place is on the lowest level of direct recognizability—namely, that the whole authorship is my own upbringing.

O my God, I am grateful—how clear you have made everything to me!—*JP* VI 6804 (*Pap.* X⁴ A 558) *n.d.*, 1852

Yes, "Either/Or"—that is where the battle is, and therefore my first words are: Either/Or. And that which is in *Either/Or* I can say of myself: I am an enigmatical being on whose brow stands Either/Or.[202]

But how this is to be understood could not be seen at once; much had to be arranged first. For this an entire productivity *uno tenore* [without interruption], an entire productivity nevertheless related to a repetition [*Gjentagelse*]: all must be taken up again. Therefore the work was under so much pressure, was so

X⁴
A 558
377

X⁴
A 558
378

Xⁿ
B 236
395

Xⁿ
B 236
396

hasty—which local sagacity regarded as very foolish—because all pointed to a repetition, as it therefore stands in the little book *Repetition*: Repetition is the category about which it will revolve.[203]

But not only did very much have to be arranged before Either/Or was really applied, but I also had to be *brought up*. This is why it says in the little book about my work as an author: The whole is my own upbringing.[204] And this is why the first words the Judge says to the Young Man are: When I see you veer etc., I think of an unbroken horse, but I also see the hand that holds the reins; I see harsh fates' lash raised over your head[205]—and this is why the last thing I have said is: There was a time when it pleased the Deity himself to be the coachman etc.[206]—*Pap.* X^6 B 236 *n.d.*, 1853

On folder with mss. of "Point of View" *and* "On My Work":

"On My Work as an Author"

N.B. see journal NB^{14} p. 10 and p. 41 [*Pap.* X^2 A 171–72, 192 (pp. 222–24, 229)].

N.B. The postscript [*Pap.* X^5 B 211 (p. 231)] to "Three Notes Concerning My Work as an Author" is essentially the same as the postscript [*Pap.* X^5 B 168 (pp. 290–94)] to "The Accounting"; thus if it is used in the one place, it cannot be used in the other.
—*Pap.* X^5 B 140 *n.d.*, 1849

From draft of Three Notes; *see 231:18–233:15:*

X^5
B 168
360

N.B. This postscript[207] is partly or essentially used in the postscript to "The Accounting" **and consequently cannot be used both places**.

Postscript to the Reader
To the typesetter:

To be set in smallest possible brevier.

My dear reader, I have wanted to and believed that I ought to say this to you, and at this very time when I am about to meet my

X^5
B 168
361

first work: the second edition of *Either/Or*, which I was unwilling to have published earlier. Direct communication, that is, by me personally *concerning* and *about* my authorship, its comprehensive plan, its objective, the placing of each individual work in the whole, and every individual part in each individual work, etc., is in a way, even where it is not a plain impossibility, against my nature, my personality—and against my work as an author, all of which is dialectics from first to last, and all of which until now at least from one side, has hitherto considered itself to be religiously committed to silence. Lest [*changed from:* God forbid, therefore, or if it should happen, may he then forgive me if] these few direct words about myself personally and about my authorship might in any way be a breach of, a weakness in relation to, what I myself have hitherto understood, namely, that I was committed to silence concerning myself personally and concerning direct communication about my authorship. If in this regard everything is in order and proper, even the little I have here communicated directly, and to you, I have not communicated, although from one side, without concern, without the concern that from this side unconditionally preoccupies me most—that I in some way might have said too much about myself and too little about Governance.

In one sense my explanation of my work as an author has a special coherence. My explaining is not like that of an author who says: This and this I have done—and then by inspecting the books is convinced that this is exactly what he has not done. No, what I explain is always something factual, is factual for the reader just as for me, is printed in the books, or if I consider the arrangement of the books, then this, too, is something factual, something anyone can verify whenever he wishes—in what order the books actually came out. Nor is my thought this, which is indeed only a simple and natural development, that in the process of working out something I gradually was better satisfied with my effort or what I want generally. This is the position taken by Johannes Climacus, who in a survey of the pseudonymous works together with my upbuilding discourses expressly states that he, who as reader kept abreast of the books, every time he had read such a published work, understood better what it was that he had wanted, he who from the beginning had himself wanted to carry out the very thing that was carried out in this

X⁵
B 168
362

authorship (see *Concluding Postscript,* p. 187 bot. [p. 251, *KW* XII.1; *SV* VII 212]). No, in my case what I myself have planned, carried out, and said—I myself sometimes understand only afterward how correct it was, that there was something far deeper in it than I thought at first—and yet I am the one who is the author. Here in my thoughts is an inexplicable something suggesting that I was, as it were, helped by someone else, that I have come to work out and say something whose deeper meaning I myself sometimes understand only afterward. This, in my view, is quite simply and God-fearingly the cooperation of Governance in such a way as everyone ought and should be able to speak of this. In other words, if the discussion of it is to be only scholarly and philosophical, it should be titled: The Relation between Immediacy and Reflection within Reflection, or The Process of Development That within Reflection Is the Transposing of Immediacy into Reflection, Here Reflected in the Work of an Author and in the Author's Corresponding Supporting Existence. The individuality in whom the same happens, if he has religiousness, and to the same degree as he has religiousness, must religiously, and to the same degree religiously attribute it to God, and all the more fervently and gratefully to the same degree as he perhaps otherwise feels unhappy and sad and, seen from another side, humble before God, feels not at all worthy or feels unworthy to have this happiness be granted to him in particular. But this can be *truly* said only in the silence of inwardness—that is, it cannot be communicated.

X⁵
B 168
363   If I myself religiously understand that I have been helped by another, what wonder, then, that I am uneasy about speaking *personally* about my work as an author and that I, when I have said only the very least thing in the first person, immediately have a great concern about having said too much about myself and too little about Governance! And, my dear reader, the difficulty involved here in speaking returns in another way: that when I personally, in the first person, make myself if possible into nothing, which in one sense I would like to do—and really let the pathos-filled emphasis of humility fall so that everything is due to Governance—then of course I run into another danger, which makes me shudder even more, that in someone's conception of me I

would be raised so high up into the extraordinary, as if in some way I had an immediate relationship with God, which, if possible, would be even more untrue and for me more appalling than if I were categorically to attribute unconditionally everything to myself, I who indeed am like an epitome of reflection.

It is difficult to speak personally here, to say in the first person what is developed there, what is in the books in their actual sequence to each other etc. This is something any third person can do without the slightest trouble at all, and what I myself as a third person can so very easily do, indeed have shown that I can do [*In margin: Note.* For example, Johannes Climacus's report on the pseudonymous writers (see *Concluding Postscript,* pp. 187–227 [pp. 251–300, *KW* XII.1; *SV* VII 212–57]) by me as third person by a third person]—since my case differs from that of most authors in that it is easiest for them to speak in the first person about their endeavor. For me it is very easy to talk about it in the third person. So it is difficult to speak, but being silent also has its difficulty. By unconditionally attributing everything to myself I can defraud Governance of what I religiously and personally must call its share. [*In margin: Note.* To give just one example of what I mean. It would be untrue if I were unconditionally to claim the whole authorship as *my intention* from the beginning, because it is also the possibility of my author-nature that has come into existence but it has not been conscious (*deleted:* from the very beginning). It would be untrue to say unconditionally that I used the esthetic productivity as maieutic from the very beginning, but for the reader the whole authorship actually will still be maieutic in relation to the religious, which in me was most basic.] But I can also defraud Governance by being silent, since in that case my reader would straightway be prompted to trace everything to me, as if I myself had envisioned everything this way from the beginning.

This is why I have chosen to say the little that I have said here. In my own innermost being on my own responsibility I understand everything easily—in my own innermost being, where before God I have my personal life, its cunning, its nevertheless God-fearing cunning in relation to my work as an author and its objective—in my own innermost being before God, where, as a

X⁵
B 168
364

beneficial tempering and correcting middle term in relation to whatever extraordinariness may possibly have been granted me, I have my personal life, its pain and sufferings, and above all its errors and sins and the consequences, its repentance and regret. But to speak about myself as someone who is dead, I cannot do or, rather, I cannot defend doing it as long as I am a living person.

Just one thing more: the little that is said in this little book about my work as an author is about the past, about what has been accomplished—something that obviously is implied in the subject itself, and something you yourself will surely become aware of during your reading, even just from the tenses that are used. With regard to the future—whether I will continue to be an author for a time, a longer or shorter time, and as before, or whether I will begin to be a different kind of author, or whether I will simply cease to be an author now—about that absolutely nothing is known, not even by me. I, who by nature am also a born dialectician and sheer reflection, have with much fear and trembling learned quite accurately, literally, and earnestly to understand that I cannot ever know whether the talents and qualifications I have possessed so far, the good fortune that has followed me so far, etc., whether all this may be taken from me in the next moment, perhaps before I have finished this sentence. Do not think that this is a depression of the kind that renders one unproductive. Under the weight of this mood—and perhaps it weighed upon me even more heavily then than it does now, since in the course of time I have become more practiced in it— I began as an author, and under the weight of this mood I have written—shall I now say the few pages I have written.

Copenhagen. Spring 1849.

S. K.

—*Pap.* X^5 B 168 *n.d.*, 1849

X^5
B 168
365

Armed Neutrality
or
My Position as a Christian Author
in Christendom

Appendix

to "The Point of View for My Work as an Author"

by

S. Kierkegaard.

SELECTED ENTRIES FROM
KIERKEGAARD'S JOURNALS AND PAPERS
PERTAINING TO
ARMED NEUTRALITY

See 129:1:

My position is armed neutrality.
—*JP* V 5341 (*Pap.* II A 770) *n.d.*, 1838

In margin: See this journal, p. 18
[*Pap.* IX A 171, 172 (pp. 222–24)].

IX
A 212
108

Surely it would be the right thing at some time to give my contemporaries a definite and nonreduplicated[208] idea of what I say I am, of what I want, etc. This was what I had in mind as the program of *Armed Neutrality*, a periodical. It was to come out simultaneously with the second edition of *Either/Or*. In it I would scrutinize Christianity piece by piece and get the coiled spring set in place.

From the very first I have dedicated myself to and belonged to the cause of Christianity. It will always be important to Christianity to have such a figure who logs the course to see where we are and whether the whole thing has not run aground in an illusion, one who presents Christianity quite uninhibitedly, yet without attacking Tom, Dick, or Harry, but leaving it up to each one to test himself.

IX
A 212
109

The trouble, however, is that by using direct communication I win people—and consequently weaken the truth. The confusion in Christendom is so great at this point (that is, Christianity has been abolished) that in order to open people's eyes it is necessary for one publicly to be put to death for the sake of the cause.

But as soon as I use direct communication my own circumstances will be eased, and, on the other hand, where will I find anyone to serve the truth in the most severe circumstances? I know of no one, literally no one. This is not arrogance, but it is an awkward matter for me; I am a penitent who in fear and trembling must be willing to humble myself under everything.

Oh, how easy it must be to place oneself at the head of a few people, and then thousands, and make a big noise—and then leave the truth in the lurch, although one fancies oneself to be serving it and is honored for doing so. My method is slower.

What makes it so difficult is the torment that my future may make it necessary for me to throw everything overboard in order to make a living. I can see my way out of all the other pressures—but to have this worry on top of everything else!

Yet it is good for me that I do nothing rash but really need God in every way.

The minute I use direct communication, the truth loses in intensity and I to some extent escape martyrdom: is this permissible, is this not deceiving God? If it is thinkable that after my death the indirect communication will give a quite different momentum to the truth I have had the honor to serve, is it not my duty to stand firm? On the other hand, may it not be pride and arrogance not to want to communicate directly? But is there not enough in what I have done to make any earnest person understand who is willing to understand? Yes, before God I dare to affirm this.

This is where the matter stands, now that I have been shaken a little by the thought that I would die very soon and that the crucial works will be published after my death.

In truth, I am heavily armed, but with all this I cannot thank God sufficiently for all the good he has done for me, so indescribably much more than I had expected.

Now under God I shall calmly do further work with the book about offense[209] that I am working on, in the confidence that God will give me a certain spirit. My personal life also requires its time—that in all this enormous work I do not forget the one thing needful—to sorrow over my own sins. This thought can clear the air immediately—and drive out all self-importance.

—*Pap.* IX A 212 *n.d.*, 1848

[margin: IX A 212 110]

"Armed Neutrality" can best be published as an appendix when the three works[210] are published as one ("Practice in Christianity, an Attempt"), but of course pseudonymously under the same pseudonym.

A pseudonym is excellent for accentuating a point, a stance, a position. It creates a poetical person. Therefore it is not as if I personally said: This is what I am fighting for—which indeed could become a duty for almost my entire life but which external conditions could make it impossible for me to fulfill, if, for example, I find it necessary to use most of my time to work for a living.—*JP* VI 6421 (*Pap.* X^1 A 450) *n.d.*, 1849

Armed Neutrality

See Journal NB^{11} [*Pap.* X^1 A 450^{211}] p. 157.

> If the three works[212] remain together under the title *Practice in Christianity, An Attempt*, this [*Armed Neutrality*] can follow as an appendix, but of course pseudonymously and under the same pseudonym [Anti-Climacus]; in any case it must be published pseudonymously.

Written at the end of '48 and the beginning of '49. If I remember rightly, this piece was written in '49 just after "From on High He Will Draw All to Himself."[213]—*Pap.* X^5 B 105 *n.d.*, 1849

From draft of Armed Neutrality; *see 129:1–4:*

Armed Neutrality
or
My Position as a Christian
Author in Christendom.
Appendix to "The Point of View for My Work as an Author"
by
S. Kierkegaard

Draft

—*Pap.* X^5 B 108 *n.d.*, 1849

X^5
B 108
301

X^5
B 108
302

From final draft of Armed Neutrality; *see 130:29:*

[*Deleted in margin:* It is said, for example, that to remain in worldly life is a higher form than to enter a monastery, but does it follow from this that everyone who remains in worldly life has made the monastic movement?]

[*Deleted in margin:* but if this dialectic is not true, what it amounts to is not a return to secular life but to outright worldly-mindedness; the dialectic is so far from being resolved that it has not even been started.]

[*Deleted in text:*] But through science and scholarship, the whole dialectical element in connection with being a Christian has confusingly been made into something annulled also in life, and thus being a Christian has been abolished. For example, the monastic movement (actual renunciation of the world) has thus been made a merely annulled movement; one lies in saying that everyone has done this in secret, in his inner being—and then one returns to worldliness.—*Pap.* X^5 B 109:2 *n.d.*, 1849

From final draft of Armed Neutrality:

?　　The title could be: Armed Neutrality, My Standpoint as the Editor of Some Pseudonymous Writings, of Which I Am the Stated Editor. (Then this pertains both to "The Sickness unto Death" and to Joh. Climacus.)
The work
"Armed Neutrality"
could perhaps be added to Anti-Climacus's "Practice in Christianity," but as an appendix by the editor, therefore by me.

Then it would have to be reworked. At the very beginning it would have to read:

Although I am only the editor of these writings, I perceive well enough that I do have a responsibility and that it is quite in order for me to give an account of my standpoint.

All the tenses would then have to be in the past, nothing about the future with regard to what I intend to do etc.—*Pap.* X^5 B 110 *n.d.*, 1849

EDITORIAL APPENDIX

ACKNOWLEDGMENTS

Preparation of manuscripts for *Kierkegaard's Writings* is supported by a genuinely enabling grant from the National Endowment for the Humanities. The grant includes gifts from the Danish Ministry of Cultural Affairs, the General Mills Foundation, Gilmore and Charlotte Schjeldahl, and the Vellux Foundation.

The translators-editors are indebted to Grethe Kjær and Julia Watkin for their knowledgeable observations on crucial concepts and terminology.

John Elrod, Per Lønning, and Sophia Scopetéa, members of the International Advisory Board for *Kierkegaard's Writings*, have given valuable criticism of the manuscript on the whole and in detail. Nathaniel Hong and Regine Prenzel-Guthrie, associate editors of *KW*, scrutinized the manuscript, and Nathaniel Hong prepared the index.

Acknowledgment is made to Gyldendals Forlag for permission to use the text and to absorb notes in *Søren Kierkegaards samlede Værker* and *Søren Kierkegaards Papirer*.

Inclusion in the Supplement of entries from *Søren Kierkegaard's Journals and Papers* is by arrangement with Indiana University Press.

The book collection and the microfilm collection of the Kierkegaard Library, St. Olaf College, have been used in preparation of the text, notes, Supplement, and Editorial Appendix. Gregor Malantschuk's marked set of *Kierkegaards samlede Værker* has been used in the preparation of the text and notes.

The original manuscript was typed by Cynthia Lund. Word processing and electronic preparation of the manuscript were done by Francesca Lane Rasmus and Nathaniel Hong. Gretchen Oberfranc was the compositor. The volume has been guided through the press by Marta Nussbaum Steele.

COLLATION OF *ON MY WORK AS AN AUTHOR*
IN THE DANISH EDITIONS OF
KIERKEGAARD'S COLLECTED WORKS

Vol. XIII Ed. 1 Pg.	Vol. XIII Ed. 2 Pg.	Vol. 18 Ed. 3 Pg.	Vol. XIII Ed. 1 Pg.	Vol. XIII Ed. 2 Pg.	Vol. 18 Ed. 3 Pg.
490	524	60	500	534	69
493	527	63	501	535	69
494	528	63	505	539	73
495	528	64	506	539	73
496	530	65	507	540	75
497	531	66	508	542	76
498	532	67	509	542	77
499	533	68			

COLLATION OF *THE POINT OF VIEW FOR MY WORK AS AN AUTHOR* IN THE DANISH EDITIONS OF KIERKEGAARD'S COLLECTED WORKS

Vol. XIII Ed. 1 Pg.	Vol. XIII Ed. 2 Pg.	Vol. 18 Ed. 3 Pg.	Vol. XIII Ed. 1 Pg.	Vol. XIII Ed. 2 Pg.	Vol. 18 Ed. 3 Pg.
514	548	80	547	585	110
517	551	81	548	586	111
518	551	81	549	587	112
519	553	82	550	588	113
520	554	83	551	589	114
521	555	85	552	590	115
522	556	85	553	591	116
523	557	86	554	593	117
524	558	87	555	594	118
525	559	88	556	595	119
526	561	89	557	597	120
527	562	90	558	597	120
528	563	91	559	598	121
529	564	93	560	599	122
530	564	93	561	600	123
531	565	94	562	601	124
532	567	95	563	603	125
533	568	96	564	603	126
534	569	97	565	605	127
535	570	98	566	606	128
536	571	99	567	607	129
537	573	100	568	608	130
538	574	101	569	609	131
539	575	102	570	611	132
540	576	103	571	611	133
541	577	104	572	613	134
542	578	105	573	614	135
543	580	106	574	615	136
544	581	107	575	616	137
545	582	108	576	617	138
546	584	109	577	618	138

Vol. XIII Ed. 1 Pg.	Vol. XIII Ed. 2 Pg.	Vol. 18 Ed. 3 Pg.	Vol. XIII Ed. 1 Pg.	Vol. XIII Ed. 2 Pg.	Vol. 18 Ed. 3 Pg.
578	619	139	599	642	158
579	620	140	600	642	158
580	621	141	601	644	159
581	622	142	602	645	160
582	623	143	603	646	161
589	631	149	604	647	162
590	631	150	605	648	163
591	633	151	606	649	164
592	633	151	607	650	164
593	634	152	608	651	165
594	635	153	609	652	166
595	637	154	610	653	167
596	638	155	611	654	168
597	639	156	612	655	168
598	640	157			

NOTES

ON MY WORK AS AN AUTHOR

TITLE PAGE, OVERLEAF, AND [PREFACE]

TITLE PAGE. With reference to the title page and pp. 1–20, see Supplement, pp. 234–37, 258, 254–56 (*Pap.* X⁵ B 143, 144, 145, 147, 252, 259, 207).

DEDICATION. See Supplement, pp. 256–58 (*Pap.* X⁵ B 261–64).

NOTE. See Supplement, p. 236 (*Pap.* X⁵ B 145).

EPIGRAPH. Gerhard Tersteegen, *Sprüche 50, Erbauliches und Beschauliches von Gerhard Tersteegen*, ed. A. Gebauer (Stuttgart: 1851), p. 97. See Supplement, p. 254 (*Pap.* X⁵ B 259).

PREFACE. See Supplement, pp. 254–56 (*Pap.* X⁵ B 207).

THE ACCOUNTING

1. With reference to the heading and the following four paragraphs, see Supplement, pp. 258–60 (*Pap.* X⁵ B 191).
2. For continuation of the text, see Supplement, pp. 260–61 (*Pap.* X⁵ B 228).
3. With reference to the following paragraph, see Supplement, p. 261 (*Pap.* X⁵ B 201).
4. The author of *The Sickness unto Death* (July 30, 1849) and *Practice in Christianity* (September 25, 1850). On the name, see, for example, Supplement, pp. 216–17 (*Pap.* X² A 147).
5. *Two Ethical-Religious Essays*, published May 19, 1849; in *Without Authority*, pp. 47–108, *KW* XVIII (*SV* XI 49–109).
6. Ibid., p. 94 (96), freely quoted.
7. Ibid., p. 84 (86).
8. See Supplement, p. 261 (*Pap.* X⁵ B 204).
9. Published May 14, 1849; in *Without Authority*, pp. 1–45 *KW* XVIII (*SV* XI 1–46).
10. Published May 14, 1849. See Supplement, p. 178 (*Pap.* X¹ A 79).
11. Published November 14, 1849; in *Without Authority*, pp. 109–44, *KW* XVIII (*SV* XI 245–80).
12. See *Eighteen Upbuilding Discourses;* pp. 5, 53, 107, 179, 231, 295, *KW* V (*SV* III 11, 271; IV 7, 73, 121; V 79). With reference to the footnote, see *Pap.* X⁵ B 219, 220.

13. Cf. "An Occasional Discourse," *Upbuilding Discourses in Various Spirits*, pp. 24–25, *KW* XV (*SV* VIII 134).

14. In the manner of a midwife, an allusion to the Socratic method. See, for example, Plato, *Theaetetus*, 150 b d; *Platonis quae exstant opera*, I-XI, ed. Friedrich Ast (Leipzig: 1819–32; *ASKB* 1144–54), II, pp. 26–29; *The Collected Dialogues of Plato*, ed. Edith Hamilton and Huntington Cairns (Princeton: Princeton University Press, 1963), p. 855 (Socrates speaking):

> My art of midwifery is in general like theirs; the only difference is that my patients are men, not women, and my concern is not with the body but with the soul that is in travail of birth. And the highest point of my art is the power to prove by every test whether the offspring of a young man's thought is a false phantom or instinct with life and truth. I am so far like the midwife that I cannot myself give birth to wisdom, and the common reproach is true, that, though I question others, I can myself bring nothing to light because there is no wisdom in me. The reason is this. Heaven [ὁ θεός, "the god" in *Theaetetus, The Dialogues of Plato*, I-II, tr. Benjamin Jowett (New York: Random House, 1937), II, p. 152] constrains me to serve as a midwife, but has debarred me from giving birth. So of myself I have no sort of wisdom, nor has any discovery ever been born to me as the child of my soul. Those who frequent my company at first appear, some of them, quite unintelligent, but, as we go further with our discussions, all who are favored by heaven make progress at a rate that seems surprising to others as well as to themselves, although it is clear that they have never learned anything from me. The many admirable truths they bring to birth have been discovered by themselves from within. But the delivery is heaven's work and mine.

15. *Concluding Unscientific Postscript to* Philosophical Fragments, see p. 59, *KW* XII.1 (*SV* VII 45).

16. Ibid., p. 617 (537).

17. *Upbuilding Discourses in Various Spirits* (March 13, 1847), *Works of Love* (September 29, 1847), *Christian Discourses* (April 26, 1848), *KW* XV, XVI, XVII (*SV* VIII 109–416, IX, X).

18. Inter et Inter, *The Crisis and a Crisis in the Life of an Actress*, in *Christian Discourses*, pp. 301–25, *KW* XVII (*SV* X 319–44).

19. *Two Upbuilding Discourses, Three Upbuilding Discourses, Four Upbuilding Discourses*, published in 1843, and three similar volumes with the same titles published in 1844.

20. *Two Upbuilding Discourses* (1843), in *Eighteen Discourses*, p. 5, *KW* V (*SV* III 11), freely quoted. See notes 12 and 19 above.

21. The manuscript of *Postscript* was delivered to the printer on December 30, 1845. After typesetting by hand and two sets of page proofs, copies were at the booksellers on February 28, 1846. See *JP* V 5871 (*Pap.* VII¹ A 2).

22. Frater Taciturnus, "The Activity of a Traveling Esthetician and How He Still Happened to Pay for the Dinner," *Fædrelandet*, 2078, December 27, 1845, col. 16653–58; *The Corsair Affair*, pp. 38–46, *KW* XIII (*SV* 422–31).

23. For deleted form of the note, see Supplement, p. 263 (*Pap.* X⁵ B 289:11).

24. *Two Ages: The Age of Revolution and the Present Age. A Literary Review* was published March 30, 1846. *KW* XIV (*SV* VIII 3–105).

25. See Supplement, p. 263 (*Pap.* X⁵ B 234).

26. See Supplement, p. 264 (*Pap.* X⁵ B 289:13).

27. See Supplement, pp. 265–66 (*Pap.* X⁵ B 208, 209).

28. See Supplement, p. 265 (*Pap.* X⁵ B 208).

29. For continuation of the text, see Supplement, pp. 264–65 (*Pap.* X⁵ B 247).

30. With reference to the following four paragraphs, see Supplement, pp. 231–32, 233, 290–94 (*Pap.* X⁵ B 211, 212, 222, 168).

31. See note 10 above.

32. With reference to the following paragraph, see Supplement, p. 266 (*Pap.* X⁵ B 258).

33. With reference to the following sentence, see Supplement, p. 284 (*Pap.* X⁴ A 85).

34. See Supplement, p. 267 (*Pap.* X⁵ B 289:21).

35. See Supplement, p. 267 (*Pap.* X⁵ B 271, 273).

36. With reference to the heading, see Supplement, pp. 267–68 (*Pap.* X⁵ B 272, 290).

37. See note 16 above.

38. *Practice in Christianity* (September 25, 1850), *KW* XX (*SV* XII i-239).

39. Ibid., pp. 7, 73, 149 (ix, 71, 139).

40. For continuation of the text, see Supplement, p. 268 (*Pap.* X⁵ B 291:17).

41. See *The* Corsair *Affair*, pp. vii-xxii, *KW* XIII.

42. For continuation of the paragraph, see Supplement, p. 268 (*Pap.* X⁵ B 293:19).

43. For continuation of the paragraph, see Supplement, pp. 268–69 (*Pap.* X⁵ B 291:41).

44. In the context of the old Slesvig-Holsten issue, Prince Frederick of Augustenburg put himself at the head of a provisional government proclaimed at Kiel in March 1848. A Danish army subdued the rebels as far as the Eider River. A new national assembly of Germany decided to incorporate Slesvig, and a Prussian army under Wrangel drove the Danes back. On August 26, 1848, an armistice was signed in Malmø and the government of the two duchies was entrusted to a commission composed of two Prussians, two Danes, and a fifth member by common consent of the four. War was renewed between March and July 1849. Germans in the duchies increased their army under General Willesen. The Danes trapped Willesen's army at Idsted on July 23, 1849, and a second armistice was signed between Prussia and Denmark. In July 1850 Prussia concluded a treaty with Denmark and gave up claim to the duchies. In London, May 8, 1852, the leading European powers signed a treaty concerning the succession after Frederik VII, and there was no further outbreak until his death in 1863. From 1848 on, the financial situation of the country was precarious and inflation rampant.

On March 21, 1848, as a result of earlier events, movements, and an enormous demonstration at Christiansborg, King Frederik VII (King Christian VIII had died January 28, 1848) agreed to the dissolution of the ministries. Thereupon the March government, the Moltke-Hvidt government, was formed and Frederik VII declared that he now regarded himself as a constitutional monarch.

45. See Supplement, p. 269 (*Pap.* X⁵ B 291:44).

46. With reference to the remainder of the sentence and the following two sentences, see Supplement, pp. 269–70 (*Pap.* X⁵ B 291:47).

47. See, for example, *Sickness unto Death*, p. 93, *KW* XIX (*SV* XI 204).

48. For continuation of the sentence, see Supplement, p. 270 (*Pap.* X⁵ B 287).

49. For continuation of the text, see Supplement, pp. 270–71 (*Pap.* X⁵ B 288).

THE POINT OF VIEW FOR MY WORK AS AN AUTHOR

OVERLEAF

EPIGRAPH. Shakespeare, *Henry the Fourth, Part II*, II, 2, ll. 195–96 (Prince Henry speaking); *Shakspeare's dramatische Werke*, I-XII, tr. August Wilhelm v. Schlegel and Ludwig Tieck (Berlin: 1839–41; *ASKB* 1883–88), II, p. 35; *The Complete Works of Shakespeare*, ed. George Lyman Kittredge (Boston: Ginn, 1936), p. 594: " . . . in everything the purpose must weigh with the folly."

EPIGRAPH. Hans Adolph Brorson, "*Op al den Ting*," st. 12, *Psalmer og aandelige Sange*, ed. Jens Albrecht Leonhard Holm (Copenhagen: 1838; *ASKB* 200), 81, p. 237.

CHR. KIERKEGAARD. Søren Kierkegaard's brother Bishop Peter Christian Kierkegaard arranged for the publication of *The Point of View* four years after the author's death.

INTRODUCTION

1. See Supplement, pp. 211–14 (*Pap.* X² a 104, 106).

2. See Supplement, p. 236 (*Pap.* X⁵ B 146).

3. See p. 12.

4. Ecclesiastes 3:7.

5. See Plato, *Apology*, 30 d–e; *Platonis quae exstant opera*, I-XI, ed. Friedrich Ast (Leipzig: 1819–32; *ASKB* 1144–54), VIII, pp. 130–31; *The Collected Dialogues of Plato*, ed. Edith Hamilton and Huntington Cairns (Princeton: Princeton University Press, 1963), pp. 16–17 (Socrates speaking):

For this reason, gentlemen, so far from pleading on my own behalf, as might be supposed, I am really pleading on yours, to save you from misusing the gift of God by condemning me. If you put me to death, you will not easily find anyone to take my place. It is literally true, even if it sounds rather comical, that God has specially appointed me to this city, as though it were a large thoroughbred horse which because of its great size is inclined to be lazy and needs the stimulation of some stinging fly. It seems to me that God has attached me to this city to perform the office of such a fly, and all day long I never cease to settle here, there, and everywhere, rousing, persuading, reproving every one of you.

6. See Xenophon, *Memorabilia*, IV, 8, 5; *Xenophontis opera, graece et latine*, I–IV, ed. Karl August Thieme (Leipzig: 1801–04; *ASKB* 1207–10), IV, pp. 264–65; *Xenophons Sokratiske Merkværdigheder*, tr. Jens Bloch (Copenhagen: 1802), p. 391; *Xenophon, Memorabilia and Oeconomicus*, tr. E. C. Marchant (Loeb, New York: Putnam, 1923), pp. 354–55.

7. See Matthew 16:26.

8. See Supplement, pp. 271–73 (*Pap.* IX B 57).

PART ONE

9. *Certain published works are not included. From the Papers of One Still Living* was a review, as was *Two Ages. The Concept of Irony* was an academic dissertation. Kierkegaard therefore considered *Either/Or* as the beginning of his authorship proper. *Point of View*, published posthumously, was written in 1848; therefore works published subsequently are not listed.

10. The second edition of *Either/Or* was published May 14, 1849.

11. *Two Upbuilding Discourses* (1843), *Three Upbuilding Discourses* (1843), *Four Upbuilding Discourses* (1843), *Two Upbuilding Discourses* (1844), *Three Upbuilding Discourses* (1844), and *Four Upbuilding Discourses* (1844). In 1845 the remaindered volumes were issued together under the title *Eighteen Upbuilding Discourses*.

12. Johannes Climacus, pseudonymous author of *Postscript*. See *Postscript*, pp. 251–300, *KW* XII.1 (*SV* VII 212–57).

13. See *Either/Or*, I, pp. 17–43, *KW* III (*SV* I 1–27).

14. Michael Pedersen Kierkegaard died August 9, 1838. See *Kierkegaard: Letters and Documents*, Letter 10, *KW* XXV; *JP* V 5335 (*Pap.* II A 243).

15. *Two Upbuilding Discourses* was published May 16, 1843, but the preface is dated May 5.

16. *Two Upbuilding Discourses* (1843), in *Eighteen Discourses*, p. 5, *KW* V (*SV* III 11).

17. *Two Upbuilding Discourses* (1844), in *Eighteen Discourses*, p. 179, *KW* V (*SV* IV 73).

18. *Two Upbuilding Discourses* (1843), in *Eighteen Discourses*, p. 5, *KW* V (*SV* III 11).

19. See Historical Introduction in *Eighteen Discourses*, pp. xviii–xx, *KW* V.

20. *Fear and Trembling*, by Johannes de Silentio, was published October 16, 1843.

21. Jakob Peter Mynster (Kts, a pseudonym formed from the initial conso-

nant of the second syllable in each name), "*Kirkelig Polemik*," *Intelligensblade*, IV, 41–42, 1844, pp. 105–06. On Mynster, see Supplement, p. 246 (*Pap.* X^3 A 249) and note 135.

PART TWO

22. The "Living Word" was Nicolai Frederik Severin Grundtvig's "matchless discovery." See, for example, *Postscript*, p. 36, *KW* XII.1 (*SV* VII 25), and note 44.

23. See p. 8 and note 16.

24. The number carried to the next column in arithmetic calculation.

25. *Mundus vult decipi ergo decipiatur* [the world wants to be deceived; so let it be deceived). Attributed to Pope Paul IV but found earlier in Sebastian Brandt, *Narrenschiff*. See Augustin Eugène Scribe, *Puf! eller Verden vil bedrages*, tr. Nicolai Christian Levin Abrahams, *Det Kongelige Theaters Repertoire* (1849). See also *JP* V 5937–38; VI 6680 (*Pap.* VII^1 A 147–48; X^3 A 450).

26. Part of "The Seducer's Diary."

27. See Romans 8:16.

28. Jens Finsteen Gi(j)ødwad (1811–91), journalist, editor of *Fædrelandet*, and the go-between for Kierkegaard with the printer and bookseller of the pseudonymous works.

29. The familiar second-person singular *du* has traditionally been used for children, family members, and close friends, rather than the formal *De*. The use of *De* has more or less disappeared in recent years.

30. *Either/Or*, II, p. 205, *KW* IV (*SV* II 184), freely quoted.

31. See p. 9 and note 21.

32. Christian Peter Bianco Luno (1795–1852), Copenhagen book printer, who printed most of Kierkegaard's works.

33. See p. 19 and note 44.

34. An allusion to *The Corsair*. See *The* Corsair *Affair*, pp. xvi-xvii, *KW* XIII.

35. Danish: *Sjouer* (day-laborer, street corner loafer, scoundrel), a term used here for an editor serving as a front for a publication in order to divert eventual legal action by the official censor, a tactic used also in *The Corsair*. See, for example, 128, March 3, 1843, col. 8.

36. Aristotle, *Rhetoric*, 1419 b; *Aristoteles graece*, I-II, ed. Immanuel Bekker (Berlin: 1831; *ASKB* 1074–75), II, p. 1419; *The Complete Works of Aristotle*, I-II, ed. Jonathan Barnes, (rev. Oxford tr., Princeton: Princeton University Press, 1984), II, p. 2268: "Irony better befits a gentleman than buffoonery; the ironical man jokes to amuse himself, the buffoon to amuse other people."

37. Meïr Goldschmidt, editor of *The Corsair*. See *JP* V 5888, 6044; VI 6282 (*Pap.* VII^1 A 99; VIII^1 A 252; IX A 432); See Historical Introduction, Corsair *Affair*, pp. vii, ix, *KW* XIII.

38. Cf. Isaiah 3:4.

39. See Historical Introduction, Corsair *Affair*, pp. xiv-xx, *KW* XIII.

40. See "The Activity of a Traveling Esthetician and How He Still Hap-

pened to Pay for the Dinner," *Fædrelandet,* 2078, December 27, 1845, col. 16658; Corsair *Affair,* p. 46, *KW* XIII (*SV* XIII 431).

41. "Victor Eremita will never die." *The Corsair,* 269, November 14, 1845, col. 14; see Corsair *Affair,* pp. 46, 96, *KW* XIII.

42. Kierkegaard's M. A. dissertation was *The Concept of Irony, with Continual Reference to Socrates, KW* II (*SV* XIII 93–393).

43. See Historical Introduction, Corsair *Affair,* pp. xxix–xxxiii, *KW* XIII.

44. Marcus Curtius. See Livy, *From the Founding of the City (History of Rome),* VII, 6; *T. Livii Patavini historiarum libri,* I-V, ed. August Wilhelm Ernesti (Leipzig: 1801–04; *ASKB* 1251–55), I, p. 410; *Livy,* I-XIV, tr. B. O. Foster (Loeb, Cambridge: Harvard University Press, 1967–76), III, p. 373:

> That same year, whether owing to an earthquake or to some other violent force, it is said that the ground gave way, at about the middle of the Forum, and, sinking to an immeasurable depth, left a prodigious chasm. This gulf could not be filled with the earth which everyone brought and cast into it, until admonished by the gods, they began to inquire what it was that constituted the chief strength of the Roman People; for this the soothsayers declared that they must offer up, as a sacrifice to that spot, if they wished the Roman Republic to endure. Thereupon Marcus Curtius, a young soldier of great prowess, rebuked them, so the story runs, for questioning whether any blessing were more Roman than arms and valour. A hush ensued, as he turned to the temples of the immortal gods which rise above the Forum, and to the Capitol, and stretching forth his hands, now to heaven, and now to the yawning chasm and to the gods below, devoted himself to death. After which, mounted on a horse caparisoned with all possible splendour, he plunged fully armed into the gulf; and crowds of men and women threw offerings and fruits in after him.

45. See p. 19 and note 44.

46. See Plato, *Phaedrus,* 230 c; *Platonis quae exstant opera,* I-XI, ed. Friedrich Ast (Leipzig: 1819–32; *ASKB* 1144–54), I, p. 152; *The Collected Dialogues of Plato,* ed. Edith Hamilton and Huntington Cairns (Princeton: Princeton University Press, 1963), p. 479.

47. *Christian Discourses,* which was delivered to the printer March 6, 1848, and was published April 26, 1848. See Supplement, p. 171 (*Pap.* IX A 375); *JP* VI 6376 (X¹ A 202).

48. The volume was published posthumously. See p. xxvii.

49. Cf. *Two Discourses at the Communion on Fridays,* in *Without Authority,* p. 165, *KW* XVIII (*SV* XII 267).

50. Shakespeare, *Richard III,* V, 4, 1. 7; *William Shakspeare's Dramatiske Værker,* I-XI, tr. Peter Foersom and P. F. Wulff (Copenhagen: 1845–50; *ASKB* U 103), VI, p. 378; Schlegel and Tieck, III, p. 372; Kittredge, p. 835.

51. Cf. *Fear and Trembling,* p. 61, *KW* VI (*SV* III 111).

52. See Adam Gottlob Oehlenschläger, *Aladdin, eller den forunderlige Lampe, Adam Oehlenschlägers Poetiske Skrifter,* I-II (Copenhagen: 1805; *ASKB* 1597–98),

II, pp. 121–22; *Aladdin or the Wonderful Lamp*, tr. Henry Meyer (Copenhagen: Gyldendal, 1968), pp. 48–49.

53. See I Samuel 15:22.

54. See II Corinthians 12:7

55. The reference is to the first Danish edition of *Postscript* (1846). See *Postscript*, pp. 252–53, *KW* XII.1 (*SV* VII 213).

56. See, for example, *Repetition*, p. 135, *KW* VI (*SV* III 176), *Stages on Life's Way*, pp. 456, 470, *KW* XI (*SV* VI 424, 437).

57. See "The Difference between a Genius and an Apostle," *Two Ethical Religious Essays*, in *Without Authority*, pp. 91–108, *KW* XVIII (*SV* XI 93–109).

58. Michael Pedersen Kierkegaard died August 9, 1838. See *Irony*, Historical Introduction, pp. ix-x, *KW* II.

59. Danish: *Faktum* [something done]. As is clear from the context, Kierkegaard has in mind here the Latin root *facere* [to act, do, make]. Cf. Supplement, p. 286 (*Pap.* X⁴ A 383).

60. On the writing and reception of *Either/Or*, see Historical Introduction, *Either/Or*, I, pp. vii-xi, xvi-xviii, *KW* III; *JP* V 5626, 5931 (*Pap.* IV A 70; VII¹ A 92).

61. See *Either/Or*, I, p. 14, *KW* III (*SV* I xvi); *Fear and Trembling*, p. 8, *KW* VI (*SV* III 59–60); *Stages*, p. 191, *KW* XI (*SV* VI 181); *Postscript*, pp. 5–6, 283, *KW* XII.1 (*SV* VII v-vi, 241).

62. See, for example, Supplement, pp. 162–63, 211–12 (*Pap.* IX A 213; X² A 104).

63. *Two Upbuilding Discourses* was published May 16, 1843, three months after *Either/Or*.

64. Cf. *Either/Or*, I, pp. 38–39, *KW* III (*SV* I 22–23).

65. See Corsair *Affair*, Historical Introduction, pp. xiii-xxii, *KW* XIII.

66. Peder Ludvig Møller (1814–1865), Danish writer and literary critic. See Corsair *Affair*, Historical Introduction, pp. x-xiii, *KW* XIII.

67. See p. 172 and note 22.

68. Cf. *JP* VI 6389, p. 146 (*Pap.* X¹ A 272), on *forlovet*.

69. With reference to "Conclusion," see Supplement, pp. 271–73 (*Pap.* IX B 57).

70. A play on *Kjøbstad* [market town] and *Kjøbenhavn* [market harbor].

71. See Ludvig Holberg, *Den politiske Kandestøber*, IV, 2; *Den Danske Skue-Plads*, I-VII (Copenhagen: 1788; *ASKB* 1566–67), I, no pagination; *Comedies by Holberg*, tr. Oscar James Campbell and Frederic Schenk (New York: American-Scandinavian Foundation, 1914), p. 85.

72. In its many caricatures of Kierkegaard, *The Corsair* repeatedly ridiculed his legs and trousers. See Corsair *Affair*, pp. 114–15, 120, 131, 133–35, 171, 186–88, 192–94, 197–99, 201, 222–24, 227, 241, *KW* XIII.

73. See *Upbuilding Discourses in Various Spirits*, p. 24, *KW* XV (*SV* VIII 133).

74. See Supplement, p. 167 (*Pap.* IX A 248).

75. With reference to the title page, see Supplement, pp. 273–74 (*Pap.* IX B

58–63:2; X⁵ B 187); to a contemplated epigraph, see Supplement, p. 275 (*Pap.* X⁵ B 170); and to the table of contents, see Supplement, p. 274 (*Pap.* IX B 63:3).

76. Socrates.

77. The text here and following is a play on the Danish *Lighed*, which means both "equality" and "similarity" or "likeness," and the suffix *-lighed*, which, as the English "-liness," means "like in appearance, manner, or nature."

78. With reference to "Note No. 1," see Supplement, pp. 151–53 (*Pap.* VII¹ A 176).

79. Cf. John 14:6.

80. Cf. 1 Corinthians 9:24; Philippians 3:14.

81. See Plutarch, "Caius Marius," 39, *Lives*; *Plutarchii vitae parallelae*, I-IX, ed. Gottfried Heinrich Schaeffer (Leipzig: 1829; *ASKB* 1829); *Plutarks Levnetsbeskrivelser*, I-IV, tr. Stephan Tetens (Copenhagen: 1800–11; *ASKB* 1197–1200), IV, pp. 318–19; *Plutarch's Lives*, I-XI, tr. Bernadotte Perrin (Loeb, Cambridge: Harvard University Press, 1968–84), IX, p. 573:

> Upon deliberation, the magistrates and councillors of Minturnae decided not to delay, but to put Marius to death. No one of the citizens, however, would undertake the task, so a horseman, either a Gaul or a Cimbrian (for the story is told both ways), took a sword and went into the room where Marius was. Now, that part of the room where Marius happened to be lying had not a very good light, but was gloomy, and we are told that to the soldier the eyes of Marius seemed to shoot out a strong flame, and that a loud voice issued from the shadows saying: "Man, dost thou dare to slay Caius Marius?" At once, then, the Barbarian fled from the room, threw his sword down on the ground, and dashed out of doors, with this one cry: "I cannot kill Caius Marius."

82. For continuation of the section, see Supplement, p. 275 (*Pap.* IX B 63:4).

83. With reference to the following article, see Supplement, pp. 154–56, 275–76 (*Pap.* VIII¹ A 482; VIII² B 190, 192).

84. See p. 172 and note 22.

85. See p. 66 and note 41.

86. With reference to the following paragraph, see Supplement, p. 276 (*Pap.* VIII² B 192).

87. With reference to the two following paragraphs, see Supplement, pp. 186–87 (*Pap.* X¹ A 152).

88. Mendel Levin Nathanson (1780–1868), editor of *Berlingske Tidende* (1838–58, 1865–66). See "*Om den norske Literatur*," *Berlingske Tidende*, 126, May 28, 1845; *Pap.* VI B 191; X² A 155.

89. Presumably a reference to P. L. Møller. "*Til Frater Taciturnus*," *Fædrelandet*, 2079, December 29, 1845, col. 16665: "You will hardly find any way of disarming the criticism other than—not to have your writings printed, whereby you will obtain what you seem to prize so highly, namely, to have only 'one reader.'" *Corsair Affair*, p. 104, *KW* XIII.

90. With reference to the following two paragraphs, see Supplement, pp. 154–56 (*Pap.* VIII[1] A 482).

91. For continuation of the paragraph and with reference to the following paragraph, see Supplement, pp. 276–79 (*Pap.* IX B 64, 65). See also Supplement, p. 279 (*Pap.* X[5] B 173).

92. *Two Ages*, pp. 60–112, *KW* XIV (*SV* VIII 57–105).

93. Gottfried Ephraim Lessing, *Emilia Galotti*, II, 4; *Gotthold Ephraim Lessing's sämmtliche Schriften*, I-XXXII (Berlin, Stettin: 1825–28; *ASKB* 1747–62), XXI, p. 216.

94. See Matthew 22:21.

95. *Either/Or*, I, pp. 19, 36, *KW* III (*SV* I 3, 20).

96. Ibid., II, p. 210, *KW* IV (*SV* II 188–89); *Postscript*, pp. 252–53, *KW* XII.1 (*SV* VII 213).

97. *Works of Love*, pp. 17–60, *KW* XVI (*SV* IX 21–62).

98. With reference to the following paragraph, see Supplement, pp. 279–80 (*Pap.* IX B 66).

99. See Supplement, p. 280 (*Pap.* VIII[2] B 195).

100. With reference to the following paragraph, see Supplement, pp. 275–76 (*Pap.* VIII[2] B 190).

101. See, for example, Plato, *Gorgias*, 474 a; *Opera*, I, pp. 326–27; *Udvalgte Dialoger af Platon*, I-VIII, tr. Carl Johan Heise (Copenhagen: 1830–59; *ASKB* 1164–66, 1169 [I-VII]), III, pp. 68–69; *Dialogues*, p. 256:

> SOCRATES: I am no politician, Polus, and last year when I became a member of the Council and my tribe was presiding and it was my duty to put the question to the vote, I raised a laugh because I did not know how to. And so do not on this occasion either bid me put the question to those present, but if you can contrive no better refutation than this, then leave it to me in my turn, as I suggested just now, and try out what I consider the proper form of refutation. For I know how to produce one witness to the truth of what I say, the man with whom I am debating, but the others I ignore. I know how to secure one man's vote, but with the many I will not even enter into discussion.

102. See Supplement, pp. 170, 280–83 (*Pap.* IX A 298, B 63:13).

103. With reference to the heading and following paragraphs, see Supplement, pp. 290–94, 231, 233 (*Pap.* X[5] B 140, 168, 211, 222). See also Supplement, p. 240 (*Pap.* X[5] B 164).

ARMED NEUTRALITY

1. The expression was used initially in international political life in 1780, when Denmark and Russia, and subsequently Sweden, entered into an agreement in Copenhagen for the defense of their rights against England in particular.

With reference to the title page, see Supplement, p. 301 (*Pap.* X⁵ B 108). See also Supplement, p. 299 (*Pap.* II A 770; with reference to the piece itself, see Supplement, pp. 209–300, 172–73, 174, 181, 194–96, 198–200 (*Pap.* IX A 212, 390; X¹ A 74, 97, 422, 510).

2. This theme is treated extensively in *Two Ages*, *KW* XIV (*SV* VIII 3–105).

3. See Supplement, p. 209 (*Pap.* X² A 80).

4. Elsewhere called "double danger." See, for example, *Works of Love*, pp. 192, 194–96, 204, *KW* XVI (*SV* IX 183, 185–86, 194).

5. For continuation of the paragraph, see Supplement, p. 302 (*Pap.* X⁵ B 109:2).

6. See Matthew 9:16; Mark 2:21.

7. See, for example, *Postscript*, pp. 561–86, *KW* XII.1 (*SV* VII 490–511).

8. Ibid., pp. 387–561 (335–490).

9. See, for example, *Works of Love*, pp. 182–191, *KW* XVI (*SV* IX 174–82).

10. See, for example, *Postscript*, pp. 170–71, 303–04, 332–33, *KW* XII.1 (*SV* VII 141, 260, 287). See also *JP* III 3665 (*Pap.* VIII¹ A 91).

11. See Diogenes Laertius, *Lives of Eminent Philosophers*, I, 12; *Diogenis Laertii de vitis philosophorum libri X*, I–II (Leipzig: 1833; *ASKB* 1109), I, p. 8; *Diogen Laërtses filosofiske Historie*, I–II, tr. Børge Riisbrigh (Copenhagen: 1812; *ASKB* 1110–11), I, p. 5; *Diogenes Laertius, Lives of Eminent Philosophers*, I–II, tr. R. D. Hicks (Loeb, Cambridge: Harvard University Press, 1980), I, p. 13: "But the first to use the term, and to call himself a philosopher or lover of wisdom was Pythagoras; for, said he, no man is wise, but God alone." See also Supplement, pp. 205–06, 245 (*Pap.* X¹ A 646; X³ A 204).

12. Michael Nielsen (1776–1846). Kierkegaard attended the secondary school for eight years. See *Kierkegaard: Letters and Documents*, Document VI, pp. 5–7, *KW* XXV.

13. "For use of the Dauphin," the eldest son of the French king. The phrase refers to expurgated editions of the Latin classics and, by extension, the use of a simple example.

14. Cf. Plato, *Phaedrus*, 229 d–230 a; *Platonis quae exstant opera*, I–XI, ed. Friedrich Ast (Leipzig: 1819–32; *ASKB* 1144–54), I, pp. 130–31; *The Collected Dialogues of Plato*, ed. Edith Hamilton and Huntington Cairns (Princeton: Princeton University Press, 1963), p. 478 (Socrates speaking):

> I can't as yet "know myself," as the inscription at Delphi enjoins, and so long as that ignorance remains it seems to me ridiculous to inquire into extraneous matters. Consequently I don't bother about such things, but accept the current beliefs about them, and direct my inquiries, as I have just said, rather to myself, to discover whether I really am a more complex creature and more puffed up with pride than Typhon, or a simpler, gentler being whom heaven has blessed with a quiet, un-Typhonic nature.

See also *Fragments*, p. 37, *KW* VII (*SV* IV 204); *Irony*, p. 177, *KW* II (*SV* XIII 260).

1. "An Occasional Discourse," Part One, *Upbuilding Discourses in Various Spirits*, p. 4, *KW* XV (*SV* VIII 116).

2. Plato, *Apology*, 18 c–d; *Platonis quae exstant opera*, I–XI, ed. Friedrich Ast (Leipzig: 1819–32; *ASKB* 1144–54), VIII, p. 104; *The Collected Dialogues of Plato*, ed. Edith Hamilton and Huntington Cairns (Princeton: Princeton University Press, 1963), p. 5.

3. This plan was not carried out.

4. This plan was not carried out.

5. Inter et Inter, *The Crisis and a Crisis in the Life of an Actress*, *Fædrelandet*, 188–91, June 24–27, 1848; in *Christian Discourses*, pp. 301–25, *KW* XVII (*SV* X 319–44).

6. See note 5 above.

7. Ibid.

8. For a time it seemed as if Rasmus Nielsen (1809–1884), professor of philosophy, University of Copenhagen, would be permitted to be a "follower" of Kierkegaard (see, for example, *Pap.* IX A 220 and X¹ A 406), but this incipient exceptional relationship was not continued. See, for example, *JP* VI 6239 (*Pap.* IX A 229); *Letters*, Letter 247, *KW* XXV.

9. *Upbuilding Discourses in Various Spirits* (March 13, 1847), *Works of Love* (September 29, 1847), and *Christian Discourses* (April 26, 1848).

10. See p. 7 and note 14.

11. See note 5 above.

12. See p. 97

13. See *Practice*, pp. 173–78, *KW* XX (*SV* XII 162–66).

14. See Supplement, pp. 271–73 (Pap. IX B 57). Eventually the Supplement to *Point of View* (pp. 101–26) contained two notes. Note no. 3 was used in the Preface to the *Two Discourses at the Communion on Fridays*, p. 165, *KW* XVIII (*SV* XII 267).

15. P. 75

16. Nytorv 2, Copenhagen. Kierkegaard inherited a substantial sum (with part of which he and brother Peter Christian bought the family house at the liquidation auction) from his father at the time of his death, August 9, 1838. During the next ten years, Kierkegaard lived fairly well on this money and paid full publication costs of his first nineteen books, only one of which sold out. F. Brandt and E. Rammel, in *Kierkegaard og Pengene*, p. 54 (Copenhagen: 1935), pointing out that Kierkegaard received a writer's honorarium from Reitzel after August 1847, reckon that Kierkegaard's total net proceeds from sales and honoraria were an average of 300 rix-dollars per year over seventeen years. This they calculate as equaling 1,500 Danish crowns in 1935, or approximately $300 annually, which in 1973 dollars would be roughly $1,500. In 1846 Kierkegaard entertained the idea of seeking a state grant, which was not uncommon as patronage of the arts and letters. He did not pursue this notion. In December 1847 the brothers sold the house (Nytorv 2), and Kierkegaard kept part of his share of the proceeds in government bonds that deteriorated badly in the war

period, put some into shares that were held through the bad times 1848–49, and kept some in cash, which also deteriorated because of rampant inflation. In the later years of his life, Kierkegaard became more stringent about his expenses. He divided what he had into units, which were placed in the custody of his brother-in-law Henrik Ferdinand Lund of the National Bank. Shortly before his death he drew out the last portion. See *JP* V 5881 (*Pap.* VII¹ B 211).

17. The corner of Rosenborggade and Tornebuskegade 156 (now 7), rented January 28, 1848, at 295 rix-dollars annually, later six rooms at 400.

18. *Christian Discourses* was published April 26, 1848.

19. The census report of February 1845 lists Anders Westergaard Christensen, servant, as living at Nytorv 2. Anders accompanied Søren Kierkegaard on the Jutland pilgrimage. In 1848 Anders was conscripted into the military. In September 1847 Kierkegaard wrote a letter of recommendation for him. See *Breve og Aktstykker vedrørende Søren Kierkegaard*, I-II, ed. Niels Thulstrup (Copenhagen: Munksgaard, 1954), II, p. 55 (tr. Bruce H. Kirmmse):

> The applicant has been in my service since May 1844. Since that time he has satisfied even my most fastidious demands so completely that I can truthfully and emphatically recommend him in every respect. Sober, moral, always mentally alert, unconditionally dependable, used to keeping quiet, not without a certain degree of intelligence, which enables one to allow him to take care of things a bit on his own: he has been so indispensable to me that I would truly be delighted to keep him in my service. To my way of thinking, that is the highest recommendation I could give anyone. If it is possible that any of these qualities, to which I have truthfully testified, could render him suited to the particular requirements of the position for which he has applied, and that these qualities could direct favorable attention to the applicant, and if my recommendation, which is admittedly from someone whom you do not know, could have any favorable influence on decisions regarding the applicant's future, this would be a source of genuine joy to me, because I feel myself highly obligated to recommend him in every way.

20. "The Sickness unto Death," "Practice in Christianity," "A Cycle of Ethical-Religious Essays," "Armed Neutrality," "The Point of View."

21. See note 8 above.

22. On December 22, 1845, P. L. Møller's *Gæa, Æsthetisk Aarbog* for 1846, was published. It contained a long piece by Møller titled "A Visit to Sorø," a large portion of which was a rather supercilious review of the pseudonymous works. Frater Taciturnus replied with "The Activity of a Traveling Esthetician and How He Still Happened to Pay for the Dinner" (Corsair *Affair, KW* XIII, pp. 38–46 [*SV* XIII 422–31]), *Fædrelandet*, 2078, December 27, 1845. The closing paragraph of the article in *Fædrelandet* constituted the opening of Kierkegaard's public attack on *The Corsair*, which carried on its political satire and destruction of personal reputations anonymously. The single Latin line, *ubi* P. L. Møller, *ibi Corsaren* [where P. L. Møller is, there is *The Corsair*], stated publicly what was known in literary circles and had already been published in Erslew's *Forfatter-Lexicon*, "Peder Ludwig Møller," II, p. 406 (Copenhagen:

1847, but published in sections from 1843)—that P. L. Møller was a writer for *The Corsair*. Møller left Denmark later in 1846 and never returned. The owner and editor, Meïr Goldschmidt, gave up *The Corsair* October 2, 1846, and traveled abroad for a year. In the meantime, *The Corsair* launched a continuing campaign of ridicule and personal attack upon Kierkegaard, which resulted in his being unable to remain the foremost peripatetic conversationalist of the Copenhagen streets. Although Kierkegaard felt this keenly, he had known the risks involved in taking on *The Corsair* single-handedly. The entire *Corsair* affair was a prolonged event consciously initiated by him, through writing as an ethical act, in order to precipitate the murkiness of anonymity and to diminish the power of journalistic intimidation, and also to separate Goldschmidt, in whom he saw real ability, from *The Corsair*. See Corsair *Affair*, *KW* XIII, passim.

23. The two subdivisions and the projected third part became the three parts of *Practice*.

24. Michael Pedersen Kierkegaard was fifty-seven when Søren was born.

25. The envisioned work "A Cycle of Ethical-Religious Essays" originally had the following parts (see *Pap.* IX B 1–6): Preface; no. 1, "Something on What Might Be Called 'Premise-Authors'"; no. 2, "The Dialectical Relations: The Universal, the Single Individual, the Special Individual"; no. 3, "Does a Human Being Have the Right to Let Himself Be Put to Death for the Truth?"; no. 4, "A Revelation in the Situation of the Present Age"; no. 5, "A Psychological Interpretation of Magister Adler as a Phenomenon and as a Satire upon Hegelian Philosophy and the Present Age"; and no. 6, "The Difference between a Genius and an Apostle." *Two Ethical-Religious Essays*, by H. H., published May 19, 1849, contains a preface and no. 3 and 6 of the above. "The Book on Adler," which remained in manuscript form, included a preface (Kierkegaard wrote eight different prefaces for it) and other parts listed above.

26. See note 16 above.

27. "Three [eventually Two] Notes" and "Armed Neutrality."

28. "Armed Neutrality," "The Point of View," "Practice in Christianity," and "A Cycle of Ethical-Religious Essays."

29. See note 25 above.

30. Ibid.

31. Ibid.

32. *The Lily in the Field and the Bird of the Air* and the second edition of *Either/Or* were published May 14, 1849. See *Letters*, Letters 154–57, *KW* XXV.

33. In addition to the two "notes" in *Point of View*, pp. 101–26, *KW* XXII (*SV* XIII 591–610), the projected "Three 'Notes' Concerning My Work as an Author" included what became the preface to the two "Friday Discourses." See preface to *Two Discourses at the Communion on Fridays*, in *Without Authority*, p. 165, *KW* XVIII (*SV* XII 267).

34. See note 18 above.

35. Essay no. III in "A Cycle" and essay no. I in *Two Essays*, "Does a Human Being Have the Right to Let Himself Be Put to Death for the Truth?"

36. The "Three 'Notes' Concerning My Work as an Author" intended to be

the Supplement to "The Point of View" were: (1) "For the Dedication to 'that Single Individual,'" (2) "A Word on the Relation of My Work as an Author to 'The Single Individual,'" and (3) "Preface to the 'Friday Discourses.'" Eventually no. 3 was omitted. A shortened version of no. 3 was used as the preface to *Two Discourses at the Communion on Fridays* (1851).

37. This term, seemingly inconsistent here, is a sample of Kierkegaard's penchant for using words in their elemental meaning. The Danish words for "art" and "artistic" are *Kunst* and *kunsterisk*, derived from the root *kunne*, "to be able" (see *Pap.* V B 53:29, p. 120; VIII² B 83; *Postscript*, pp. 349–60, *KW* XII.1 [*SV* VII 303–12]). In this elemental sense, the art is to live, the existential thinker's life is a being-able, a making, a doing, an embodying in personal being of what he understands.

38. Hans Christian Andersen, who, for example, clearly used his own personal history in "The Ugly Duckling."

39. The last two pieces became no. 1 and no. 2 (of three) of *Practice in Christianity*, published September 25, 1850.

40. See note 36 above.

41. *The Lily in the Field and the Bird of the Air, Three Devotional Discourses,* published May 14, 1849.

42. See note 41 above.

43. Ibid.

44. Regine Olsen. See note 159 below.

45. *Postscript*, p. 147, *KW* XII.1 (*SV* VII 120–21), freely quoted.

46. *Two Upbuilding Discourses,* preface dated May 5 (Kierkegaard's birthday) and book published May 16, 1843. "The Accounting" became the main part of *On My Work as an Author*, pp. 5–11.

47. Not used in the printed version of "On My Work."

48. See, for example, *Practice,* pp. 173–79, *KW* XX (*SV* XII 162–66).

49. Socrates.

50. See Mark 9:49.

51. See Luke 7:47.

52. See *JP* VI 6178 (*Pap.* IX A 106). The two preceding paragraphs constitute Kierkegaard's thumbnail autobiography: his Christian upbringing and vision of Christ, his view of Socrates, his engagement, the *Corsair* affair, his relationship with his father, all in the context of his sense of vocation, penitence, and mature religious life.

53. *Two Ethical-Religious Essays,* by H. H., published May 19, 1849.

54. "The Accounting."

55. Part IV of *Christian Discourses* (See note 18 above).

56. See note 41 above.

57. No. 1, 2, and 4 of "Cycle." See note 25 above.

58. Carl A. Reitzel (1789–1852), Copenhagen publisher and bookseller.

59. See note 55 above.

60. See note 16 above.

61. Danish *Livslede*, life-weariness with an admixture of sadness and disgust.

62. Kierkegaard regarded all differentiating talents as esthetic differences. Genuine human equality is found only in the realm of ethical-religious possibility independent of personal gifts.

63. See Luke 12:49.

64. The publication of "The Collected Works of Completion." See Supplement, pp. 172–73 (*Pap.* IX A 390) and writings on his work as an author.

65. See Supplement, pp. 172–73 (*Pap.* IX A 390).

66. For Kierkegaard's distinction between "upbuilding" and "for upbuilding," see *JP* V 5686 (*Pap.* IV B 159:6).

67. *The Sickness unto Death*, by Anti-Climacus, was published July 30, 1849.

68. See note 78 below.

69. See note 67 above.

70. No. I, II, and III of *Practice.*

71. Terkild Olsen, father of Regine Olsen.

72. See Corsair *Affair*, Historical Introduction, pp. xxi–xxii and Index entry "Kierkegaard, S. A.: trousers," p. 318, *KW* XIII.

73. No. I and II of *Practice.*

74. Part Four of *Christian Discourses*, pp. 247–300, *KW* XVII (*SV* X 245–317).

75. Anti-Climacus.

76. See *Practice*, pp. 278–80, *KW* XX (Pap. X¹ A 510) and *Eighteen Discourses*, note 3, pp. 503–05, *KW* V.

77. *Sickness unto Death*. On "for upbuilding," see note 76 above.

78. *Sickness unto Death* (title page), *KW* XIX (*SV* XI 113) and *Practice*, pp. 5 (*SV* XII xiii), 283, 295–96, 309 (*Pap.* X¹ A 520, X⁵ B 76, X¹ A 251), *KW* XX.

79. *Sickness Unto Death* and *Practice.*

80. See *Fear and Trembling*, p. 121, *KW* VI (*SV* III 166).

81. P. 137 and note 11.

82. *Practice in Christianity* was eventually published September 25, 1850, under the pseudonym Anti-Climacus.

83. No. 3 of *Practice.*

84. *Pap.* IX B 68, together with *Christian Discourses* and *Crisis*, in *Christian Discourses*, *KW* XVII.

85. The reference is presumably to Part IV of *Christian Discourses* (See note 18 above). See Supplement, p. 193 (*Pap.* X¹ A 351).

86. N. C. Møller, Kierkegaard's favorite bookbinder. See H. P. Rohde, "*Søren Kierkegaard som Bogsamler*," *Auktionsprotokol over Søren Kierkegaards Bogsamling* (Copenhagen: Royal Library, 1967), p. xxvi.

87. *The Sickness unto Death* or *Practice in Christianity*. Kierkegaard worked on both of the Anti-Climaus volumes during 1848. The journal entry is from September 1848.

88. Anti-Climacus was the pseudonym used.

89. *Practice, Three Discourses at the Communion on Fridays, Armed Neutrality,* and *Point of View.*

90. See pp. 129, 132–33, 134, 138–39.

91. This eventually became Part III of *Practice in Christianity*, by Anti-Climacus, published September 25, 1850.

92. See Supplement, pp. 178, 207–09 (*Pap.* X^1 A 95, X^2 A 66).

93. Anti-Climacus, pseudonymous author of *Sickness Unto Death* and *Practice*.

94. Cf., for example, *Fear and Trembling*, p. 121, *KW* VI (*SV* III 166).

95. See note 72 above.

96. See Supplement, p. 172 (*Pap.* IX A 390).

97. See *JP* VI 6429 (*Pap.* X^1 A 497).

98. Terkild Olsen, Regine's father, died the night of June 25–26, 1849.

99. For example, the Young Man and Constantin in *Repetition*, *KW* VI (*SV* III 171–264), and Quidam and Frater Taciturnus in *Stages on Life's Way*, *KW* XI (*SV* VI).

100. Jakob Peter Mynster (1775–1854), Bishop of Sjælland.

101. See "The Moral," *Practice*, pp. 67–68, *KW* XX (*SV* XII 64–65).

102. Here the name of the author of *Postscript* designates the book.

103. Thomas à Kempis, *Om Christi Efterfølgelse*, tr. Jens Albrecht Leonhard Holm (Copenhagen: 1848; *ASKB* 273); *Of the Imitation of Christ*, tr. anon. (New York: Appleton, 1896), p. 175.

104. See note 90 above.

105. "Poetic" in the sense that it is not accurately descriptive of the one who writes but is an ideal presentation. See, for example, *Practice*, pp. 293–95, *KW* XX (*Pap.* X^2 A 184); *JP* VI 6497 (*Pap.* X^2 A 45).

106. Johan Nicolai Madvig (1804–1886), Danish classical scholar and politician, at one time Minister of Church and Education, and Jakob Peter Mynster, Bishop of Sjælland.

107. Carl A. Reitzel (1789–1853), Copenhagen publisher and bookseller.

108. Terkild Olsen, father of Regine Olsen.

109. In *Sickness unto Death*.

110. See Supplement, pp. 172–73 (*Pap.* IX A 390).

111. See note 98 above.

112. The paper is not extant. See Supplement, p. 242 (*Pap.* X^2 A 427).

113. See note 159 below.

114. See Matthew 3:3; Mark 1:3.

115. Published May 16, 1843, about three months after *Either/Or*.

116. *The Lily in the Field and the Bird of the Air*, published May 14, 1849. The motto was not used.

117. See Supplement, p. 172 (*Pap.* IX A 390).

118. See Supplement, p. 235 (*Pap.* X^5 B 144).

119. See Supplement, p. 234 (*Pap.* X^5 B 143).

120. Cf. Supplement, pp. 271–72 (*Pap.* IX B 57, p. 348). The quoted clauses were omitted later.

121. See pp. 55–56.

122. *Two Discourses at the Communion on Fridays*, published August, 7, 1851. See *Without Authority*, pp. 165–66, *KW* XVIII (*SV* XII 267).

123. *Pap.* X⁵ B 208, which with changes became "The Accounting," pp. 5–11 (*SV* XIII 493–99).

124. See note 122 above.

125. "The High Priest" — "The Tax Collector" — "The Woman Who Was a Sinner." *Three Discourses at the Communion on Fridays*, published November 14, 1849.

126. See note 159 below; Historical Introduction, p. xix.

127. See Supplement, p. 230 (*Pap.* X² A 215).

128. See note 159 below; Historical Introduction, p. xix.

129. Peder Ludvig Møller, "*Et Besøg i Sorø*," *Gæa* (1846), pp. 144–87; Corsair *Affair*, Supplement, pp. 96–104, *KW* XIII.

130. See *The Corsair*, 269, November 14, 1845, col. 14; Corsair *Affair*, p. 96, *KW* XIII.

131. To Kierkegaard, his confronting *The Corsair* was an ethical, social act of general benefit. He felt abandoned by the commoners on the streets, who after the incessant ridicule by *The Corsair* avoided or taunted him, and also by the literary-political elite, who although now relieved as objects of the *Corsair's* attacks in turn gave Kierkegaard the silent treatment, criticized the action as rash, or called the whole thing a trifle not worth thinking about.

132. "Practice in Christianity," "On My Work," "Point of View," and "Armed Neutrality."

133. P. 137.

134. Presumably Peter Wilhelm Lund (1801–1880), brother of Johan Christian Lund and Henrik Ferdinand Lund (married to Kierkegaard's sisters Nicoline Christine and Petrea Severine), paleontologist, natural scientist. Peter Lund returned to Brazil in January 1833.

135. Jakob Peter Mynster (1775–1854), from 1811 a pastor of Frue Church in Copenhagen and from September 9, 1834, Bishop of Sjælland. Mynster was a friend of the Michael P. Kierkegaard family, so that young Søren came to know him at home and throughout his life associated Mynster appreciatively with his father. Kierkegaard read Mynster's writings regularly, just as he had heard Mynster's sermons read aloud at home. In later years he visited Mynster periodically, although he became critical, and increasingly so, of Mynster's cultural accommodation of Christianity but withheld open critique until after Mynster's death. See, for example, *JP* V 5637, 5864, 5961; VI 6749 (*Pap.* IV A 71; VII¹ B 75, A 221; X⁶ B 173).

136. Luther, "Sermon on the Fourteenth Sunday after Trinity" (Luke 17:11–18); *En christelig Postille*, I–II, tr. Jørgen Thisted (Copenhagen: 1828; *ASKB* 283), I, p. 513.

137. *Postscript*, p. [626], *KW* XII.1 (*SV* VII [546]).

138. See pp. 5–11.

139. Michael Pedersen Kierkegaard died on August 9, 1838.

140. See Luther, "Sermon on Fourth Sunday after Easter," James 1:17–21; *En christelig Postille*, II, pp. 248–55; *Church-Postil*, II, 146–52.

141. James 1:17–21.

142. *Practice.*

143. See Luther, "Sermon on Fourth Sunday after Trinity," Romans 8:18–23; *En christelig Postille,* II, pp. 339–49; *Church-Postil,* III, pp. 50–61.

144. See Romans 8:18–23.

145. September 8, 1840, the day of the proposal; Regine accepted the proposal on September 10.

146. See Matthew 6:24–34.

147. Regine Olsen. See note 159 below.

148. See note 145 above.

149. Matthew 6:24–34. See Supplement, p. 247 (*Pap.* X^3 A 391).

150. A German hymn by Paul Gerhardt, "*Befiel du deine Wege,*" no. 573 in *Gesangbuch* (Berlin: 1829; *ASKB* 205), translated into Danish by E. Stevensen, *Roskilde-Konvents Psalmebog,* 42 (Copenhagen: 1850; *ASKB* 198). The text in English (tr. Henry Mills, *Evangelical Lutheran Hymnal,* 411 [Columbus, Ohio: 1888]) reads:

1. Commit thy way, confiding,
   When trials here arise,
   To Him whose hand is guiding
   The tumults of the skies.
   There clouds and tempests, raging,
   Have each their path assigned;
   Will God, for thee engaging,
   No way of safety find?

2. Trust in the Lord! His favor
   Will for thy wants provide;
   Regard His word!—and ever
   Thy work shall safe abide.
   When sorrows here o'ertake thee,
   And self-inflicted care,
   Let not thy God forsake thee!
   He listens for thy prayer.

3. Should Satan league his forces,
   God's purpose to withstand
   Think not their rage and curses
   Can stay His lifted hand!
   When He makes known His pleasure,
   The counsel of His will,
   That, in its utmost measure,
   Will He at last fulfill.

4. Hope on then, weak believer,
   Hope on, and falter not!
   He will thy soul deliver
   From deeps of troubled thought.

Thy graces will He nourish.
With hope thy heart employ,
Till faith and hope shall flourish
And yield their fruits of joy.

5. Well blest, His grace receiving,
God owns thee for a son!
With joy, and with thanksgiving,
Behold the victor's crown!
Thy hand the palm-branch raises,—
God gives it thee to bear;—
Then sing aloud His praises.
Who has removed thy care.

6. The sorrows, Lord, that try us.
O bring them to an end!
With needed strength supply us!
Thy love to us commend!
That we, till death pursuing
Thy best, thy chosen way,
May then, our life renewing,
Praise Thee in endless day.

151. Hans Peter Kofoed-Hansen (1813–1893), curate at Frelsers Church, 1849–54, author of *Dialoger og Skizzer* (under the pseudonym Jean Pierre) and various other works for which Kierkegaard was the greatest single influence and at times the subject. He wrote perhaps the first penetrating review of a Kierkegaard work (*Either/Or*) in *For Literatur og Kritik: Et Fjerdingsaarsskrift udgivet af Fyens Stifts literære Selskab*, October 1843, I, 4, pp. 377–405

152. Eventually published the following year, August 7, 1851.

153. Kierkegaard considered the possibility of a cryptic dedication to Regine. See Supplement, pp. 257–58 (*Pap.* X^5 B 263, 264); the dedication to *Two Discourses at the Communion on Fridays*, in *Without Authority*, p. 163, *KW* XVIII (*SV* XII 265).

154. Published September 25, 1850.

155. Eggert C. Tryde (1781–1860), pastor, friend of Johan Ludvig Heiberg, and Royal Chaplain after 1854.

156. See *Practice*, pp. 233–36, *KW* XX (*SV* XII 213–16).

157. Peter's words to Christ. See Luke 5:8.

158. See the dedication to *Two Discourses at the Communion on Fridays*, in *Without Authority*, p. 163, *KW* XVIII (*SV* XII 265). No dedication is used in "The Accounting." Cf. *JP* VI 6332 (*Pap.* X^5 A 153).

159. Regine Olsen (January 23, 1822–March 18, 1904), daughter of Terkild Olsen (1784–1849) and Regine Frederikke Olsen (1778–1856). Kierkegaard met Regine Olsen at T. S. Rørdam's house in Frederiksberg just outside Copenhagen sometime between May 8 and May 16, 1837. On September 8,

1840, Kierkegaard proposed to her, and on September 10 she gave her acceptance. On October 11, 1841, the engagement was definitely terminated following Kierkegaard's return of the engagement ring on August 8, 1841. The two main reasons for Kierkegaard's breaking the engagement were: his love for Regine in the context of an awareness that he most likely would crush her and his sense of a life-task that would preoccupy him. The possibility of a renewal of a friendly relationship was always in Kierkegaard's mind, but out of consideration for Regine and Johan Frederik Schlegel (to whom she became engaged in July 1843 and married November 3, 1847) he did not want to take the first step. The closest he came was a letter to Schlegel (November 19, 1849) accompanied by a letter (written and rewritten many times) to Regine after her father's death (June 25–26, 1849). Schlegel returned unopened the letter addressed to Regine. See *Letters*, Letter 239, *KW* XXV.

160. See notes 158, 159 above.

161. Ibid.

162. Ibid.

163. Cf. "An Occasional Discourse," *Upbuilding Discourses in Various Spirits*, pp. 26–27, *KW* XV (*SV* VIII 136).

164. See Supplement, p. 266 (*Pap.* X⁵ B 209).

165. Published May 14, 1849.

166. *Two Upbuilding Discourses* (1843), in *Eighteen Discourses*, p. 53, *KW* V (*SV* III 271).

167. "Discourses at the Communion on Fridays," Part Four of *Christian Discourses*, pp. 247–300, *KW* XVII (*SV* X 245–317).

168. *Christian Discourses*, p. 249, *KW* XVII (*SV* X 251).

169. An allusion to Paul. See II Corinthians 12:7.

170. See p. 19 and note 44.

171. Ibid.

172. *Two Ages: The Age of Revolution and the Present Age. A Literary Review*, *KW* XIV (*SV* VIII 3–105).

173. *JP* VI 6663 (*Pap.* X⁶ B 93); *Pap.* X⁶ B 94–102. See note 8 above.

174. *Sickness Unto Death* and *Practice*.

175. Presumably pp. 91–95:12 (Epilogue), 95:13–97 (Conclusion).

176. See *Two Discourses at the Communion on Fridays*, pp. 165–66 (*SV* XII 267), and Supplement, p. 272, *KW* XVIII (*Pap.* IX B 63:14).

177. See note 33 above.

178. See p. 254.

179. See p. 2.

180. See pp. 118–19.

181. See Supplement, pp. 276–79 (*Pap.* IX B 64).

182. The preface was written for but not used in *For Self-Examination*, published September 10, 1851.

183. P. 12.

184. *On My Work as an Author* and *Two Discourses at the Communion on Fridays*, August 7, 1851.

185. See Luke 5:8–9.
186. See note 135 above.
187. See note 184 above.
188. The extended review of Thomasine Gyllembourg-Ehrensvaard's *Two Ages* is the chief instance of Kierkegaard's implementation of an idea for ceasing to be an author *without ceasing to write* (see *JP* V 5877; VI 6334 [*Pap.* VII¹ A 9; X¹ A 90]). His first book, *From the Papers of One Still Living*, a long review of Hans Christian Andersen's *Kun en Spillemand* [Only a Fiddler] was of the same order, although prior to his idea formulated in *Pap.* VII¹ A 9.
189. P. 19.
190. Michael Pedersen Kierkegaard died August 9, 1838.
191. See *JP* VI 6748, p. 396 (*Pap.* X⁶ B 171, p. 263 fn.).
192. See note 22 above.
193. Mynster praised Goldschmidt (see *JP* VI 6748, 6750, 6751 [*Pap.* X⁶ B 171, 188, 194]), founder and original editor of *The Corsair*, as "one of our most talented writers." See J. P. Mynster, *Yderligere Bidrag til Forhandlingerne om de kirkelige Forhold i Danmark* (Copenhagen: 1851), p. 44.
194. See note 22 above.
195. See note 135 above.
196. *Flyve-Posten*, 215, September 16, 1851, p. 1, col. 3.
197. *Postscript*, pp. [625–30], *KW* XII.1 (*SV* VII [545–49]).
198. P. 7
199. "Editor's Preface," *Practice*, p. 7, *KW* XX (*SV* XII xv).
200. See *Two Ages*, p. 107, *KW* XIV (*SV* VIII 99–100).
201. Cf. p. 12.
202. Cf. *Either/Or*, II, p. 159, *KW* IV (*SV* II 145).
203. Cf. *Repetition*, p. 149, *KW* VI (*SV* III 189).
204. See p. 12.
205. See *Either/Or*, II, p. 6, *KW* IV (*SV* II 6), loosely quoted.
206. See *For Self-Examination*, p. 86, *KW* XXI (*SV* XII 369).
207. See Supplement, pp. 231, 233 (*Pap.* X⁵ B 211, 222). The postscripts in *Pap.* X⁵ B 168 and 211 were not used in *On My Work* or *Point of View*.
208. Here *nonreduplicated* means "direct" as contrasted to indirect communication or the mode of double-reflection, as in the pseudonymous works, which are works of reflection intended to occasion a second reflection—the reader's. For Kierkegaard, *reduplication* usually means "existing in what one understands." But here "nonreduplicated" refers to a direct mode of written expression without the implication that the writer exemplifies the ideality delineated in the writing.
209. *Practice in Christianity*, which was eventually published September 25, 1850.
210. The three parts of *Practice*. See note 209 above.
211. See Supplement, p. 301 (*Pap.* X¹ A 450).
212. See note 209 above.
213. *Practice*, III.

BIBLIOGRAPHICAL NOTE

For general bibliographies of Kierkegaard studies, see:

Jens Himmelstrup, *Søren Kierkegaard International Bibliografi*. Copenhagen: Nyt Nordisk Forlag Arnold Busck, 1962.

International Kierkegaard Newsletter, ed. Julia Watkin. Launceton, Tasmania, Australia, 1979–.

Aage Jørgensen, *Søren Kierkegaard-litteratur 1961–1970*. Aarhus: Akademisk Boghandel, 1971. *Søren Kierkegaard-litteratur 1971–1980*. Aarhus: privately published, 1983.

Kierkegaard: A Collection of Critical Essays, ed. Josiah Thompson. New York: Doubleday (Anchor Books), 1972.

Kierkegaardiana, XII, 1982; XIII, 1984; XIV, 1988; XVI, 1993; XVII, 1994; XVIII, 1996.

Bruce H. Kirmmse, *Kierkegaard in Golden Age Denmark*. Bloomington: Indiana University Press, 1990.

François H. Lapointe, *Sören Kierkegaard and His Critics: An International Bibliography of Criticism*. Westport, Connecticut: Greenwood Press, 1980.

Søren Kierkegaard's Journals and Papers, I, ed. and tr. Howard V. Hong and Edna H. Hong, assisted by Gregor Malantschuk. Bloomington, Indiana: Indiana University Press, 1967.

For topical bibliographies of Kierkegaard studies, see *Søren Kierkegaard's Journals and Papers*, I-IV, 1967–75.

INDEX

abolition: of being a Christian, 129–31

adherents: winning Christian, 51

Adler, Alfred P., 178, 181, 183, 324

admission(s): and individual, 17–18; and Mynster, 287

age, the: of disintegration, 119, 276–79; and ideality, 206; Kierkegaard's view of, 180; misfortune of, 104; of passion and sagacity, 163; present demoralized, 264; religion and, 47–50

age (old): and youth, 218–19

alienation: of Kierkegaard, 162; of public, 10

America: forests of, 75

analogy: backward pupil, 191–92; ballast, 19; birds, wild and tame, 202; coachman, 290; diligent pupil, 96; excavation of fossils, 245–46; fisherman's float, 249; fish in air, 20; fishing bait, 182; fish on line, 84; girl in love, 221; Guadalquibir River, 194, 199, 202, 204; invisible writing, 54; knotting thread, 20; legal documents, 131–32; mushrooms, 180; overripe fruit, 277; patient, 179; plow, 9, 263–64; policeman, 78; sewing, 20; smoke-abatement, 125; spider, 6; stepfather, 192; street inspector, 78; sword, two-edged, 279–80; tacking, 286; teacher, 49–50; Thermopylae, 118, 154; Titans, 122; unbroken horse, 290; unclaimed property, 121; wound, 280; yellow bunting, 96

Andersen, Hans Christian, 185; *Kun en Spillemand* [Only a Fiddler], xxiii, 332; "The Ugly Duckling," 325

anonymity: of daily press, 57; of "4651," 287–88

apologetics: as the old science of arms, 52

apostle: as constrained, 230; Kierkegaard not an, 78

aristocrat(s): and Kierkegaard, 157

Aristotle: *Aristoteles graece*, 316; on irony, 64; *Rhetoric*, 316

armed neutrality: idea of, 136–41, 320; as Kierkegaard's position, 129, 183, 299

authority: crowd as, 112, 275; human race as, 122–23; and number, 126; and ordination, 261

author(s): approach of, 43–44, 47, 53; as Christian, xi; idea of, 211; Kierkegaard on becoming an, 84–90; as polemical, 67–68; writing for, 153–54. *See also* writer; writing

authorship

and Christianity, 7, 55–56, 88, 90, 92, 272–73

Kierkegaard's, 212–17

aim of, 235, 256

awareness as goal, 12, 58, 124, 224–25, 253, 256

best things in, 171

central issue of, 8, 63, 90, 92, 235

comprehensive plan of, xviii, 6–12, 41–97, 55–56, 76–77, 165–67, 182, 185, 193, 213, 217, 283, 286

contemplated lectures on, xiii

coherence of, xiii